The Politics of Internet Communication

The Politics of Internet Communication

Robert J. Klotz

ROWMAN & LITTLEFIELD PUBLISHERS, INC.
Lanham • Boulder • New York • Toronto • Oxford

ROWMAN & LITTLEFIELD PUBLISHERS, INC.

Published in the United States of America
by Rowman & Littlefield Publishers, Inc.
A wholly owned subsidiary of The Rowman & Littlefield Publishing Group, Inc.
4501 Forbes Boulevard, Suite 200, Lanham, Maryland 20706
www.rowmanlittlefield.com

P.O. Box 317, Oxford, OX2 9RU, UK

British Library Cataloguing in Publication Information Available

Library of Congress Cataloging-in-Publication Data

Klotz, Robert J., 1969–
 The politics of Internet communication / Robert J. Klotz.
  p. cm.
Includes bibliographical references and index.
 ISBN 0-7425-2925-8 (Cloth : alk. paper) — ISBN 0-7425-2926-6 (Paper : alk. paper)
 1. Internet—Political aspects. 2. Internet—Political aspects—United States. I. Title.
HM851 .K57 2004
303.48'33—dc22   2003014126

Printed in the United States of America

⊗™ The paper used in this publication meets the minimum requirements of American
National Standard for Information Sciences—Permanence of Paper
for Printed Library Materials, ANSI/NISO Z39.48-1992.

Contents

Contents

Tables

TABLES

Acronyms

ACLA	American Coalition of Life Activists
ACLU	American Civil Liberties Union
ACPA	Anti-Cybersquatting Consumer Protection Act
AIDS	acquired immunodeficiency syndrome
AOL	America Online
ARPA	Advanced Research Projects Agency
ARPANET	ARPA Network
AT&T	American Telephone & Telegraph
AUP	Acceptable Use Policy
BBN	Bolt, Beranek & Newman
CDA	Communications Decency Act
CD-ROM	compact disk-read-only memory
CIA	Central Intelligence Agency
CIPA	Child Internet Protection Act
CNN	Cable News Network
COPA	Child Online Protection Act
COPPA	Children's Online Privacy Protection Act
CSS	Content Scrambling System
DMCA	Digital Millennium Copyright Act of 1998
DMV	Division of Motor Vehicles
DNet	Democracy Network
DSL	digital subscriber line
DVD	digital video disk
EEOC	Equal Employment Opportunity Commission
EFOIA	Electronic Freedom of Information Act

EPA	Environmental Protection Agency
EU	European Union
FCC	Federal Communications Commission
FDIC	Federal Deposit Insurance Corporation
FEC	Federal Election Commission
FOIA	Freedom of Information Act
FTC	Federal Trade Commission
GAO	General Accounting Office
GDP	gross domestic product
GILS	Government Information Locator Service (formerly FILS—Federal Information Locator Service)
GPO	Government Printing Office
HTML	HyperText Markup Language
IADAS	International Academy of Digital Arts and Sciences
ICANN	Internet Corporation for Assigned Names and Numbers
IIS	Integrated Information Systems, Inc.
IP	Internet Protocol
IRS	Internal Revenue Service
ISP	Internet service providerI
ITFA	Internet Tax Freedom Act
ITU	International Telecommunication Union
KACST	King Abdulaziz City for Science & Technology
KOOL	Kentucky Offender Online Lookup
MSNBC	Microsoft Network NBC
NASA	National Aeronautics and Space Administration
NCES	National Center for Education Statistics
NIST	National Institute of Standards and Technology
NPR	National Public Radio
NSF	National Science Foundation
NSFNET	National Science Foundation network
NSI	Network Solutions Inc.
OECD	Organisation for Economic Co-operation and Development
OMB	Office of Management and Budget
PARC	Palo Alto Research Center (of Xerox Corporation)
PC	personal computer
PETA	People for the Ethical Treatment of Animals
TCP/IP	Transmission Control Protocol/Internet Protocol
UDRP	Uniform Domain Name Dispute Resolution Program
UN	United Nations
VAT	value added tax
VCR	videocassette recorder
WIPO	World Intellectual Property Organization
WWF	World Wrestling Federation

Preface

My introduction to the politics of Internet communication began with surprise as I listened to a political consultant instinctively discourage me from posting on the Web a detailed political proposal on which there would be a referendum. Once the consultant conceded that the proposal must be placed online, the talk then turned to whether page numbers should be put on the document. After asking if I had ever attended a meeting where pages weren't numbered and everyone was on a different page, he proceeded to describe a scene in which people were confused and had difficulty criticizing a proposal. I recognized this as an argument against including page numbers. Even though most people would not read the proposal, and we felt we had a good product, the openness of the Internet was still a scary prospect. Ultimately, we decided to post the document—page numbers and all—and take our chances with an empowered public. This incident of the democratizing potential of the Internet motivated an extended investigation of the broader relationship between the Internet and politics.

This book is the result of that investigation. I found a medium that has been inextricably linked to politics since its origin within the Department of Defense. I found a medium that is systematically enhancing democracy. The Internet's capacity for information dissemination and mobilization has profound consequences for politics. Dramatic developments like the online fundraising success of Howard Dean and the online movement encouraging the candidacy of General Wesley Clark during the 2004 campaign punctuate a steady expansion of the political use of the Internet. Although this is serious business for politics, there is also a refreshing lighter side to Internet politics. I found much humor in the politics of Internet communication, ranging from vociferous positions on imaginary legislation to the animal rights group PETA's attempt to take peta.org from "People Eating

Tasty Animals." The blend of a serious and lighter side to Internet communication is well captured by a Tina Fey story on *Saturday Night Live*'s "Weekend Update": "A new website started last year gives married couples in four states the option of divorcing online; for an extra $5 they'll even send an e-mail to your children telling them it's not their fault."

In writing this book, I have received assistance from others. The book uses data sets from the Pew Research Center for the People and the Press, the Pew Internet & American Life Project, and the U.S. Census. These outstanding organizations would like me to remind you that they are not responsible for any conclusions that I have drawn from their data. The book would not have been possible without Jennifer Knerr, Renee Legatt, April Leo, and the talented team at Rowman & Littlefield. In the early stages of writing, I benefited from interaction with students in my Internet politics class at the University of Southern Maine, especially Sheila Cohen, Bodie Colwell, and Amber Smith. I have received support from the USM libraries, Computing Center, and Political Science Department. I have learned much from conversations with Steve Ceccoli, Randy Glean, Oliver Woshinsky, and Internet users throughout the world. I received many valuable written comments, especially from Anna Broome, John Klotz, Lynn Kuzma, and the anonymous peer reviewers. On a broader note, I am grateful for having been taught by dedicated teachers throughout my life, especially William Danforth, James Davis, Doug Estell, Marjorie Hershey, Bill Lowry, and Robert Salisbury. Above all, I thank my family for their support.

Introduction

The Internet has been embraced for political purposes, even as politicians have trouble expressing how. Awkward expressions of the conjunction of the Internet and politics span time and place. When asked by Wolf Blitzer to distinguish himself from his year 2000 Democratic primary opponent Bill Bradley, Al Gore explained that he "took the initiative in creating the Internet." In a high-profile Senate debate against Hillary Clinton in October 2000, Rick Lazio described federal bill 602p to impose a tax on e-mail as an example of "government's greedy hand" even though no such bill has ever existed. In a 1998 debate, Senator Frank Murkowski described himself as the "seventh friendliest Web page user" in Congress. Bob Dole made history in 1996 by becoming the first presidential candidate to mention his website in a presidential debate, but he omitted a critical part of the address of his website.

An eagerness to embrace a new technology for political use is a long-standing tradition. When a new medium emerges, invariably claims are made that it can dramatically improve politics. The telegraph, for instance, was thought to be able to reduce political conflict and promote world peace by generating a shared understanding. The Internet is no different. Political consultant and former adviser to President Clinton, Dick Morris, has said that the Internet will "make better candidates."[1]

The temptation to see technology as a leap forward for democracy is strong. Consider the following statement by M. H. Aylesworth. No new technology could live up to his expectations:

[It] is destined to be used more and more widely every year as a public forum . . . [and] may eventually be the means of making our country what it was theoretically supposed to be when its government was established—an ideal democracy.[2]

In this case, Aylesworth was writing about the new medium of radio in *The Century Magazine* in June 1929. History tells us that no new technology is going to lead to an ideal democracy. We aren't ideal citizens.

If, however, the optimists about new technology take things too far, so also do the pessimists. Throughout time, new media have been widely approached with a natural suspicion. This suspicion was articulated as early as the writing of Plato in fourth-century B.C. Greece. In his dialogue *Phaedrus,* Socrates and Phaedrus are comparing the new medium of writing to speaking. Socrates is suspicious of writing. Compared to the time-honored tradition of speaking, writing had all kinds of faults. Writing only reminded people of what they already knew. Writing would lead to the decline of memory. Later, echoing Plato, legendary political sociologist Paul Lazarsfeld described the virtues of reading for imparting political knowledge over a new form of speaking—radio: "Reading permits a person to dwell upon printed material, to reread it, and one cannot do this while listening to broadcast material."[3] The Internet, too, has received a fair share of pessimism. Longtime CBS news anchor Walter Cronkite, for instance, has described the Internet as a "frightful danger to all of us."[4]

Indeed, if history seems to repeat itself, it is because all media, especially the Internet, build on each other. The Internet is a combination of previous advances in technology. It is a computer-enabled integration of printed, audio, and visual material in a personal and mass medium. The combination of all these media is more than the sum of its parts. It has resulted in a medium that represents a tremendous increase in the ability to disseminate information and mobilize. Any medium that enhances information dissemination and mobilization is going to be adopted in a competitive political environment. This use of the Internet for political purposes is an important part of the politics of Internet communication.

Thus, an examination of how the Internet is being used in politics is one important dimension of this book. It explores how candidates, interest groups, political parties, and government officials are using the Internet. The book also takes an in-depth look at how the Internet is affecting the journalists who report on politics. Systematic analysis of politics on the Internet will be supplemented by identifying compelling examples of Internet use.

The politics of Internet communication, however, is about more than politics conducted on the Internet. It is about the underlying politics that affects Internet communication even when the communication is about a subject that has nothing to do with politics. It is about the legal structure that frames Internet communication, whether someone is e-mailing a friend or downloading music files. The politics of Internet communication also includes the political meaning of Internet experiences. It is about how nonpolitical use becomes an issue in politics. It is about the building of social capital. It is about the political implications of whether or not the Internet is enhancing private life.

As the book explores both politics on the Internet and the politics of the Internet, it strives to move beyond the initial climate of hopes and fears about the Internet. Two pursuits are critical in this endeavor: placing the Internet in its historical context and generating systematic data about its actual use. Placing the Internet in a historical context can help pinpoint what is and what is not new about the medium. Understanding the underlying patterns and historical progression of the Internet can help make sense of novelty and lead to a reasoned assessment.

Generating systematic data is crucial to moving discussion beyond nonrepresentative anecdotes. Numbers, it should be recognized, do arise with some frequency in discussions about the Internet. Even Jay Leno's *Tonight Show* monologues are able to use numbers to leave an impression about the Internet experience: "86 percent of *Cosmo* readers have tried online dating . . . and of those that dated people they met on the Internet, 61 percent said the experience was good; the other 39 percent are still missing."[5] While forgoing Leno's pollster, the book will take advantage of the immense amount of data available about the Internet. In fact, compared to other media at a similar stage, the World Wide Web provides an unbelievable opportunity to base assessments on systematic data. Six years after the first commercial station went on the air in the United States, there were 16 television stations. Six years after its introduction, the Web already had over one million sites. In 1955, after nearly fifteen years of commercial American television, candidate spot advertising was mainly identified with forty similar ads filmed by Dwight Eisenhower in 1952. One can extrapolate only so much from forty Eisenhower ads. In well under a decade, the Web had transmitted communication from literally thousands of candidates. To make sense of all these data, the book is committed to presenting compelling statistics in an accessible manner.

The theme of the book is that politics and the Internet are integrally related. Once viewed as a convenience, Internet use is becoming a necessity for political participants. Competitive advantages go to those who use the Internet well; disadvantages go to those who do not. Like politics on the Internet, the politics of the Internet has intensified. Once viewed as the Wild West, the Internet is becoming home to a substantial body of law. Internet regulation presents opportunities and constraints to communicators. As the book progresses, the many layers of the relationship between politics and the Internet will be uncovered.

For politics, this relationship represents a net gain for democracy. The analysis reveals something more than a relativistic conclusion that optimists and pessimists both exaggerate. The Internet does alter the political landscape. It offers information dissemination and mobilization on a scale impossible by other means. The Internet is strengthening the relationship between citizens and their leaders. It will be a long-term process, but there are already important consequences.

STRUCTURE OF THE BOOK

The book's structure reflects its goal of providing the first comprehensive analysis of the intersection between politics and the Internet. The book begins with a background chapter covering the nature and development of the Internet. The characteristics of the Internet are placed in the context of previous advances in personal and mass communication. The contributions of the public and private sectors to Internet development are assessed.

In Part I, the politics of Internet access is explored. The evolution of the user base of the Internet is documented. A systematic analysis of online activities reveals the extent of commerce, education, entertainment, health, religion, and sex on the Internet. The portrait of who is using the Internet and how it is being used establishes the context for a consideration of government policy regarding Internet access.

Parts II and III explore the Internet communication of major participants in politics. Advocacy by candidates, political parties, interest groups, and citizens is analyzed. The e-government initiatives of public officials are examined. Journalists are found to have unique opportunities and challenges on the Internet. Applying data about the content and consumption of online news, the implications of the Internet for the accuracy and availability of news are considered.

Part IV examines the legal context in which Internet communication occurs. Identifying the fundamentals of cyberlaw sets the stage for contemplating specific areas of law. An assessment of content regulation pays special attention to pornography, spam, and employee communication. While content regulation concerns what is communicated, domain name law regulates where communication occurs. Building on content and location regulation, the law of Internet piracy and privacy is explored.

Part V places the previous chapters, which emphasize the American Internet experience, in a global context. The politics of Internet communication in democracies and non-democracies around the world is examined. By the end of the book, a systematic understanding of the integral relationship between the Internet and politics will emerge.

1

Characteristics and Development of the Internet

The Internet is at once like no other communication device and like every other communication device. It is a personal and mass medium of communication. It is capable of transmitting communication in any format—print, audio, or video. Of course, these dimensions of communication have been available previously—just not through the same medium. By harnessing the power of the computer to previous communication advancements, the Internet has become the most versatile of media.

In fact, it is the computer protocol that technically defines the Internet. According to the Federal Networking Council, the Internet has the following characteristics:

> "Internet" refers to the global information system that—(i) is logically linked together by a globally unique address space based on the Internet Protocol (IP) or its subsequent extensions/follow-ons; (ii) is able to support communications using the Transmission Control Protocol/Internet Protocol (TCP/IP) suite or its subsequent extensions/ follow-ons, and/or other IP-compatible protocols; and (iii) provides, uses or makes accessible, either publicly or privately, high level services layered on the communications and related infrastructure described herein.[1]

Of course, when most people think about the Internet, they do not have in mind the unique protocol that allows the networking of computers. More likely, they think of the Internet in terms of the international network of computers that can transmit information to each other. In the landmark case *Reno* v. *ACLU,* the Supreme Court defined the Internet as "an international network of interconnected computers."[2] Both the technical definition of the Federal Networking Council and

1

the simple definition of the Supreme Court capture the essential feature of the term *Internet*: it refers to the global information infrastructure at the broadest level.

Within the broader Internet, a number of different types of communication take place. Many of the dimensions of the Internet have widely recognized identities in their own right: e-mail, chat rooms, newsgroups, listservs, and the World Wide Web. At present, electronic mail and the Web are the most significant aspects of the Internet. E-mail refers to the broad array of techniques used to transmit messages over a computer network. While e-mail was prevalent in the infancy of the Internet, the Web is a relative newcomer to the Internet. The Web rose from the 127th most popular dimension of the Internet in 1993 to the 5th most popular in 1994 to the most popular dimension by early 1995.[3] The Web is the universe of documents and files written in hypertext that are accessible from servers connected to the Internet. Technically, the Web is just one highly visible component of the Internet.

The distinction between the use of the term *Internet* and its various dimensions is a useful one, but it can be easily exaggerated. Exaggerating the distinction between these terms suffers from an excess of refinement and ignores the benefits of word variety. After all, people are likely to simply say that they are going to turn on the "radio" regardless of whether they intend to listen to AM, FM, or shortwave. Thus, while acknowledging the distinction between the Internet and the Web, this book does not maintain a rigid demarcation of the terms. This approach is consistent with the common vernacular, which has increasingly used Internet and Web interchangeably, if not merged them into an even broader, amorphous term—cyberspace. It also recognizes the increasing use of the Web as a seamless avenue into many of the other dimensions of the Internet.

FUNDAMENTAL FEATURES AS A MEDIUM

At a fundamental level, the Internet can be viewed as a combination of a personal and mass medium for any format of communication. It is a personal medium through which people can communicate one-to-one in a private manner. The Internet is also a mass medium by which one person can communicate simultaneously with many others in a public manner. It can also support communication in any format, whether it be text, audio, or video.

The versatility of Internet communication represents a combination of centuries of innovation in communications technology. Innovations prior to the Internet had tackled one at a time the problems of communicating in any format through personal and mass media. These earlier innovations represent landmark developments in human communication: telegraph, telephone, videophone, printing press, radio, and telephone. Table 1.1 outlines the communications advances prior to the Internet based on type of medium and format.

Table 1.1   Innovations in Communication

Format	One-to-One	One-to-Many
Text	Telegraph	Printing Press
Audio	Telephone	Radio
Video	Videophone	Television

Major innovations in the personal media of communications have been the telegraph, telephone, and videophone. The invention of the telegraph allowed a sender to transmit a coded text message over a wire to a receiver. Taking its name from the Greek words for distance and writing, the telegraph meant that physical or visual contact was no longer necessary for one person to transmit a message to another. News that had previously taken weeks to be transmitted could arrive in minutes. Distance was no longer an impediment to rapid, one-to-one communication of text. The unknown implications of shattering the barrier of distance are symbolized by the message sent in 1844 by Samuel Morse during the first major public demonstration of the telegraph: "What hath God wrought?"

The telephone further reduced the barrier of distance in personal communications. It enabled nearly instantaneous audio communication at a distance. While a telegraph was typically decoded by an operator, then physically delivered to somebody, a ringing telephone would instantly bring one-to-one audio communication into the home. The ability of the telephone to intrude and summon audio communication is symbolized by the first sentence transmitted by telephone: "Mr. Watson, come here, I want you." Uttered spontaneously by Alexander Graham Bell as a response to having spilled battery acid on himself, the message lacked the gravity of the words of Morse. Thomas Watson, however, saw a certain poetry in this utterance:

> Not expecting such a sudden advance in the talking power of his telephone that evening, however, he [Bell] had not prepared a suitable sentiment for the occasion. His shout for help on that night of March 10, 1876, doesn't make as pretty a story as did the first sentence, "What hath God wrought," which Morse sent over his new telegraph from Washington to Baltimore about thirty years before, but it was an emergency call—therefore typical of the great service the telephone was to render to mankind. What could have been more appropriate.[4]

The videophone enabled one-to-one transmission of video at a distance. The first device was built by AT&T in 1956 and introduced as the Picturephone in 1964. Unlike the telegraph and telephone, which enjoyed enormous popularity and fundamentally changed how people communicate, the videophone had almost no immediate impact. This advance in personal communications may have been a bit too personal. People seemed to enjoy engaging in audio communication even when they might not relish being in video communication at the same time. The videophone did not find acceptance until being integrated with the computer for videoconferencing. Thus, there is no famous first message transmitted by videophone. If one were to exist, the most symbolic message would have been an exasperated "Who cares?"

Advancements in mass media have followed a similar progression in breaking down distance as a barrier to the transmission of text, audio, and video messages. The major innovations in mass media have been the invention and advancements in the printing press, radio, and television. While personal communications over a distance generally utilized a secure wire, the development of mass media required transmission over something other than a wire. To reach mass audiences, these developments were dependent on mass production or transmission through air.

Advances in technology gradually made printing into a mass medium. Depending on the preferred definition of one-to-many communication, it could be argued that ancient Asian inventions of paper and ink or perhaps the later Asian innovation of movable text had propelled printing into a mass medium. Certainly, these early advances allowed some printed works to be widely circulated well before the use of any advanced techniques of mass production. It was, however, the invention of the printing press that most clearly marks the emergence of printing as a mass medium. While previous multiple distribution was dependent on painstakingly slow methods of production, the printing press mechanized the printing process and led to massive increases in the distribution of printed works.

The invention of the radio greatly expanded the capacity for one-to-many audio communication. Mass audiences no longer needed to be physically present to receive audio communication. Communication could occur as radios received sound in the form of reflected radio waves that had been projected into the air. Although the signal grew weaker with distance, a radio could project audio to an infinite number of people within a fixed geographic area. As long as people had the radio equipment and antennae to receive a signal, they would receive the audio feed.

The one-to-many communication of audio was quickly followed by the capability of transmitting video from one-to-many. The development of the television meant that video signals could be received by an infinite number of people within a fixed geographic area. The use of affiliates to broadcast the same television programming in different areas enabled a shared visual experience for millions of people who had televisions and were within a broadcast area. Over time, developments in technologies such as satellite and cable expanded the number of stations and the distance over which they could be received.

As a combination of these previous media, the Internet is more than the sum of its parts. It offers the potential to do things that were impossible before. Combining previous media changed them. The Internet becomes the most versatile of media. This versatility applies to its use in politics. As a medium for politics, it offers advances over previous media. In particular, Internet technology represents a giant leap forward in interactivity. Communication occurs in both directions.

Elites can initiate communication with citizens, and citizens can initiate communication with political elites. The Internet represents a significant advancement for political elites seeking to disseminate information and mobilize. The medium has the flexibility for disseminating information of all types—text, audio, and video. Unlike previous media in which information dissemination is limited by cost and audience size, the Internet allows information dissemination at minimal cost to a potentially unlimited audience. The Internet does not require expensive paper or broadcasting time. Yet, information can potentially be seen by anyone with access to the Internet. Further, this information can be directly geared to mobilization. The Internet's existence as both a personal and mass medium is ideal for this task. Communication on a mass level can be supported with individualized appeals for action.

The Internet also facilitates citizen interaction with government. Citizens can initiate communication with government on an individual basis. They can make their opinion known. They can contribute money to political causes. Beyond advocacy, the personal nature of the Internet allows individual business to be conducted with government. Government interactions can be made more efficient. Indeed, this was the original use of the Internet's precursor, the ARPANET, which linked the Defense Department to the institutions it did business with. The Internet can facilitate routine interactions with government.

Interactivity makes the Internet a formidable medium for politics. Disseminating information, mobilizing, and citizen interaction lie at the heart of politics. The Internet is, therefore, well suited for political use. How is it being used? Throughout this book, the political uses of the Internet will become apparent. They will be illuminated with real-world examples and systematic data.

GOVERNMENT ROLE IN PREVIOUS TECHNOLOGICAL ADVANCEMENTS

Governments have a substantial interest in new methods of communication. The power of a nation partly depends on its communication infrastructure. Superior communications can bestow military, economic, or other advantages. A nation can obtain a military advantage over its competitors if its troops have a better way of obtaining information. The timely reception and transmission of information about market conditions can enhance the economic performance of a nation. A good communications structure can enhance education within the general populace, thereby fostering the sharing of ideas and encouraging innovation. The potential interest of government in communications technology is limitless. Considering their fundamental interest in communication, governments predictably have been quick to become involved in new communications technology.

Despite its interest in communication improvements, government did not have a major role in creating the telegraph, telephone, videophone, printing press, radio, or television. Not one of these inventions was a result of a government-sponsored initiative. Government, however, quickly took an interest in the new technologies. It quickly assumed the role of regulator.

The invention of the telegraph was enabled by a series of advances in electricity and electromagnetism. Building on these advances, innovators in Britain and the United States demonstrated operational telegraphs at about the same time. American Samuel Morse's 1837 patent using a series of dots and dashes had the most enduring legacy. In the early stages of his work, Morse depended entirely on private funds. He marshaled his own resources along with private partners to make an operational telegraph. Once he was confident it could work, Morse took a proposal to Congress requesting funds for a telegraph line between Washington, D.C., and Baltimore. Congress refused. After more success, he returned to Congress and by the slim margin of 89–83 was given funds to demonstrate a Baltimore–D.C. line. The first substantive information passed over the new line was information from the 1844 Whig Convention in Baltimore. Morse successfully received the names of nominees Henry Clay and Theodore Frelinghuysen, but had not heard of Frelinghuysen. Despite the success, Morse's request for additional funds for a New York line was denied.[5] New lines would be fueled by private investment.

Working with the assistance of machine shop engineer Thomas Watson, the inventor Alexander Graham Bell patented the telephone in 1876. The experiments of Bell had been dependent on the financial backing of two independent businessmen. In fact, Bell did not make a penny from his invention until 1878, when he was paid to give a lecture on the telephone.[6] Soon after the invention of the telephone, Bell's financial backers had tried to sell his patent; but Western Union declined the offer, seeing no potential in the telephone. Bell, Watson, and a growing organization eventually produced a service that people were willing to buy. The company they formed, American Telephone & Telegraph, spearheaded the development of the telephone and later the videophone.

The conversion of printing into a mass medium was driven by private sector initiative. Johannes Gutenberg, a German goldsmith working in a small lab, integrated a number of earlier technologies into a viable printing press in the 1440s. He was backed financially by a lawyer who loaned him money to build a press. Gutenberg would need to find a different lawyer after being sued for failing to return the money.

The private sector is also responsible for the development of radio and television. Both inventions were the product of a number of developments made by researchers in the private sector. The man typically viewed as providing the largest advance in the radio, Italian Gugliano Marconi, struggled to find financial backing and did most of the work on his "wireless telegraph" in the home of his parents. Vladimir Zworykin made his seminal advances in electronic television while working for Westinghouse. If anything, the role of the federal government was to slow the progress of the technology by freezing development of radio and television during World War I and World War II, respectively.

GOVERNMENT ROLE IN INTERNET DEVELOPMENT

Compared to prior innovations, the development of the Internet was closely tied to government. The public sector played a critical role in nearly all stages of Internet development. Many years of groundwork had been laid before the withdrawal of government from the development of the Internet.

The development of the computer, which is central to the Internet, also relied heavily on government. The first two supercomputers were both commissioned by government. The Colossus, which became operational in 1943, was developed by the British as a means of decoding German messages in World War II. Thus, not only was the machine developed by the government, but its purpose was tied to the imperatives of government. The first American supercomputer, ENIAC, was commissioned by the federal government and created at the University of Pennsylvania. The development of the first commercial computer in the United States, UNIVAC, was commissioned by the U.S. Census.

Although many advances in computer technology contributed to the birth of the modern Internet, it is helpful to think of a time line of four major events. The first of these is the 1969 initial connection of two nodes in ARPANET communicating through packet-switching technology. In 1972, the first e-mail was sent over the ARPANET network. In 1974, a common language allowing different networks to communicate, TCP/IP (Transmission Control Protocol/Internet Protocol), was released. In 1983, when the ARPANET adopted Internet Protocol (IP), the Internet was officially born. Each of these four major events was accomplished largely at the behest of the United States government.

The main institutional player in the development of the Internet was the Advanced Research Projects Agency, or ARPA. A division of the Department of Defense, ARPA was established in 1958 during the Eisenhower administration in response to the Russian launch of Sputnik. ARPA was given significant discretion to fulfill a broad mission to conduct scientific research. One project that intrigued ARPA was networking computers. Money was dedicated for an ARPANET that would link the Defense Department to the institutions with which it did business. The description by ARPA research head, Bob Taylor, of how the new ARPANET was started captures the agency's flexibility: "The decision to start the ARPANET was mine with very little or no red tape."[7]

One common myth is that ARPA sought to establish a network that could maintain communication under a nuclear attack. As in many myths, there is an element of truth. The possibility of withstanding nuclear attack, however, was only one of the ideas entertained by those active in the network's design. Of the projects commissioned on networking, only a project by the research institute RAND explicitly pursued the goal of nuclear resistance.[8]

The perseverance of the nuclear myth is no doubt partly a product of how it appears to be a plausible motivation for the crucial Internet innovation of packet switching. Packet switching is a key innovation that lies at the heart of how data are communicated over the Internet. Since packet switching involves breaking down information into small packets and using redundant channels, a nice story about nuclear war resistance can be devised. Packet switching certainly reduces the risk that communication will be interrupted because one part of a communication line is down. The advances of packet switching, however, occur whether that line is down for nuclear war or for the more pedestrian reasons on the minds of the researchers who developed packet switching. The circuit might already be in use. There might be a mechanical problem along the way.

Packet switching is just a more effective way to send data. With the previous circuit model, one uninterrupted connection between the origin and destination must be maintained. Unlike the telephone circuit, which must be continuously re-served for the end users, packet switching requires a connection only long enough to send the small packet of data. Later packets may take different paths. They take the fastest available path to the destination. Packets arriving out of sequence are reassembled at the destination. ARPA was able to incorporate packet-switching technology into the innovative ARPANET.

With the development of packet switching as a way to transmit data, it was time to construct a network. The center of the network was ARPANET in the Department of Defense. The goal of the project was to develop an open architecture by which computers in the network could retain individual-level attributes but be linked with macro-level protocol. In establishing a workable protocol, the government took bids and ultimately contracted with Bolt, Beranek & Newman (BBN). Anticipating the request for a proposal from the Defense Department, BBN had been working on the matter before the federal contract was issued. This helped BBN to produce an operational router for the network on schedule. Written by Bob Kahn, the specification of how the computers would communicate was released in April 1969. The next step was installation.

In October 1969, the landmark first connection of two nodes on the ARPANET was made. The first two nodes were located at UCLA and Stanford. The role of both universities was fostered by federal research funds. With the connection made, files from one university could be retrieved from the other. The ARPANET was born.

The first message transmitted over the network that would become the Internet was "lo." The message lacked the drama of "What hath God wrought" or the urgency of "Come here, Dr. Watson, I need you." There is, however, a certain poetry in "lo." Historically used to attract attention, the word *lo* represents an ironic start for an event that attracted little fanfare at the time. Further, "lo" was not the intended message. The computer crashed before the intended phrase was transmitted. It took a second attempt to finish: "login." "Login," too, is an appropriate start since the Internet is not the end itself but allows one to log in to a vast array of resources.[9]

The next landmark in Internet history was the sending of the first e-mail over a network in 1972. Under contract from the federal government, BBN set about to devise a program to send e-mail over a network. The primary developer of the first e-mail was Ray Tomlinson. One of his earliest decisions was the choice to use the "at" (@) sign for showing where a person was located on the network. As an interactive medium, the usefulness of e-mail depends on how many other people have e-mail. The first person pioneering e-mail would not be expected to have much use for it. It would be very lonely. Tomlinson's first e-mail message was to himself: "Testing 1–2–3."[10]

The success of ARPANET was followed by the creation of a number of separately functioning networks. These networks were all self-contained. They utilized computer networking capability built up over time. Many of these networks were entirely within the private sector. The problem was that the networks couldn't talk to each other. Before all these networks could combine into one Internet, there must be a way, or protocol, for networks to interact. Thus, work began on writing a protocol to allow different networks to communicate. At ARPA, the effort to find such a protocol fell under an "Internetting" program.[11]

By 1974, the goal was attained with the release of the Transmission Control Protocol/Internet Protocol (TCP/IP), which allowed the different networks to communicate with each other. It was co-written by Robert Kahn and Vinton Cerf, whose work has earned them the title "Inventors of the Internet." Their development of Internet Protocol was created largely at the behest of the United States government. Robert Kahn was the head of ARPANET at the time. He was working with Stanford Professor Vinton Cerf, who had experience with Defense Department systems and would later join Kahn at ARPA. Under government contract, a number of researchers set about to implement the new protocol. It took a while for the protocol to be adopted. Until the various networks used Internet Protocol, there was technically no Internet.

The birth of the modern Internet occurred with the 1983 adoption of TCP/IP by the ARPANET. It was a fairly dramatic transition from one protocol to another, planned well in advance. On January 1, 1983, the network hosts had to switch to TCP/IP or be left scrambling to find other ways to connect. Although it resulted in some people wearing "I survived the TCP/IP transition" buttons, the basic backbone of the growing network was now using TCP/IP. The Internet was born. In 1985, the NSFNET (National Science Foundation network) required use of TCP/IP. Other major segments of the network soon adopted TCP/IP.

Throughout development of the Internet, the federal government played a prominent role in facilitating Internet research. This role prompted Internet co-inventors Bob Kahn and Vinton Cerf to characterize the U.S. government as "a real hero" in the story of Internet development.[12] Although government-facilitated, this research was certainly not a top-down directive. Government provided the home for the initial backbone of the network as well as sponsored direct research on networking. It also helped fund projects of those working in academic settings. Government contracted with the private sector for key projects. The private sector, meanwhile, had been making huge advances in the development of personal computers. The ability to network these PCs was facilitated by the development of Ethernet networking technology at the Xerox Palo Alto Research Center (PARC). At heart this was a bottom-up project benefiting from independent contributions from many in the research community who were loosely connected. The federal government played a critical role in providing an institutional base and incentives for many of these contributions.

After 1983, the preeminent role of the government in Internet research was drawing to a close. It would continue significant funding and backbone provision for another decade. The Al Gore–sponsored 1991 High Computing Act, for example, dedicated funds to bringing agency supercomputers together. Yet, government was slowly turning over more responsibility to other institutions. A key event in the shift was a 1985 conference at which ARPA shared much of its research with private vendors.

In 1985, however, the incentives for private applications were somewhat limited. This was the year in which the National Science Foundation (NSF) replaced the Defense Department as the part of the federal government responsible for the major Internet backbone. The conversion to the NSFNET backbone was accompanied by significant speed and capacity increases. The NSFNET ushered in an era of Internet growth, although the main backbone remained limited to research and educational purposes. The NSF policy was formulated in its Acceptable Use Policy (AUP). As codified, the general principle of the AUP was clear: "NSFNET Backbone services are provided to support open research in and among U.S. research and instructional institutions, plus research arms of for-profit firms when engaged in open scholarly communication and research. Use for other purposes is not acceptable."[13] This policy applied to traffic over the main NSFNET backbone. Despite the flourishing of private networks outside the main backbone, there was concern that the AUP was slowing growth of the Internet.

A key stage in government withdrawal was to allow commercial traffic on the main backbone of the Internet. Beginning in1988, the NSF began to experiment with ways of increasing commercial traffic on the Internet. Congress, for its part, sought to enhance the NSF efforts. In June 1992, Representative Rick Boucher (D-VA) introduced a bill (HR5344) to amend the National Science Foundation Act to relax the AUP to allow commercial traffic. Although the bill passed the House, it was never taken up in the Senate. Following his initial failure, Boucher continued trying to allow commercial use of the Internet. His proposal was ultimately incorporated nearly word for word into a NASA authorization bill. Unlike Boucher's original bill, the NASA authorization bill passed both chambers and became Public Law 102–588. The law framed commercial use in terms of the original mission:

The [National Science] Foundation is authorized to foster and support access by the research and education communities to computer networks which may be used substantially for purposes in addition to research and education in the sciences and engineering, if the additional uses will tend to increase the overall capabilities of the networks to support such research and education activities.

Ironically, congressional debate on the legislation that changed a key Internet policy included a discussion of the government's role in searching for alien lifeforms, but did not mention the Internet. It was, after all, attached to a NASA authorization bill. The NASA bill was a consensus bill that became law with no formal votes. It was called up by unanimous consent and passed by voice votes in both the House and Senate. The paragraph on the Internet was not brought up in the floor debate. The primary objection voiced against the bill was that it did not eliminate the approximately $13 million NASA was authorized to spend for its Search for Extraterrestrial Intelligence program. Senator Richard Bryan (D-NV) lamented in the floor debate on October 7, 1992, that NASA "will begin surveying the skies for signs of extraterrestrials next Monday."[14] As a postscript, extraterrestrials have not been located, and Congress canceled the program when Senator Bryan got a last-minute amendment added to a bill in September 1993.

Within a couple years, the federal government privatized the network backbone. Following the 1992 law, the NSF changed its policies consistent with the legislation to ease the Acceptable Use Policy. With commercial traffic increasing, the U.S. government passed the National Information Infrastructure Act of 1993, paving the way for privatization. In 1995 the NSFNET formally dissolved. The backbone of supercomputers channeling Internet traffic on the NSFNET was replaced by network access points operated by telecommunications companies.

By the time the World Wide Web arrived, the private sector was responsible for nearly all innovation. The network had largely been built. With the infrastructure in place, the Internet was ready to take off once it became more accessible to the average person. People were certainly using e-mail, but e-mail alone wasn't propelling the Internet into the lives of high percentages of Americans. What ultimately caused the Internet to rapidly grow into a majority medium was the development of the Web. Although there are many developments making the Web possible, there are two landmark events in its history: the invention of the Web in 1991 and the creation of a browser providing a graphical interface to the Web in 1993.

The most significant development in the formation of the Web was the use of hypertext to link documents on different computer networks. The Web was invented by Tim Berners-Lee in 1991. He developed the idea over the course of a decade while consulting for CERN, a physics lab in Geneva, Switzerland. In 1993, CERN moved the Web into the public domain by graciously relinquishing any claim that it might have had. The project had not been a high priority at CERN, where it originated as an organizational telephone directory. More surprisingly, the Web was not immediately hailed in the hypertext community. The use of hypertext, or using words to link files, had existed for some time as a way to call up related files on one computer or within one computer database. Annual conferences were held to discuss advances in hypertext. For the "Hypertext '91 Conference," Tim Berners-Lee submitted a paper outlining the Web's use of hypertext in a network context. His paper was initially rejected, in part because it "didn't make enough references to work in the field."[15] Berners-Lee had indeed come up with something new. Berners-Lee describes in his own words what was new about the World Wide Web:

> What was really new with the Web was the idea that you could code all the information needed to find any document on the network into a short string of characters. These strings, originally called universal document identifiers, are now known as universal resource locators, or URLs. The notion that all these tagged documents from computers all over the world could share a common naming and addressing "space" was what made hypertext links so much more powerful.[16]

The critical development in popularizing the Web was the invention of a browser, which reduced the technical competence required to interface with the material at a particular address. The most prominent figure in the development of a popular browser was Marc Andreessen. In 1992, he was earning $6.85 an hour working part-time at a campus supercomputing facility while an undergraduate at the University of Illinois. Andreessen had become interested in the Internet and the newly invented World Wide Web. Bored by his part-time work, Marc on his own initiative decided to see if he and a friend could add a visual element to the Web. Surviving on "Marc's cookies and milk" and his partner Eric Bina's "Skittles and Mountain Dew," the two worked virtually nonstop for months to ultimately release the Mosaic browser in 1993.[17] It represented a huge improvement over primitive browsers by allowing images and easier navigation. Later, Andreessen teamed with Jim Clark to form Mosaic Communications to create a better browser. In October 1994, the Netscape browser was released. Its user-friendly interface had instant results for the popularity of the Web.

A high-caffeine university setting is also widely credited with providing the first live image on the Web in 1993. The image was a coffee pot in a computer lab at Cambridge University. Frustrated with a long walk to discover an empty coffee pot, Scientist Quentin Stafford-Fraser focused a camera on the pot to be able to monitor it from afar. The device came to attract an audience beyond its original purpose. In its eight years in operation, the site was estimated to have attracted over two million visitors.[18]

In addition to improved images, Web users also benefited from the development of comprehensive search engines. A search engine is a tool that generates a list of websites containing selected keywords. The first major search engine "Yahoo!" went online in 1994. It was created in a Stanford University trailer by two graduate students in electrical engineering, David Filo and Jerry Yang. The name was an acronym combining the conventional "Yet Another" software moniker with "Hierarchical Officious Oracle." Assigning traditional subject headings to websites, Yahoo! required a substantial amount of personnel to keep up with the burgeoning number of sites. Later search engines emphasized computer algorithms that comprehensively searched the Web for requested terms.

While the browser made things easier for the user, significant advancements were also made by information providers, or servers. The increasing use of graphics made websites more and more accessible. The widespread use of Java-based programs allowed for moving images and eye-catching features. Programs were developed to minimize the need to write in HyperText Markup Language (HTML). Auxiliary progress in computer technology in graphics, sound, and images led to an explosion in what a website could provide.

While the government was withdrawing from Internet development and the private sector presided over a period of rapid innovation, the government began to take on its more traditional role as overseer of the new medium. Regulators would find this a difficult medium to regulate because of its decentralized and international nature. Later chapters in this book will consider Internet regulation in substantial detail.

CONCLUSION

Looking broadly at the Internet as a medium, the Internet is a combination of the capabilities of earlier media. As such its development owes a lot to previous innovations. Painstaking effort and risk taking by innovators of the telegraph, telephone, videophone, printing press, radio, and television had—one step at a time—conquered barriers to personal and mass communication of text, audio, and video. Bringing together these capabilities into one medium was a large undertaking in which the private and public sectors each played a significant role. It was an undertaking that was critically dependent on advances in computer technology. Born in the Department of Defense and a select few research universities, a network of computers sharing textual data emerged. Within a couple decades, the capabilities of this small network expanded to the extent that the Internet became a personal and mass medium capable of communicating text, audio, and video.

P A R T   O N E

POLITICS OF INTERNET ACCESS

2

User Base of the Internet

Virtually unknown in 1993, the Internet is now a fundamental means of communication in modern America. The majority of Americans are online. They go online from home, work, school, the library, and other locations. Yet, there are other Americans who are not online. Assessing the nature and size of these populations is a critical first step in understanding the impact of the Internet. Who is going online?

This question is best answered by placing current use in historical context. This chapter traces Internet diffusion from relative anonymity to its current existence as a majority medium. To ensure a consistent statistical portrait, the data are drawn primarily from two highly respected sources. The first data source is Pew Research, including both the Pew Internet & American Life Project and the Pew Research Center for the People and the Press. The second source is census data from the Department of Commerce. The data from these sources reveal that the diffusion pattern of the Internet is similar to that for previous media.

ERAS OF INTERNET USE

Internet use falls into distinct eras. In the first era, the Internet was an exclusive medium used by less than 10 percent of the population. In the second era, it was a significant minority medium used by more than 10 percent of the population but less than half of the population. Currently, the Internet is in a third era of being a majority medium used by over half the population but not everybody. The overall diffusion of the Internet is shown in table 2.1. Potentially, the Internet may reach a fourth era—a universal medium in which use approaches 100 percent.

Table 2.1   Diffusion of the Internet

Year	Percentage of Americans Using the Internet
1993	3
1994	8
1995	14
1996	23
1997	36
1998	41
1999	49
2000	55
2001	62
2002	66
2003	67

Source: Pew Surveys.
Notes: Q: "Do you ever go online to access the Internet or World Wide Web or to send and receive email?" Table uses the available data closest to July of the given year. Data for 1993 and 1994 are derived from when people in July 1996 started going online.

The first era of Internet use is the Exclusive Era from 1983 to 1994. It began with the Internet being used in select technical populations but unknown to the larger population. In the Exclusive Era, the Internet grew from a medium used by 0 percent of the population to one that had reached a 10 percent threshold, from which it was ready for a rapid takeoff in the larger population. The number of users remained at less than one percent for much of the period. A prolonged period of slow growth began to accelerate by 1990, reaching approximately 3 percent of the population by early 1993. Internet use had grown to approximately 8 percent by early 1994 and was on the threshold of 10 percent by the end of 1994.[1]

The Exclusive Era of the Internet began in 1983. Of course, the origin for Internet diffusion is debatable. An argument could be made for a date as early as the 1969 expansion of the ARPANET beyond the Defense Department to a university setting. Others may select the 1972 sending of the first e-mail or the 1974 creation of Internet Protocol (IP). The year 1983, however, seems the most appropriate date because that was when the ARPANET adopted IP. This adoption marked the birth of the modern Internet and, therefore, approximates the notion of invention. It should be acknowledged that this starting point gives the Internet a head start of sorts. By 1983, there was already a significant infrastructure in government and educational environments.

The slow growth of the Exclusive Era can be seen in how the Internet was introduced to the broader population in 1988. Online service providers moved in stages. The behavior of Prodigy is illustrative. Prodigy was formed as TRINTEX by IBM, Sears, and CBS in 1984. By 1988, it had been renamed Prodigy and began introducing a new online service. The initial product was focused on high-tech California cities, but over a two-year period it was expanded into large cities throughout the United States. By 1990, Prodigy was nationwide.

Throughout the Exclusive Era, Internet technology was difficult for many people to use. It was a text-based medium requiring complex commands for accessing resources. Thus, the Exclusive Era continued as the World Wide Web was made public in 1991, and online service providers moved from closed online communities to ones that provided gateways to the Internet by 1993. Even with these advances, effective use of the Internet required a knowledge of computers that most people didn't have. By the late stages of the Exclusive Era, the text-based nature of the Internet had changed. In 1993, the Mosaic browser introduced a graphical interface to the Internet. By October 1994, an improved Netscape browser was released. The experience of the Internet would now be a visual one less reliant on text-based material. The Internet was ready to enter a second era of use.

Around the start of 1995, the Internet began an era as a significant minority medium. The Significant Minority Era was a period of rapid growth. While it took twelve years for the Internet to reach 10 percent, it took about five years to move from 10 percent to 50 percent. In one year, growth exceeded 60 percent as Internet use went from 14 percent in June 1995 to 23 percent in July 1996. Double-digit growth rates continued throughout the Significant Minority Era.

By the beginning of 2000, the Internet crossed the 50 percent threshold to become a majority medium. The beginning of the Majority Medium Era brought a significant reduction in growth rates. The basis for slowed growth was demonstrated early in the era by a Pew poll of those who had never used the Internet. Asked if they would "like to start using the Internet and e-mail," only 16 percent replied "Yes."[2] Although slowed, growth does continue in the Majority Medium Era. About two-thirds of Americans are now Internet users.

Throughout all eras of Internet use, there have been a variety of places to use the Internet. People can use the Internet from home, work, school, library, and other locations. Looking only at the population of Internet users, there is an 80 percent chance of home use, 36 percent chance of work use, 22 percent chance of school use, and 10 percent chance of library use.[3] The dominance of home use is a long-standing phenomenon. Over time, however, an increasing number of people have been using the Internet both at home and outside the home. In 1998, 16 percent of Americans used the Internet only from home, 11 percent only outside the home, and 7 percent both at home and outside the home. Over the next three years, almost all the growth was among multiple-location users. During 2001, 19 percent used the Internet only from home, 10 percent only outside the home, and 25 percent from both.[4]

ACCESS TO THE INTERNET

While the first section of this chapter considered Internet use, this section will look at the subtly different measure of Internet access. In conversation, *access* and *use* are often used interchangeably. Yet there are important distinctions. Use is a measure of behavior. It measures whether an individual goes online. Access, on the other hand, is a measure of ongoing status. It measures whether an individual has the capacity to go online. Specifically, Internet access refers to the condition in which an individual has a computer readily available for use with the necessary permissions to initiate a connection to the Internet.

In the home and workplace, access and use are closely related and do not require independent consideration. A household that has access to the Internet is unlikely to go to the trouble and expense if there is no intention to use it. Similarly, an employer is unlikely to provide Internet access to an employee if it is not somehow useful to job performance. Thus, the interchangeable use of the terms *access* and *use* would be justified if the Internet existed only in the home and workplace.

The importance of the distinction between access and use, however, becomes apparent in the context of public places. There is a huge gap between the many people who have access in public places and the few who actually use it in public places. Since use is low, it might be tempting to ignore the Internet in public places. This would be a mistake on two levels. First, use in public places, although comparatively low, does represent a significant number of people. Second, access itself is important. Access is a condition of being able to use the Internet. There is no reason to require that this condition be met in the home.

Nearly all Americans have Internet access in at least one public facility. Indeed, by 2000 access in public libraries was approaching universality, although only 2 percent of Americans used the Internet in public libraries.[5] The move to universality was rapid in both schools and libraries. From 1994 to 2000, the number of public schools having public access grew from 35 percent to 98 percent.[6] The number of public libraries providing access also grew rapidly. In fact, there are significant parallels between the number of schools and libraries connected to the Internet at various points in time. In 1998, for instance, 89 percent of public schools had Internet access compared to 84 percent of public libraries.[7] Well on the way to universality in 1998, a library connection to the Internet was actually slightly more likely in a library serving high-poverty populations than in the average library.[8]

DIGITAL DIVIDE

Having documented aggregate Internet use, it is important to consider how use varies within the population. The aggregate numbers mask a lot of diversity. Internet use and access are not distributed randomly. Every person does not have an equal likelihood of being an Internet user. Depending on the characteristics of an individual, Internet use is statistically more or less likely.

The term *digital divide* is used to represent the systematic differences between those who have access and use of digital technologies and those who do not. Each component of the definition suggests the breadth of the term. The notion of systematic differences is broad. There are many reasons why differences might emerge. The differences include some of the most common ways of distinguishing the population. Attention has primarily been focused on whether there is a digital divide based on socioeconomic status, age, race, location, or gender. The term also refers to a broad conception of digital technologies, including any new innovations associated with the Internet. Finally, *digital divide* places no limits on location. It includes home, work, and public facility Internet access and use.

A digital divide has been a persistent, if declining, feature of American Internet life. As its name implies, the Exclusive Era passed quietly with a pronounced digital divide. During the Significant Minority Era, the existence of a digital divide became a high-profile subject among journalists, pollsters, and scholars. In 1997, the federal government incorporated the term *digital divide* into the title of its regularly updated census data on technology and distributed these reports on the website www.digitaldivide.gov. As the Significant Minority Era progressed, growth rates were tremendous—especially among groups starting with a low base and much room to grow. Thus, as early as 1998, some prominent scholars released a study of Internet use under the title "Web Users are Looking More Like America."[9] The growth across all groups prompted the Department of Commerce to invoke an image of a potentially universal medium in its October 2000 report: "I am pleased that the data in this report show that, overall, our nation is moving toward full digital inclusion."[10] By February 2002, the Department of Commerce eliminated the term *digital divide* from its report on Internet diffusion. The new report was called "A Nation Online" and noted that "all segments of our Nation are included in this ongoing information revolution."[11] Yet, the nation was only moving toward the goal of full digital inclusion. Well into the Majority Medium Era, the nation continues to move toward this goal.

A compelling portrait of the digital divide is provided by U.S. Census data. Table 2.2 compares the user base of the Internet at important stages in two eras. In 1997 the Significant Minority Era was well under way, with Internet use having just exceeded 20 percent. By September 2001, Internet use had reached a preliminary stabilization point in the Majority Medium Era. This noteworthy stabilization point is confirmed by Pew Research data revealing no increase in Internet use from April 2001 to April 2002.[12] In both eras, it is clear that not all Americans have been equally likely to be Internet users.

A consideration of the components of the digital divide necessarily begins with socioeconomic status. The reasons for hypothesizing a relationship between socioeconomic status and Internet use are clear. The Internet costs money and requires technical knowledge. Thus, the better educated and more affluent seem most likely to access and use the Internet.

As expected, the wealthy and well-educated have better access to Internet technology. The Department of Commerce data in table 2.2 demonstrate this clearly. College graduates use the Internet at double the rate of those who have not continued their education beyond high school graduation. With every increase in income level, Internet use is more likely. The independent effect of both income and education is confirmed by multivariate analysis.[13]

Table 2.2   Trends in Percent Online by Socioeconomic Characteristics

	1997	2001
All Americans	22	54
Gender:		
Male	24	54
Female	20	54
Ethnicity:		
White	25	60
Black	13	40
Hispanic	11	32
Asian	26	60
Annual Household Income:		
< $15,000	9	25
$15,000–$24,999	12	33
$25,000–$34,999	17	44
$35,000–$49,999	23	57
$50,000–$74,999	32	67
$75,000 +	45	79
Last Year of Education:		
< High School Graduate	2	13
High School Graduate	10	40
Some College	25	62
College Graduate (B.A.)	41	81
Graduate School	52	84
Age:		
9–17	33	69
18–29	30	65
30–49	27	64
50–64	18	51
65–79	4	22
80 +	1	8

Source: U.S. Census Bureau, "CPS Computer and Internet Use Supplement," Data Sets; Department of Commerce, A Nation Online (2002).

Historically, Internet use has been strongly associated with both income and education. In 1997, those with a college degree were twelve times more likely than those without a high school degree to have household Internet access. Similarly, those making over $75,000 were almost ten times more likely than those making under $15,000 to have household access in 1997. The ratio of the top to the bottom categories has declined steadily. Yet at the end of the Significant Minority Era, the ratio of the top category to bottom category was still six to one.

Much of the bias associated with income and education can be understood in light of an individual's orientation to a personal computer. Since use of a com-

puter is necessary to gain Internet access, it is not surprising that biases in computer use will be reflected in Internet use. Higher levels of education make people more comfortable with basic computer functions, whether that be setting up
a machine or interfacing with an existing connection. Higher levels of income
make it easier to afford a high-quality computer. The long-standing relationship
between computer ownership and socioeconomic status is depicted in table 2.3.

The digital divide for use based on education and income is less than the digital divide for household access. This is a long-standing finding. As an example,
during the Significant Minority Era in 1998, use and household access at high income levels were almost identical. On the other hand, at low levels of income, use
nearly doubled household access. Thus, a 60 percent to 7 percent advantage for
the over $75,000 income cohort compared to the under $15,000 cohort in household access was only 59 percent to 14 percent in use.[14]

The reason for the gap is greater use in public places by people of lower income
and education. In other words, there is a reverse bias of income and education on
Internet use in public places. The intuition is clear. Those with home or work access seem unlikely to forgo the convenience of home or work access to use the Internet in public places. There is strong empirical support for this intuition. In its first
rigorous study of location of use conducted in 1998, the Census Bureau found less
affluent and less educated Americans to be the most likely to use the Internet in public places. Persons in households making under $15,000 were over three times more
likely to use the Internet at a public library than those making over $75,000.[15] Sim-
ilarly, those who did not complete high school were 285 percent and 60 percent
more likely to use the Internet at a public library than college graduates and high
school graduates, respectively. The unemployed were more likely than the average

Table 2.3   Trends in Profile of Computer Owners

	1984	*1989*	*1994*	*1998*	*2001*
Education:					
Elementary	1	2	3	8	16
Some High School	2	5	6	16	28
High School Graduate	6	9	15	31	47
Some College	11	18	29	49	65
College Graduate	16	31	48	69	80
Income:					
< $10,000	2	5	7	14	22
$10,000–$19,999	4	6	10	18	28
$20,000–$34,999	10	13	18	32	46
$35,000–$49,999	17	23	33	50	64
$50,000–$74,999	22	32	46	66	78
$75,000 +	22	44	61	80	89

Source: U.S. Census Bureau, "CPS Computer and Internet Use Supplement," Data Sets; Department of
Commerce, *Falling through the Net* (1999).

American to use the Internet in a public library. Later studies confirmed the initial finding. Three years later, those making under $15,000 continued to use the Internet at public libraries at approximately three times the rate of those making over $75,000.[16]

Another important component of the digital divide is age. The Internet is a medium that has a strong foundation in work and school environments. Internet skills are often learned at school or work. Less likely to be in these environments, retired individuals will have to take a greater initiative to become familiar with the Internet than those who have it integrated into their school or work life. Having lived many years in a world without the Internet, the elderly can remember a world without the Internet and are less likely to perceive it as one of life's essentials. In addition, age-related problems such as declining eyesight and arthritis offer challenges to actions such as viewing a monitor or manipulating a mouse that others may take for granted.

It is, therefore, not surprising to find a significant divide between the young and the elderly. Internet use declines with every advancing age group. The most likely users of the Internet are those between the ages of 9 and 17.[17] The decline is, however, fairly slow until 65 years of age. Those over the age of 65 are by far the least likely to use the Internet. The number of those older than 80 online is well below 10 percent. Reflecting on the lack of seniors online, a prominent survey of online activity by seniors was subtitled "A Fervent Few."[18] Senior citizens are three times less likely than 18- to 29-year-olds to go online. Although the digital divide based on age remains large, there are strong signs of greater use by seniors in the future. The fact that use of the Internet by 50- to 64-year-olds is only slightly below the overall rate of use by the average American has prompted the Pew Internet & American Life Project to predict a "silver tsunami" of increasing use by seniors as the current 50- to 64-year-olds retire.[19]

The significant age gap is long-standing. It appears to be changing more slowly than other aspects of the digital divide. In June 1995, a Pew study found 1 percent of those over 65 years of age to have Internet access, while 9 percent of those between 18 and 30 were online.[20] Five years later in 2000, Pew found only 13 percent of those over 65 years old to have Internet access, while 65 percent of those between 18 and 30 years of age were online. The data revealed that 65 years was the key dividing line. With 41 percent access, the 50–64 age bracket was closer to the 18–30 age bracket than the over-65 group.[21]

Another component of the digital divide is disability. Those with disabilities are less likely to be Internet users. This has been a consistent finding since the first large-scale study on the Internet and disabilities conducted by the Census Bureau in 1999. It found that those with disabilities were about half as likely to have Internet access as those without disabilities. The extent of the divide varied by type of disability. Especially low use was found among those with visual and walking disabilities. Their Internet access rate of 16 percent trailed the overall access rate of 22 percent for the disabled.[22]

One bias in the user base of the Internet that received significant early attention was gender. Early studies showed that men used the Internet significantly more often than women. In late 1994, men outnumbered women online by about four to one.[23] In June 1995, men were still more than twice as likely to be online than women.[24]

The digital divide between genders, however, had disappeared for all practical purposes by 1998. It was a rapid decline. By mid-1996 men represented only 58 percent of Internet users.[25] By early 1998, Bruce Bimber found no independent effect of gender on Internet access and the Internet population split evenly between men and women.[26] Other studies briefly showed a small residual gap. The U.S. Census Bureau, for example, not controlling for other factors, found a 3 percent gender gap in 1998.[27] By August 2000, the Census Bureau showed an unadjusted gender gap of less than one-half percent.[28] A milestone was officially reached a few months later when women surpassed men on the Internet. After becoming new users at three times the rate of men in 2001, women constituted 52 percent of all Internet users.[29] The combination of the female majority and faster growth rates suggested for the first time the real possibility of a gender gap favoring women in the not-too-distant future.

The digital divide based on race is essentially a manifestation of socioeconomic status. Indeed, there is no theoretical reason to believe that race on its own would affect Internet use and access. Racial groups, however, do differ in Internet use. Whites regularly show higher rates of Internet use than blacks. These differences, however, largely disappear when controlling for differences in income and education. This was apparent early in the diffusion of the Internet. A 1997 survey arrived at the conclusion that "the Web population now reflects a racial breakdown statistically indistinguishable from Census data for the general population."[30] In 1998, Bruce Bimber found race to have no independent effect on Internet access.[31] Although not offering a theoretical reason for an independent effect of race, a few studies have found a residual gap by race even after controlling for other factors.[32]

One potential basis for a digital divide that draws much attention but is basically nonexistent is political affiliation. Theoretical support and evidence are both lacking. There seems to be no plausible theory to suggest that the Internet inherently favors communication by identifiers of a particular political party. There is also no empirical evidence to support a partisan bias. Typically, where a small party advantage exists, it disappears when other factors are held constant.[33]

If there is support for a political orientation among Internet users, it would be marginally higher support for freedom of expression. Although now minimal, a libertarianism of expression was prominent in the early days of the Internet. A 1995 Times Mirror study, for instance, showed that only 24 percent of online users agreed that "books that contain dangerous ideas should be banned from school libraries" compared to 45 percent of nonusers.[34] In 1996, Libertarian candidate Harry Browne reportedly defeated Bill Clinton and Bob Dole in a majority of Internet straw polls in the presidential campaign.[35] There is some evidence that this libertarianism of expression may have been tied to a broader liberalism. If, however, adherents to any political philosophy had hopes of holding an advantage on the Internet, they were quickly dashed. By 1995, Al Gore was invoking a historical comparison to lament the lack of an identifiable political orientation on the Internet: "If you could have transplanted this technology back into the 1960s, you would have seen activists on the left dominating it."[36]

Another potential source of a digital divide is location. Related to socioeconomic status, differences based on location do exist. Rural areas trail urban areas, although the difference has declined substantially. While there was a 4.6 percent gap between urban and rural Internet use in 1997, the gap had dropped to 1.3 percent in 2000.[37] Variations by state have been a long-standing feature of Internet diffusion. During 1998 in the middle of the Significant Minority Era, Internet use varied from 44 percent in Alaska to 14 percent in Mississippi.[38] By late 2001, the Census Bureau found every state to have over 40 percent Internet use and all but nine over 50 percent. The same survey showed that Alaska's 69 percent use made it the first state to exceed two-thirds online.[39]

OVERALL USE OF THE INTERNET

The way in which Internet use has spread from an exclusive group to the broader population is consistent with the diffusion of other media and innovations generally. As demonstrated by scholars working in a variety of disciplines, innovation diffusion follows a pattern.[40] In the early stage, the innovation is concentrated within an exclusive population. Due to the initial expense of the innovation and general risk aversion, the innovation may remain in this exclusive stage for some time. At some point a successful innovation will drop in price, pass a threshold of exclusivity, and enter a stage of rapid adoption. As the innovation becomes widespread, the growth rate necessarily slows and will ultimately reach a saturation point at which no more growth occurs.

The general pattern is often characterized as an S-curve of diffusion plotted over time. As plotted, the y-axis represents the percentage of users who have adopted the innovation and the x-axis represents time. The tails of the letter *s* represent the slow growth in the early and late stages, and the center of the *s* represents the rapid rise in adoption after the initial threshold is reached and before the adoption nears saturation. In reporting on Internet use, the Department of Commerce has adopted this terminology: "The pattern exhibited thus far by household access to both computers and the Internet accords with the S-curve pattern typically observed in the adoption of new technologies."[41]

As shown in figure 2.1, the eras of Internet use can be seen as segments of the S-curve. The Exclusive Era represents the tail of the letter *s,* in which growth is slow and the user base remains small. Using the 10 percent threshold as the takeoff point, the Significant Minority Era is characterized by tremendous growth. Shortly

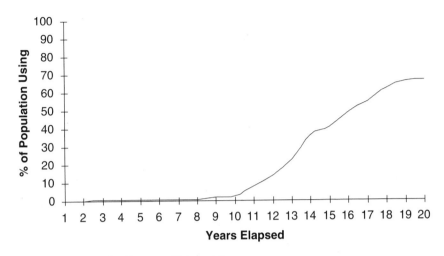

Figure 2.1: Diffusion Pattern of Internet Use
Note: Origin is 1983; adapted from Pew Research with missing data estimated.

after the Internet becomes a majority medium, the growth rate slows considerably, in part by the mathematical imperative of less room to grow. Based on existing data, the slow growth stage of the second tail of the *s* will be an extended one.

The diffusion pattern of the Internet is consistent with previous mass media. The telegraph, telephone, videophone, printing press, radio, and television all started out primarily with higher socioeconomic users. In each case, improved technology gradually reduced price and increased availability. A new technology tends to move from the more affluent to the less affluent. A technological divide, therefore, is not a new phenomenon. It has existed with all technologies. It would have been possible, for instance, to speak of a wired divide for the telegraph in the sense that the wealthy were better able to afford telegrams.

Of course, if a product fails it never spreads to lower socioeconomic users. This was clearly the case with the videophone in the 1960s. Use of the videophone never extended beyond a small base of affluent users who could afford the product. The wealthy get the new product first, but the poor don't get stuck with the high-priced clunkers. If a new product has potential, the poor also benefit from wealthy individuals buying the primitive design. These early purchases provide important revenue to a company that can be invested in improving the product. These improvements can reduce price and eventually widen distribution of the product.

No high-priced clunker, the Internet has a respectable diffusion rate even if it hasn't set any records. The growth rate of television clearly exceeds that of the Internet. Television grew from 10 percent of households in 1950 to 50 percent in

1954 and surpassed 90 percent in 1963. Radio diffusion was slower than television, going from 10 percent in 1925 to 50 percent in 1931 to over 90 percent in 1947.[42] On the other hand, the telephone constitutes a classic example of a medium that diffused slowly. Telephones were in 10 percent of households by around 1902, did not reach 50 percent until 1946, and reached 90 percent in 1970.[43]

As it stands now, cable television may be the best comparison for the Internet. The two media have several practical similarities. Both represent enhancements of an existing medium. A television is required for cable, while a computer is required for the Internet. A television retains a significant function without cable in the same way that a person can get much out of a computer without the Internet. Both media are distributed primarily as subscriber services. The actual service is not a one-time purchase, but a repeated event. People can choose at any time to discontinue the service.

Cable diffusion represents a slower version of the S-curve than Internet diffusion. Beginning with the first subscription system in 1950, cable did not reach 10 percent of American households until 1972.[44] Although not as dramatic as the impact of the Web on the Internet, the 1975 satellite delivery of Home Box Office and subsequent relaxing of Federal Communications Commission (FCC) regulations ushered in a period of rapid growth for cable. In 1988, cable finally reached the 50 percent plateau.[45] A partial explanation for the slower diffusion of cable is that it required extensive wiring to be completed incrementally when an area appeared to support a profitable service. Internet diffusion, on the other hand, was facilitated by building on a nearly universal telephone infrastructure. This advantage of the Internet was partly offset by lower diffusion of the computer than the television.

The greatest insight of the cable model may be into a potential saturation point. The era of rapid growth for cable ended well before universality. In fact, cable had its last year of 5 percent annual growth during 1988–1989. Since that time, annual growth rates have been less than 5 percent, and at times growth appears to have stalled completely. Over the four-year period 1997–2000, the percentage of cable subscribers increased from 67.3 percent to 68 percent. The potential clearly exists for an absolute decline in use if more people disconnect cable rather than install it. Without a dramatic change, it can be argued that the market for cable television has saturated at around 70 percent.[46] Cable, then, stands as a modern-day example of incomplete diffusion. The Internet, too, may find its diffusion stalling well before 100 percent. In both cases, the impetus for nonuniversal diffusion is only partly related to the price of the product. Many people believe that these media do not measurably improve their lives and may, in fact, introduce influences that detract from life. By 2000, the Pew Internet & American Life Project found that a majority of nonusers had no plans to go online. The Pew survey showed that significantly more people agreed with the statement that the "Internet is a dangerous thing" than with the statement that "Internet access is too expensive."[47] Posing a slightly different question in 1998, the Census Bureau found that price was not the major reason households were not using the Internet. The most common reason for not having Internet access was "don't want it." It outnumbered "cost, too expensive" as a reason for not subscribing by a margin of 26 percent to 17 percent.[48]

NEW CYCLE

Internet diffusion is not a one-dimensional phenomenon. For any new Internet-related innovation, there is a diffusion pattern. The prevalence of any innovation can be measured over time. It will begin within an exclusive group. Some Internet-related innovations, such as RealAudio, will become widely diffused. Others will never take off. Internet technology doesn't stand still. At any point in time, many innovations exist; and each will have a diffusion pattern. New cycles of diffusion are always beginning. Consistent with other innovations, users having higher income and education levels will generally be in a better position to adopt them. A new divide will form between those using and not using the innovation.

A number of different innovations to an existing medium might be worthy of consideration as distinct phenomena. Continuing the cable comparison, the cable-related innovation of digital services certainly warrants independent consideration. The digital cable experience is substantially different than the basic cable experience. Digital cable requires additional equipment and offers a magnitude of choices far greater than basic cable. The diffusion of digital cable can be tracked as a separate phenomenon. It began an era as a significant minority medium at 10 percent in early 2001. This represented a more than 600 percent increase since being at less than 2 percent in 1998.[49]

The major Internet-related innovations relate to speed. Faster service means less waiting and more of the desired activity. The precise speed differential that justifies consideration as a distinct Internet experience is difficult to ascertain. Yet, it is clear that at some point in time a substantial difference in the Internet experience exists. There are a variety of possible distinctions. In the early years of Internet diffusion, pollsters asked the question in terms of modem speed. The world has changed since June 1995, when Pew found the population to be split about evenly between those with a modem of 9600 baud or slower and those with faster connections.[50]

The major speed-related innovation in the modern era is broadband access. The term *broadband* is used to refer to Internet service delivered through a means broader than conventional telephone service. It includes digital subscriber line (DSL) enhanced telephone service, cable, and some fast wireless services. The first major survey of broadband diffusion was conducted in August 2000 by the Department of Commerce. It showed broadband was an exclusive service present in only 4 percent of American households. This exclusive era was marked by a modest digital divide. Of Internet users, 10 percent of those under $5,000 annual income had broadband compared to just 14 percent of those over $75,000.[51] By

2001, broadband entered its own significant minority era. A year of rapid growth resulted in slightly over 10 percent of American households having broadband in 2001. A cable modem was the most common broadband vehicle, accounting for about 65 percent of all broadband service.[52]

CONCLUSION

There is nothing new about the primary contours of Internet diffusion. It is a pattern that parallels earlier technologies. The Internet existed in an exclusive era for some time. It took off and experienced a period of rapid growth that ultimately led to it becoming a majority medium. Its growth was not evenly distributed in the population. Some people, especially those of higher socioeconomic status, were better positioned to adopt the new technology. This is consistent with the adoption of innovations generally. It is a pattern that will be repeated with future Internet-related innovations.

3

Impact of Internet Use

When the Department of Commerce reported that the Internet had become
a majority medium, Jay Leno joked that half of Americans are online while
the other half have a live sexual partner.[1] Indeed, the presence of sex-related activities on the Internet has taken on mythic proportions. Many have contributed
to exaggerating the importance of sex as a component of life on the Internet. Although sex is certainly one dimension, it is a small part of Internet life. The big-
ger picture reveals a medium that is facilitating communication and increasing information.

While the previous chapter examined who is using the Internet, this chapter examines how they are using it. The major components of Internet use are identified. Political use is a small but significant part of online activity. Once activities
are outlined, the chapter explores the impact of Internet use on the lives of Americans. The analysis reveals that early concern about socially negative effects has
largely evaporated into an overall positive view of the impact of the Internet.
Lastly, the impact of the Internet on citizenship is contemplated.

MAJOR INTERNET ACTIVITIES

A consideration of impact begins with an understanding of what it is that people
are actually doing online. The best way to identify what online activities are most
prevalent is through surveys. A pioneer in Internet research, the Pew Internet &
American Life Project asks about the frequency and nature of online activity in
great detail. As shown in table 3.1, Pew surveys reveal that Americans undertake
a wide variety of activities on the Internet. Many of these are not daily activities,

31

Table 3.1   Percent of Internet Users Doing Various Online Activities

Online Activity	Ever	Yesterday
Send e-mail	93	49
Search for map or driving directions	79	4
Find information on hobby or interest	77	19
Get news	71	26
Check weather	69	17
Look for health or medical information	66	6
Surf the World Wide Web for fun	65	22
Buy a product	61	5
Visit a government site	56	10
Conduct education-related research	53	10
Buy or make travel reservations	53	1
Conduct job-related research	52	19
Look for information about a job	47	4
Send instant message	46	11
Check sports scores or information	44	12
Get financial information	42	10
Find political news or information	40	13
Play a game	37	7
Bank online	30	7
Share computer files	28	4
Find religious or spiritual information	28	4
Chat in chat room or online discussion	25	4
Participate in an online auction	22	4
Buy or sell stocks and bonds	12	1
Go to a dating website	10	2

Source: Pew Internet & American Life Project Surveys (August 2001–present), at pewinternet.org.
Notes: Q: "Please tell me if you ever do any of the following when you go online. Do you ever . . . "? Responses include "Yes, did this yesterday," and "Yes, have done this, but not yesterday."

as evidenced by the gap between those who have "ever" undertaken an activity and those who did it "yesterday."

Combining these data with other studies produces an overall hierarchy of online activities. Obviously there is some overlap and discretion in choosing specific categories. Nonetheless, it is helpful to think about a general ordering of online activities. The predominance of e-mail is long established. The second most common online activity is entertainment. Third, people participate in online commerce either as an employee or as a consumer. One must go down to fourth place to find political activity. In descending order, people online are next focused on health, education, and religion. One category that must be considered, although difficult to measure, is sex-related activity.

The perennial, most common online activity is sending and receiving e-mail. With the first network e-mail sent in 1972, this was one of the earliest applications of the Internet. To some extent, the growth of e-mail was slower than expected.

In 1981, the General Accounting Office predicted that e-mail would cause a two-thirds cut in the postal workforce by 2000.[2] While the predicted decline in regular mail has not materialized, e-mail has become a fundamental means of communication for most Americans. E-mail is used regularly for both personal and professional functions. Of those online, over 90 percent have used e-mail. Approximately half of the online population uses e-mail every single day.[3]

The second most common online activity is entertainment. The frequency of going online for entertainment is seen clearly in the popularity of game playing. Many are also entertained by going where their mind takes them on the World Wide Web: they surf for fun. The Web is a great place to learn about a variety of entertainment industries. In short, people go online for pleasure. The prominence of pleasure certainly is inconsistent with the original goal of the Internet to facilitate Defense Department business. It is also inconsistent with the emphasis on research in the Exclusive Era. The advent of the Web and its multimedia format paved the way for entertainment. As late as 1995, about one-third of the online population went online only for work purposes. By late 1996, the number of those using the Internet only for work had been cut by more than half to 14 percent.[4] The opportunities for entertainment continue to grow.

The third most common category of Internet activity is commerce. Interpreted broadly, commerce includes use of the Internet as part of a person's role in the economy as an employee or as a consumer. An increasing number of people are using the Internet as part of their job. In absolute numbers the period of fastest growth was between August 2000 and September 2001, when use of the Internet at work increased from 26 to 42 percent. As late as 1997, less than 18 percent of people had used the Internet at work. By 2001, Internet use in managerial and professional occupations exceeded two-thirds.[5]

In addition to use as an employee, people engage in online commerce as a consumer. One early high-profile activity was buying stocks. Taking advantage of lower commissions and seemingly ever-rising stock values, stock trading shifted quickly online. By 1998, online trades had passed the 50 percent threshold of all trades at broker Charles Schwab.[6] With the bursting of the stock bubble, the focus of online commerce turned to more traditional purchases. This effort was facilitated by major advances in secure credit card technology. These improvements laid the groundwork for an explosion in electronic commerce. By 2000, over half of Internet users had shopped online. Over 80 percent of online shoppers believe that it saves time.[7]

Government-related activity constitutes the fourth most common use of the Internet. Placed in the context of overall use, politics is certainly not the highest priority for most Internet users. Yet, the number of people who undertake some political activity is impressive. Clearly, the most common political use of the Internet is to obtain news about government-related matters. Since much general "news" is related to government, the increase in online news consumption translates directly into more political use. Besides news, people may interact directly with government through a website. A landmark was identified in 2000 when Pew Research found that over half of online users had visited a government website.[8] Less frequent, but still significant, people are involved in online advocacy.

The Internet is also used for health-related activity. There is a tremendous amount of health information online. People use the Internet to learn about new treatments and practices. Over 70 percent of health information seekers report that online information influenced how they treated an affliction. Convenience, anonymity, and the opportunity for additional information are each important reasons for over 80 percent of the people seeking health information online. While obtaining health information is common, interactive health uses are growing slowly. About 5 percent of Americans have communicated with health professionals by e-mail or bought health products online.[9]

The distinct category of health demonstrates that defining categories is imprecise and entails significant overlap. Government agencies are a frequent source of online health information. In fact, one study found that health information was what Americans wanted most from government websites.[10] Similarly, health and commerce overlap. Health products are an important component of online commerce. One well-publicized aspect of online health commerce is the purchase of prescription drugs from online sources outside the United States. Since the price of prescription drugs in the United States often exceeds the price in other nations, consumers have an incentive to purchase them from international sources. The Internet has made this a feasible alternative.

The use of the Internet in education is also significant. For those in school, schoolwork constitutes the largest online activity. Over 90 percent of online users aged 18–24 in school use the Internet for schoolwork. Similarly, using the Internet for schoolwork is the single largest online activity and is undertaken by over 80 percent of online users between 10 and 17 years old. For 10- to 24-year-olds, schoolwork exceeds even e-mail as the single largest use. The frequency of Internet educational use declines significantly after the age of 24.[11] Used beyond traditional educational settings, the Internet has been successfully incorporated into distance learning environments.[12]

Lastly, the Internet is used for religious activity. The Internet offers a variety of ways to undertake spiritual activity. The most common religious activity online is to find information. Information is available from the most established churches to the least conventional faiths. While most people go online for information about their own faith, the number of people seeking information about other faiths is only about 25 percent less. Another frequent religious activity is using e-mail to communicate prayer requests. A landmark in religious activity occurred in response to the September 11, 2001, attacks when 41 percent of Internet users received or sent a prayer request by e-mail.[13]

No discussion of major online activities would be complete without considering the frequency of sex-related activity. Online material ranges from sexual health to child pornography. People can go online to receive sexual health information in much the same manner as they would obtain any health information. The male anti-impotence drug Viagra, in particular, has used the anonymity of the online environment to become a top-100 search term and a popular drug to purchase on-line.[14] Information about sexual health, however, can be difficult to find online because it must compete for the attention of search engines with other sexual content lacking a health focus. Much of this material is conventional pornography. Unfortunately, a small part of this material is the product of child abuse. The nation has been reminded of this illegal content by major busts of child pornography on the Internet. The highly publicized "Operation Candyman" set a new standard for the breadth of an investigation as more than 7,000 people in the Candyman e-mail group (including 2,400 outside the United States) were investigated for over a year, leading to approximately 100 arrests being made in March 2002.[15]

Measuring the extent of sex-related activity on the Internet poses significant challenges to social scientists. The two most common techniques of data collection have significant drawbacks for measuring this activity. Survey research, which has proved reliable for many other behaviors, is notoriously unreliable for sexual matters. It is very difficult to get people to be honest about their sexual activities. Survey respondents, who are often in the presence of others at the dinner table or elsewhere, are unlikely to describe sexual behavior, especially unconventional behavior, when answering a telephone survey. Thus, in most cases, pollsters simply don't ask the question.

Similarly, experimental research has significant shortcomings for measuring sexual activity. Hawthorne effects, which result from people behaving differently when they know they are being studied, are particularly large for sexual activity. These effects are significant whether online behavior is being directly observed or monitored electronically. Finding a random sample for an experiment may also be difficult. There is no group of people, for instance, lining up to wear the standard eyeball-measuring apparatus to help researchers discover how people view pornography online. As with survey research, good experimental research is possible but the challenges are substantial.

The lack of reliable scientific research on sexual activity allows misinformation to spread about the frequency of sexual activity on the Internet. Myths can survive even when opposed by overwhelming scientific evidence. They are even more resistant when conflicting evidence is difficult to find. Thus, most people have probably heard in some form the myth that pornography dominates the Web. There is plenty of blame to go around in perpetuating the myth. There is also a kernel of truth.

The most prominent misinformation about sexual activity online is probably a July 1995 cover story in *Time* magazine. With over four million readers of an average issue in 1995, *Time* constituted a substantial platform for the spread of information. The cover story, titled "Cyberporn: On a Screen Near You," made broad generalizations about the frequency of cyberporn. The article described online porn with phrases such as the colloquial "awful lot of porn online," the alliterative "popular, pervasive, and surprisingly perverse," and the scholarly "ubiquitous." Banner headlines outside the text indicated that "Carnegie Mellon researchers found 917,410 sexually explicit pictures," and the "Biggest demand is not for hard-core sex pictures but for 'deviant' material including pedophilia, bondage, sadomasochism and sex acts with various animals."[16] The primary support for these statements was a study conducted by a research team identifying itself with Carnegie Mellon University. *Time* had been given the study prior to its publication in a legal journal. The article highlighted the finding that 83.5 percent of images on adult bulletin boards were "pornographic."

The *Time* article received significant attention. It had dramatic findings. *Time* was a huge forum. The findings of the research were absorbed into popular culture. The article became a key piece of evidence in the debate over online child pornography in Congress. Senator Grassley, for example, quoted the study on the floor of Congress in June 1995. As in the *Time* article, the senator drew broad implications from a narrow finding. He used the credibility of Carnegie Mellon and *Time* to lament the dominance of pornography online:

> I want to emphasize that this is Carnegie Mellon University. This is not a study done by some religious organization analyzing pornography that might be on computer networks. The university surveyed 900,000 computer images. Of these 900,000 images, 83.5 percent of all computerized photographs available on the Internet are pornographic. Mr. President, I want to repeat that: 83.5 percent of the 900,000 images reviewed—these are all on the Internet—are pornographic, according to the Carnegie Mellon study.[17]

The eventual discrediting of the *Time* article did not obtain the forum of the original work. After the *Time* article was published, doubts about the research emerged. It soon became obvious that *Time* had made a substantial blunder. What had been presented to *Time* as the work of a research team at Carnegie Mellon was essentially the work of one undergraduate at Carnegie Mellon named Martin Rimm. Published in the *Georgetown Law Journal,* the work had never been peer-reviewed to determine if scholars vouched for its merit. The 83.5 percent figure turned out to be a specific measure of content on adult bulletin board sites that may or may not have been connected to the Internet. It certainly could not be interpreted to mean that 83.5 percent of all Internet content was pornographic.[18] Finally, in its July 24 issue, *Time* issued a de facto correction. It acknowledged that the Carnegie Mellon study was the "centerpiece" of the article and that there were "serious questions" about its methods, ethics, and author.[19] The correction ran on page 57.

What, then, is the frequency of sex-related activity on the Internet? Exact measures are difficult. Enough is known, however, to dispel the myth of a sex-dominated cyberspace. Yet, the most reliable indicators suggest that there is a significant amount of sexual material online.

The popularity of sex on Internet search engines captures both the reality and the basis for mythology. Major search engines such as Yahoo! and Lycos automatically register all searches. They face none of the methodological problems faced by experimental or survey research on sexual matters. When the subject of the most common searches is compiled, a better picture of the extent of sex on the Internet is possible. According to a comprehensive two-year study, *sex* is the most frequent search term. Since *sex* tops the list of most common searches, it might appear to support the idea of sex as dominant on the Web. Yet, when one looks further, the most popular term says little about systematic behavior. The top search term represents less than one-half of 1 percent of all searches.[20]

Other content studies show that pornography is a small but significant part of the Web. It is ironic that within the same 1995 study picked up by *Time* magazine, there was evidence of low overall sexual content. The study found that less than one-tenth of 1 percent of websites were pornographic.[21] As a percentage of overall content, pornography is routinely shown to be quite low. While pornography represents about 1 or 2 percent of Web content,[22] it has a visibility that far exceeds its actual occurrence. One reason for this is the frequency with which adult content sites send mass unsolicited e-mail, or spam. By 2001, over half of Internet users had received spam from an adult site, while 20 percent said that it occurred "often." This spam is almost universally regarded as "annoying."[23]

Finally, the ability of pornography to make money also shows how a myth can emerge. It is well known that pornography was among the first enterprises to regularly make a profit from Internet-only content. Effectiveness in selling a product to a dedicated group of consumers, however, cannot be taken as an indication of the behavior of the broader population. The reality is that most people visit sites that do not require subscriptions.

OVERALL SOCIAL IMPACT

Having outlined the nature of online activity, it is now appropriate to assess how this activity is affecting people's lives. Central to the question is whether Internet use increases overall well-being. The answer depends on factors such as whether the Internet is enhancing relationships, improving efficiency, and increasing knowledge. One key contributor to overall impact is what activities the Internet is replacing. People have limited time. The impact of the Internet would be very different depending on whether the Internet is squeezing out less or more productive activities. Is the Internet enriching lives?

The short answer is, yes, the Internet is enriching lives. In general, social science has found the Internet to have a positive effect on people's lives. Communication is vital to well-being, and the Internet is providing another medium of communication. It is a particularly rapid and unobtrusive medium. It is, therefore, not surprising that people almost invariably believe it is improving their communication with others. The Internet has also made it possible to get information efficiently and conduct transactions on matters that span the range of human interest.

While the preponderance of social science evidence suggests that the impact of the Internet is to increase well-being, scholars have some lingering areas of concern. There is concern, for instance, that electronic communication is less effective in building bonds than face-to-face interaction.[24] While the Internet can reduce stress for some, it is also possible that Internet use may increase stress for others.[25] The evidence suggests that high levels of Internet use can be problematic.[26] Clearly, the nature of online activities has much to say about impact.

Scholarship on the broad social impact of the Internet follows a clear historical pattern. When this scholarship began, the conventional wisdom was that the Internet had a positive impact. The Internet was widely viewed as a classic example of a technology that was improving lives by facilitating communication. Considering this backdrop, the first major study of the broad social impact of the Internet came as a bombshell. It suggested that the Internet might actually reduce overall well-being. After the initial bombshell, most major studies have found positive effects of the Internet on overall well-being. Scholars have caught up to conventional wisdom.

The first study of the social impact of the Internet, published in *American Psychologist,* was highly anticipated. As the first broad study, it naturally attracted interest. The interest was multiplied by the reputation of the authors and funders of the study. The authors were at well-respected Carnegie Mellon University. They represented an interdisciplinary team of scholars including the social sciences, computer science, and business. The organizations that funded the study included the National Science Foundation, Apple Computer, AT&T Research, Intel, Hewlett-Packard, Lotus Development, Markle Foundation, and the U.S. Postal Service.

The researchers spent approximately $1.5 million[27] on an elaborate research design. The scholars identified a sample of ninety-three families in Pittsburgh who did not have a computer or Internet access. Each family was given a computer, Internet access, and a morning's training. In return for receiving the equipment, the families agreed to participate in the study and have their Internet use monitored. Demographic information was collected about each of the participants. At the beginning of the study, participants were given a questionnaire about their social patterns and general disposition. The nature and extent of Internet use was monitored for one to two years. At the end of the experimental period, participants were questioned again about their social patterns and general disposition.[28]

In August 1998, the release of the Carnegie Mellon study dropped a bombshell. While the Internet was expected to be improving lives, the study provided evidence to the contrary. The study found that Internet usage was related to an increase in loneliness and depression. The authors stated their main finding as a paradox: "The paradox we observe, then, is that the Internet is a social technology used for communication with individuals and groups, but it is associated with declines in social involvement and the psychological well-being that goes with social involvement."[29] This was a shocking finding in an academic journal. The audience for the study, however, would extend well beyond a professional audience. The framing of results in terms of loneliness and depression made the study accessible to the public. The story garnered huge media attention.

The second major study of broad social impact gave additional support to the Carnegie Mellon study. While not the bombshell of the first, a study by Stanford University released in 2000 continued the stir caused by the Carnegie Mellon findings. Again, this study was conducted by a highly prestigious research team using strong scientific methods. Unlike the experimental research at Carnegie Mellon, the research by the Stanford Institute for the Quantitative Study of Society used surveys. The scope of the Stanford study was impressive. A national random sample of over two thousand Internet users was surveyed. This gave the survey a smaller margin of error than the average poll. There was also great depth to the questions. The researchers asked many questions about how the Internet was being incorporated into people's lives. Perhaps the key question was whether electronic communication replaced face-to-face interaction: "Has using the Internet changed the amount of time you spend with your friends?"[30]

Although often perceived as reporting a negative impact, the Stanford study also presented a substantial positive side. The most widely cited finding was that people believed that Internet use prompted them to spend less time with people in their social network. About 10 percent of Internet users reported spending less time with their friends and family as a result of their Internet use.[31] The decline in face-to-face communication became a concern to many social scientists, who believe that verbal and visual cues give face-to-face communication a richness that electronic communication does not have. The study's lead researcher, Norman Nie, for instance, commented that he enjoyed receiving e-mails from relatives; but they provided "none of the emotional quality of spending an evening with them."[32] Drawing conclusions from his research, Nie warned that the Internet may have substantial social costs: "The Internet could be the ultimate isolating technology that further reduces our participation in communities even more than television did before it."[33] While the Internet may be reducing time with friends and relatives, the small magnitude of the results could be viewed as a positive. The Stanford study found that over 85 percent of people reported that Internet use had left "unchanged" the amount of time spent with family and friends.[34]

Although the studies were conducted by prestigious scholars with sound methodologies, there was still reason for skepticism about generalizing from these early findings. The design of the studies seemed limiting. First, the Carnegie Mellon study was not a random sample. Participants were selected from people who did not have a computer or Internet service. Although this population has advantages for considering a sort of "blank slate" impact of the Internet, it also has a drawback. These are people who had already made a calculation that based on what it would do for their lives, a computer and Internet access were not worth purchasing. This population, then, was likely to obtain fewer benefits from the Internet than a population who actually anticipated that the Internet would have a benefit for their lives. The experimental design did not reflect the way in which people acquired these goods in the real world. Second, although the findings technically reached a level of statistical significance, the magnitude of the changes was not great.

The Stanford study also had a significant limitation. It focused on the important task of finding out what the Internet was replacing. Social interaction was found to be one of the activities being replaced by the Internet. Saying that people spend marginally less physical time with friends, however, is not equivalent to saying that people believe the quality of their relationship is declining. Thus, after publication of the study, lead researcher Norman Nie said that if he could do it over again, he would have inquired more into what people thought the Internet did for the quality of their relationships.[35] Was it possible that even though the Internet reduced face-to-face time, social relations could still be affected positively?

This was indeed the conclusion of the next major study of social impact by the Pew Internet & American Life Project. The study released in May 2000 was a substantial survey of 1,690 Internet users. It addressed the key lingering issue from the Stanford study. This was whether relationships were improving despite small declines in face-to-face interaction. The overwhelming conclusion of the study was that, yes, people thought the Internet improved relationships even if it led to spending less face-to-face time. Most of the Internet users surveyed said that e-mail "improved their connections" to family members and friends.[36]

The Pew study began a trend that has culminated in a generally positive view of the social impact of the Internet. This is true of both experimental and survey research. A 2002 *Journal of Social Issues* article, for instance, reported the results of an experimental study monitoring Internet use by 406 new Internet subscribers. Although warning that the Internet seemed to increase stress levels, the authors found a generally positive social impact of Internet use including increases in overall well-being, an expanding social circle, and greater community involvement.[37]

Symbolically, the most important of the experimental studies identifying a positive impact is the continuation of the original Carnegie Mellon study. After the release of the first study, the Carnegie Mellon researchers continued their study for another year. Receiving a small percentage of the media coverage of the original study, the follow-up study reported a significant change in the results. The additional year had reversed the major findings. With the longer time frame, Internet use had become positively related to social involvement and well-being.

In thinking about why the results changed, the authors concluded that the Internet itself had changed between the end of the original and follow-up studies.[38] Because participants in the original study gained Internet access early in the diffusion process, they were often using an interactive medium for which they might be the only person connected in their social circle. Note to self: this can be very lonely. Over time, others in their social circle went online. During the same time frame, opportunities on the Web increased tremendously. Because the Web continues to expand, this interpretation predicts an increasingly positive impact.

The greatest evidence of positive impact is from survey research. When people are asked about how the Internet has affected their lives, they routinely say it has a positive impact. The magnitude of the positive response is staggering. A Gallup poll, for instance, found Internet users were thirty-six times more likely to say that the Internet has improved their lives rather than making them worse.[39] The overwhelmingly positive view of the Internet expressed in surveys is strong evidence for positive impact. People using the Internet in the real world should be the best judge of whether they feel that life is being improved.

One perennial question related to overall social impact is what activity the Internet replaces. People have a finite amount of time. Time spent on the Internet was previously spent elsewhere. What activity is being squeezed out by the Internet? Clearly, the Internet is taking some time away from a number of activities. Overall, however, there is a consensus that the primary activity being replaced by the Internet is television viewing.

The replacement of television viewing is a long-standing finding. The landmark Stanford survey in 2000 received media attention for reporting that people were spending less time in social interaction because of the Internet. The replacement of television viewing, however, was of far greater magnitude. While only 10 percent reported less time with family and friends, 47 percent reported that the Internet was directly leading to less time watching television.[40] In 2003, a UCLA study found that Internet users watched 4.8 hours of television per week less than nonusers.[41]

The replacement of television is somewhat comforting to many social scientists. Television viewing, particularly excessive viewing, is often seen as having socially negative consequences. The high-profile work *Bowling Alone* by Robert Putnam is typical of the negative perspective of social scientists on television viewing. Putnam identifies the isolating effects of television as the major culprit for why Americans are less likely to join the civic and social organizations that can ultimately lay the groundwork for solving collective problems—a phenomenon he calls declining social capital.[42]

Others are not convinced that people use the Internet differently than they use the television. A CNN headline once posed the question: "Web Surfers versus TV Watchers: Who's Lazier?"[43] Other studies show significant similarities in how people use television and the Web, especially when the Web is used for entertainment. Ferguson and Perse, for instance, found a high comparability of "Website repertoire to television-channel repertoire" in terms of the different content producers that users encountered on a regular basis.[44]

IMPACT ON CITIZENSHIP

Does the Internet enhance citizenship? Looking at the hierarchy of Internet activities, it is clear that politics is never going to eclipse entertainment or commerce in the virtual world. Of course, it doesn't in the physical world either. Yet activities that foster citizenship constitute a significant amount of online activity. The Internet is providing an additional medium through which individuals can pursue the privileges and obligations of citizenship. It is being used both for political participation and for receiving government-related information.

The Internet marks a substantial gain in the ability of citizens to receive information, mobilize, and interact with government. Just six years after the introduction of the Netscape browser, more people were going online for news at least once a week than were regularly watching the nightly network television news.[45] The online search for news extends to information related to the key citizenship task of voting: four of ten Internet users report that information received over the Internet affects their voting decision.[46] Citizen interaction is also facilitated by government websites, which have been visited by about half of all Internet users.

Although political use of the Internet is primarily by the already politically active,[47] the Internet has demonstrated the ability to bring in new participants. In particular, young adults are being energized. The least involved by nearly any measure of political involvement, young adults have been encouraged to participate through a medium that they find accessible. Compared to those over 65 years of age, 18- to 29-year-olds are half as likely to enjoy following the news, half as likely to read a newspaper, and one-third as likely to watch network television news. Yet these same young adults are far more likely to obtain political information online.[48]

Even when not serving explicitly as a vehicle for political activity, the Internet enhances citizenship by strengthening social capital. As documented by Robert Putnam in *Bowling Alone*, social networks that foster reciprocity are critical to the overall health of a nation.[49] The empirical evidence that the Internet promotes group participation is strong. A survey of 1,700 Internet users by the Pew Internet & American Life Project finds that 84 percent use the Internet to engage in some group activity. As shown in table 3.2, almost half of all Internet users believe that the Internet has helped them at least "some" in making social connections with people who share their beliefs or interests. It is, however, not just like-minded people who are coming together online.

In an essay in *The Civic Web*, David Anderson describes the Internet as more than a place for similar people to bond: "The possibilities for new coalitions in issue advocacy are endless when you consider how the Internet facilitates communication among people who would otherwise have difficulty finding each other."[50] Strong empirical support for Anderson's intuition is found in table 3.2, which shows that 45 percent of Internet users believe the Internet has helped them at least somewhat in connecting with people of either different ages or generations, ethnicities, or economic backgrounds. Despite the international nature of the Internet, almost one-fourth of Internet users believe that the Internet has helped them at least some in connecting with local groups.

Table 3.2   Internet Use for Making Various Social Connections

	Similar People	Different People	Local Groups
All Internet Users	47	45	23
Gender:			
Male	52	49	25
Female	43	43	21
Ethnicity:			
White	47	44	22
Black	49	53	28
Hispanic	50	50	28
Annual Household Income:			
< $20,000	48	49	24
$20,000–$74,999	50	48	24
$75,000 +	50	48	26
Education:			
< College Graduate	46	45	21
College Graduate	50	47	26
Age:			
18–29	53	55	26
30–64	47	43	22
65 +	28	31	19
Know Names of Neighbors:[a]			
Know All Names	46	45	24
Know Only Some Names	48	46	23
Don't Know Any Names	47	47	23

Source: Pew Internet & American Life Project, "Communities and the Internet," Data Set.
Notes: Q: "Please tell me how much, if at all, the Internet has helped you do each of the following things. Has the Internet helped a lot, some, only a little, or not at all?" Positive responses are "a lot" or "some." *Similar people* is a positive response to either "finding people or groups who share your interests" or "finding people or groups who share your beliefs." *Different people* is a positive response to either "connecting with people of different ages or generations," "connecting with people from different racial or ethnic backgrounds," or "connecting with people from different economic backgrounds." *Local groups* is a positive response to "connecting with groups and organizations that are based in your local community." Margin of error for all Internet users is ± 3.
[a]Q: "Do you know the names of your neighbors who live close to you, or not?"

Within the population of Internet users, there is little difference between those using and not using the Internet to build social capital. As shown in table 3.2, socioeconomic characteristics do not significantly affect whether an Internet user will make social connections online. A minimal measure of local social connection outside cyberspace, whether people know the names of all, some, or none of their neighbors, also does not help predict Internet connections. In fact, whether or not one controls for other factors, no single characteristic is statistically significant for all three social capital activities.[51]

CONCLUSION

Conventional terminology notwithstanding, the Internet does not really create a
new world. It gives people an opportunity to communicate better in the physical
world. Indeed, interpersonal communication through e-mail is the most common
use of the Internet. Other activities undertaken online generally reflect people's
interests and experience. Entertainment and commerce-related activities are now
preeminent on the Web. Politics is a significant but less common online activity.
The Internet is also frequently used for health, education, and spiritual activities.
The overall social impact of this online activity is positive, as evident from Internet users who consistently report that the Internet has improved their lives. A
small but significant part of this improvement is in their lives as citizens.

4

Internet Access Policy

The portrait of who is using the Internet and how it is being used, which was developed in the previous two chapters, sets the backdrop for government policy on Internet access. Depending on the landscape of Internet diffusion, government officials might want to take action. Should the government do anything about Internet access? In answering this question, policymakers have a tremendous amount of data about Internet diffusion. The first step for policymakers is to decide whether the nature of Internet access makes it something other than an ordinary product or service in which the government has no particular interest. If there is a legitimate governmental interest in Internet access, there are a variety of potential policy directions to take.

This chapter explores how American policymakers have resolved these issues. It begins by discussing a range of five general orientations that government can take toward any product or service: fundamental civil wrong, disfavored, ordinary, favored, or fundamental civil right. The general orientation of government to Internet access is contemplated in terms of these five categories. The predominant orientation is shown to be that Internet access is not an ordinary good, but one that receives a positive orientation from government. Having adopted a positive orientation to Internet access, government officials have consistently pursued policies to broaden Internet access. The chapter will outline the two main strategies used by government: ensuring that taxation does not prevent a barrier to home access and guaranteeing public access. The major legislation implementing each strategy is identified and its progress traced over time.

GOVERNMENT ROLE OVERVIEW

For any product or service produced in a society, including Internet access, government can be viewed as potentially having five general orientations. The orientations from least to most desired are fundamental civil wrong, disfavored, ordinary, favored, and fundamental civil right. Many factors influence the orientation taken. As articulated in the Declaration of Independence, one fundamental consideration is how a product or service relates to "life, liberty, and the pursuit of happiness." Politics, too, plays an important role as producers and consumers lobby government on behalf of the desirability of their product or service. Each orientation is associated with a general government policy. It is important to note that products and services may not fall neatly into one category, and indeed government may adopt multiple orientations with ostensibly contradictory policies.

On the negative side, government may regard a product or service as disfavored or even a fundamental civil wrong. If disfavored, government may provide a variety of disincentives such as negative tax repercussions for the product or service. If rising to the level of a fundamental civil wrong, government policy involves trying to deny the product or service. The product of heroin, for example, is regarded as a fundamental civil wrong that can lead to a loss of liberty for those associated with it.

Perhaps the most common orientation is for government to regard something as an ordinary product or service. For ordinary products and services, the natural policy of government is to withdraw and allow the market to operate. It becomes a matter of individual choice. An example would be the purchase of a Joe Walsh compact disc. Outside of a possible generic sales tax, government does nothing to encourage or discourage this ordinary purchase. There is no governmental interest.

On the positive side, the orientation of government to products or services may be favored or even a fundamental civil right. Having adopted a favored orientation, government can offer a variety of subsidies or tax incentives to encourage providing the product or service. A good example of a favored product is a charitable contribution, which is encouraged by a variety of tax preferences. A fundamental civil right, on the other hand, is regarded as so essential to life, liberty, and the pursuit of happiness that government guarantees the provision of the product or service. If incentives for provisions are not sufficient, government itself provides the good. A classic example is a primary school education, which government not only guarantees but compels.

In making policy for the Internet, the issues outlined in the previous two chapters become crucial. Policymakers will want to know about Internet diffusion. They will also want to know how it is being used. These factors will be important to how government orients itself to the Internet. If, for example, the Internet is found to be a medium that makes shopping more convenient, government might regard it as something favored. If the Internet is a frequent avenue for interacting with government, uneven diffusion might have implications for equality as citizens. Perhaps the Internet should be favored by government, if not guaranteed as a fundamental civil right. If, on the other hand, the Internet is a medium more often used to simulate sex than voting, government will not regard it as favored. If the Internet is a medium that draws people away from more productive activities and relationships, government might want to discourage some aspects of its use. Perhaps the Internet should be regarded as an ordinary good, with positive and negative uses, that warrants government withdrawal. How should government treat Internet access?

In weighing these considerations, policymakers can draw from the mixed message of government policy toward previous media. Government has generally withdrawn from the consumer purchase of media. Americans cannot, for instance, write off on their taxes the purchase of a radio or television set from an electronics store. Government does not subsidize the purchase of cable television. The key exception, however, is the provision of telephone service. Government has a long-standing policy of requiring telephone companies to subsidize residential phone service with long distance and business service. Government has instituted a universal service fee that assists Americans living in remote areas or having low incomes in obtaining telephone service. As a combination of previous media, the Internet could potentially fall under any of these models.

ORIENTATION TO THE INTERNET

Government has consistently demonstrated a positive orientation to Internet access. It has not been seen as an ordinary good. Whether Internet access is merely favored or rises to the level of a fundamental civil right depends on the type of access being discussed. For access in the home, government has adopted a favored orientation. Home access is encouraged, but not guaranteed. On the other hand, government policy regarding Internet access in public places demonstrates many of the characteristics of guaranteeing a fundamental civil right.

The argument for guaranteeing Internet access in public places as a civil right was outlined while the Internet was still a minority medium. In his 1996 State of the Union address, President Clinton said "every classroom in America must be connected to the information superhighway" and challenged the nation to have all classrooms and libraries online by the year 2000. Speaking at the 1998 MIT commencement, President Clinton said that it was government's responsibility to ensure Internet access. He painted a picture of universal Internet access reducing social disparities:

> We can reap the growth that comes from revolutionary technologies and use them to eliminate, not to widen, the disparities that exist. . . . [W]e have to make sure that the opportunities of the Information Age belong to all our children. Every young American must have access to these technologies.[1]

On the anniversary of the assassination of the Reverend Dr. Martin Luther King Jr. in 2000, President Clinton gave an address about guaranteeing Internet access, saying that Reverend King would find it a "righteous cause."[2] Al Gore continued the theme in his 2000 presidential campaign. He referred to computer literacy as a "fundamental civil right."[3] In making the case for a fundamental civil right orientation, politicians have tied Internet access to equal opportunity. The argument of Senator Maria Cantwell is typical: "No child should be placed at a disadvantage because he/she is not offered the opportunity to learn in a modern, wired and safe classroom."[4]

While not rising to the level of a fundamental civil right, home Internet access has been favored by government. Politicians using the phrase "fundamental civil right" generally are referring only to access in public facilities. For home access, the language is about encouragement, not a guarantee. The argument is usually that home access offers convenience and strengthens the economy.

Acting on this positive orientation, government has pursued two distinct policy tracks. The goals of guaranteeing public access and encouraging home access have been pursued separately. Government policy to guarantee public access has primarily entailed the federal government subsidizing the wiring of public facilities. The major program supporting this goal is the E-Rate. On the other hand, encouraging home access has been pursued by minimizing the extent to which government taxation presents a barrier to Internet access. The major policy supporting this goal is the Internet Tax Freedom Act.

GUARANTEEING ACCESS IN PUBLIC PLACES

The major federal program for guaranteeing access in public places, the E-Rate, has an eventful history with three distinct stages. The E-Rate has gone from an awkward start to high-profile success to becoming an established program. From the outset, the E-Rate was envisioned as a "temporary" program. It was almost very temporary.

The E-Rate was established in the 1996 Telecommunications Act. It was a small part of a sweeping reform of telecommunications that passed with strong bipartisan support. As established in the law, the program was not associated with a particular line item. It was not specific to the Internet but took in an array of "evolving technologies." The amount of funding was blank.

The underlying principle of the legislation establishing the E-Rate was to broaden the scope of the existing "Universal Service" program. It represented a classic example of the political system incorporating the Internet into existing frameworks. In this case the framework was from the 1930s. The landmark Communications Act of 1934 introduced the goal of universal service for telephones. To promote universal service, the telephone companies have long subsidized less profitable residential telephone service with business and more profitable residential telephone service. The model of universal service for telephones would now be applied to "evolving technologies" including the Internet.

Although the basic principle was well established, the mechanics of the E-Rate were unorthodox. Typically, Congress funds a program by dedicating a certain amount of money from general tax revenue. The E-Rate, however, was designed differently. First, the amount of money spent up to a specified cap would be determined by the Federal Communications Commission (FCC). Second, the revenue source was not general tax revenue, but a subsidy system to be established by the FCC. Ultimately, the FCC decided to impose fees on long-distance companies to help wire schools and libraries for the Internet. This unusual design would form the basis for political and legal challenges.

One way the FCC and other program supporters hoped to minimize the political challenge was by making the tax invisible to consumers. The Telecommunications Act included a variety of tax and regulating provisions that affected telephone companies. The E-Rate program was the most visible provision raising costs for the companies. Other provisions of the law were expected to decrease costs. Hoping for a net reduction in costs, the FCC expected telephone companies to fold E-Rate costs into an overall reduced cost of service. Consumers theoretically would see a minor reduction in price, and the new tax would be invisible.

The long-distance companies, however, did not see it the same way. To the surprise of the FCC, the long-distance companies in May 1998 added a new line item to telephone bills to reflect the cost of the E-Rate program. AT&T, for instance, clearly marked the cost of the program on the bill: "Last year, the FCC set up a new Universal Service Fund to . . . give schools and libraries access to advanced services like the Internet. AT&T must contribute to this fund and will assess a universal connecting charge of about 5% on your monthly bill starting in July."[5] The disclosure of the new tax drew the ire of some consumers. For its part, the FCC criticized the telephone companies for highlighting the new tax.

The unexpected visibility of the new tax and the FCC response led to the E-Rate coming under political and legal attack. Senator John McCain sent an open letter urging the FCC to "refrain from interfering with a carrier's prerogative to truthfully identify any consumer bill increases as a Commission imposed tax required to subsidize identified programs." Senator Conrad Burns, a Communications Subcommittee Chair, said that "nothing in the Telecommunications Act suggested that the Universal Service Fund should become a cash cow for Internet access."[6] Others criticized Internet technology as unproven in enhancing the quality of education. Some critics adopted the name "Gore tax" for the tax to reflect the vice president's support for the program.

The strength of the criticism is symbolized by the strength of the criticism voiced by House Majority Leader Dick Armey. He challenged the program on political and legal grounds: "Every time you make a call, you'll pay a surcharge imposed by FCC bureaucrats. And every time you look at your phone bill, you'll have the Vice President [Al Gore] to thank. . . . This new tax is unconstitutional."[7]

Building on the argument that the tax was unconstitutional, various parties—including the telephone companies—initiated a lawsuit. The seriousness of the legal and political challenge prompted a strong response by the supporters of the program. Not surprisingly, supporters launched an Internet-based effort to demonstrate support for the E-Rate. The effort was further helped by the release of a Department of Commerce report showing a pronounced digital divide. President Clinton also made a concerted effort to defend the program. He had, after all, made wiring every classroom an explicit goal in his 1996 State of the Union address. In defending the E-Rate, President Clinton tied Internet access to broader participation in the American dream:

> [The E-Rate is] the most crucial initiative we've launched to help connect our schools, our libraries, and our rural health centers to the Internet. Now some businesses have called on Congress to repeal the initiative. They say our nation cannot afford to provide discounts to these institutions. . . . I say we cannot afford not to have an e-rate. . . . If we really believed that we all belong in the Information Age, then, at this sunlit moment of prosperity, we can't leave anyone behind in the dark.[8]

With backing from the president the program was able to survive, albeit in a modified form. Originally hoping to spend $2.25 billion for the program's first year of implementation beginning January 1, 1998, the FCC reduced the amount to $1.3 billion. Although it didn't disburse its original goal, the FCC did get the checks out to public facilities. The E-Rate program had survived.

Following its awkward start, the E-Rate program entered a period of high-profile success from 1999 to 2001. The first disbursements began the process of building a constituency of schools and libraries that benefited from the E-Rate. This constituency translated into popular support. FCC Chair William Kennard defended the program by pointing to a poll showing 87 percent support for the E-Rate program.[9] Building on the new climate, the FCC in 1999 raised the amount spent to over $2 billion, just short of the original goal of $2.25 billion.

This money was going disproportionately to the poorest schools. Federal subsidies were triggered by a local contribution. The amount of the subsidy varied from 20 to 90 percent depending on the resources of the school. Thus, the poorest schools received the most federal aid for their contribution. Wealthy schools still benefited from the program, albeit at a lesser federal subsidy.

Support for the program was further enhanced by the beginning of political credit claiming. There were tangible results for the program in the form of schools and libraries that were wired. These facilities were located throughout the country. They were in every congressional district. Political officeholders could point to federal money helping local facilities. Although formulated by a bureaucratic agency, the program had a classic design by which all congressional districts would benefit. A May 2000 press release by Connecticut senator and future vice-presidential candidate Joseph Lieberman demonstrates how well suited the program is for credit claiming: "Joe Lieberman . . . today announced that 47 Connecticut schools, libraries, and districts will share more than $650,000 to provide access to the Internet and upgrade computer and communications networks . . . as part of the national E-rate initiative."[10]

At times, credit claiming became very enthusiastic. The ultimate in credit claiming for expanding access perhaps was attained by Virginia Senator Charles Robb. He took typical credit claiming one step further by speaking about the wiring that he had not only authorized, but personally had done. Senator Robb served as a volunteer with a nonprofit that wired schools. His campaign highlighted this personal involvement in expanding Internet access: "So far, Senator Robb and his staff have personally wired schools in the counties of Fairfax, Roanoke, Chesterfield, and Augusta."[11] Indeed, for incumbents, it was a can't-lose proposition. Some facilities in every state had benefited. While a number of incumbents were claiming credit for the E-Rate program, criticism of the program could not be found in campaigns.

The political success was accompanied by important legal victories. By 1999, the lawsuit challenging the design of the program had reached the federal appellate level. On July 30, 1999, the U.S. Court of Appeals for the Fifth Circuit upheld the core of the E-Rate program as a "new wrinkle to the concept of universal service."[12] The court acknowledged that the FCC had probably overstepped its authority, but ruled that there was enough ambiguity in the law to allow the FCC actions to withstand constitutional scrutiny. Although the FCC might have preferred a more ringing endorsement, a win is still a win. The program had cleared a major legal hurdle. Of course, there was one more hurdle. The plaintiffs appealed the decision to the Supreme Court. Their efforts, however, were unsuccessful; the Supreme Court dismissed the case in November 2000.

The E-Rate program maintained its political support after the change to the Bush administration in 2001. Early in the administration, Education Secretary Rod Paige defended the E-Rate. The defense of the E-Rate by the Bush administration was noteworthy considering the 2000 campaign. George Bush had defeated Al Gore, the individual most associated with the program. Critics had been calling the revenue mechanism the "Gore tax." Yet, President Bush defended the program. This prompted Adam Thierer, writing in the *National Review,* to lament that the "Administration's reluctance to pursue serious reform now paves the way for the E-Rate program to become a full-blown national entitlement program."[13] Thierer closes his article with a tongue-in-cheek recommendation about the person President Bush should appoint to oversee the program: Al Gore.

The period of high-profile success culminated with the release of data documenting nearly universal Internet access in public schools. In May 2001, the National Center for Education Statistics released its study of Internet access in public schools. The report highlighted dramatic progress in reaching universal access. Starting with 35 percent in 1994, the number of public schools in the United States with Internet access had approached 100 percent by the end of 2000. With 98 percent of schools shown to be wired for the Internet, the study revealed a near fulfillment of the goal of universal access. The digital divide had disappeared on the broad measure of school connectivity. Despite the dramatic reduction of the digital divide, the report demonstrated some continued disparities in Internet access. The percentage of classrooms wired varied from 64 percent in high-poverty schools to 85 percent in the schools with the lowest poverty rates.[14]

The E-Rate received some of the credit for the progress in wiring schools. Of course, it was only one contributor. Many schools had been wired long before the E-Rate program began distributing funds. The program, however, distributed a significant amount of money in a short period to facilitate universal access. After the initial-year reduction to $1.3 billion, the program disbursed over $2 billion in each of the next two years. By March 2001, $5.8 billion had been distributed through the program.[15] Studies showed a direct link between the program and school wiring. The Benton Foundation, for example, described the E-Rate as a "refreshing case of federal dollars well-spent" after it was found to be responsible for significant infrastructure improvement in Chicago, Cleveland, Detroit, and Milwaukee schools.[16]

With its most visible goal essentially achieved, the E-Rate entered a new era as an established program. It had a strong constituency. Even if the major measure of school access had been achieved, there were continuing projects to fund. Disparities persist on subsidiary measures of Internet access, such as faster connections. The E-Rate continued with less fanfare but with institutionalized support.

With the high-profile political fight over the E-Rate grabbing much attention, care must be taken not to overlook the role of state government in wiring schools. The federal role existed alongside state efforts. In some cases, the state role significantly preceded the federal role. This is not surprising considering that the federal government accounts for such a small portion of overall education funding. In fulfilling their dominant role in education, state and local governments saw Internet access as an important initiative. The state efforts also reflect a broad commitment to Internet access in public places as approaching a fundamental civil right. States have tried to guarantee Internet access for their schools.

There are many noteworthy efforts, but a few merit special attention. In 1994, Missouri became the first state to have all its schools networked.[17] Under Governor George Bush, Texas undertook the nation's largest initiative to wire schools and libraries in 1995.[18] California has also been a leader in state-based programs to wire schools. The Digital California Project spent over $3.5 million annually to wire all schools in a broadband network.[19]

ENSURING THAT TAXES DO NOT IMPEDE HOME INTERNET ACCESS

The second major government Internet access policy is minimizing the extent to which government taxation presents a barrier to Internet access. The strategy has a different focus than the E-Rate. While the E-Rate emphasizes public access, the tax minimization strategy emphasizes private access. The E-Rate involves government spending, while this component involves government agreeing not to do anything. The motivation for the policy is that the decision to purchase Internet service is based on a calculation of costs and benefits. One potential cost that could enter the calculation is a tax imposed on Internet activity. The less taxes enter into the calculation, the more likely it is that access will be provided.

The most direct tax on the Internet would be a tax on Internet access itself. This would constitute a classic excise tax levied on a specific commodity. The federal government already levies an excise tax on products such as gasoline, alcohol, tobacco, and airline travel. Falling under the category of interstate and indeed international commerce, Internet access can clearly be taxed by the federal government. The federal government also has a history of quickly taxing new modes of communication, including the telegraph and radio. One possible model is the taxation of telephone service. Excise taxes on telephone service at all levels of government make it one of the most heavily taxed services in modern America. Considering that Internet access was initially provided almost exclusively through telephone wires, government policy on Internet access might have used telephone service as a model. An excise tax, however, might reduce the incentive for Internet access.

Policymakers have a choice. Internet access can be used as a reliable source of revenue for government. Alternatively, government can forgo revenue from taxing Internet access with the expectation that the greater good is served by a potential increase in online commerce. Over time, policymakers have tended to resolve this choice by forgoing revenue in favor of promoting online commerce. It is a policy choice that generally has low visibility in American politics. Occasionally, however, it has been able to draw the attention of policymakers.

This choice first drew the attention of policymakers at the state level. Well before the federal government entered the policy domain, many states had already been there. By 1998, nine states had provisions to impose a tax on Internet access. The states were Connecticut, Iowa, New Mexico, North Dakota, Ohio, South Dakota, Tennessee, Texas, and Wisconsin. Other states, however, were reluctant. Following the initial enthusiasm, a trend in the opposite direction was emerging. A number of states passed laws precluding a tax on Internet access. This included the largest state of California, whose 1998 law against taxes on Internet access took effect at the beginning of 1999.[20]

The first major federal action related to the taxation of Internet access was the Internet Tax Freedom Act of 1998. The legislation was sponsored by Christopher Cox (R-CA) in the House and Ron Wyden (D-OR) in the Senate. The key component of the legislation was a moratorium, or temporary suspension, of government authority to institute Internet-specific taxes. The act was largely motivated by a desire to make sure that the government didn't do anything to slow the growth of the new technology. Proponents of the measure were concerned about

the potential effect of state-level taxes. By suspending the authority of all levels of government to impose new taxes on the Internet, the Internet Tax Freedom Act was designed to prevent government from taking any rash action when so little was known about how the Internet might develop.

The Internet Tax Freedom Act of 1998 gained wide political support. As part of his administration's Framework on Electronic Commerce, President Clinton had come out in favor of a moratorium on any Internet-specific taxes. In Congress, the legislation had bipartisan support. It became law as part of an omnibus appropriations bill in 1998.

The Internet Tax Freedom Act of 1998 had several major provisions. First, although initially introduced with a five-year moratorium, the length of the moratorium was reduced to three years before final passage. The moratorium on new Internet-specific taxes covered the period October 1, 1998, to October 21, 2001. Second, the states with Internet access taxes could choose to keep them under a grandfathering provision. The state of Texas quickly announced its intention to abandon its tax and not claim the exemption. Third, the legislation set up an Advisory Commission on Electronic Commerce to explore future policy options.

With the end of the moratorium approaching, Congress revisited the issue in the summer of 2001. The House passed a strengthened version of the original act with a bipartisan majority of 352 to 75. The House legislation extended the moratorium for an additional five years. Under the House version, the grandfather provision would be eliminated for the states already imposing an access tax. With the Senate not taking action, the House passed a scaled-down version of the bill reducing the moratorium to two years ending in November 2003. The scaled-down version also reinstated the grandfather provision for states already taxing access. The Senate still did not respond.

The tax moratorium was allowed to lapse. On October 22, 2001, states again could contemplate taxes on access. Advocates of the tax moratorium made dire predictions about what would occur if the lapse continued. The House sponsor, Christopher Cox, suggested that "all hell may break loose."[21] The Senate sponsor, Ron Wyden, noted the potential for "considerable economic mischief" in the intervening period.[22] Before it was over, the legislation had lapsed for over a month before the Senate agreed to the scaled-down House bill. No state took advantage of the gap to institute a new tax on access.

As President Bush signed the legislation on November 28, 2001, he drew a clear link between government policy and enhanced Internet access. President Bush wasn't altogether satisfied with the two-year moratorium; he preferred five years. He, however, described it as a victory for access. On one hand, his statement on the legislation represents a rather unusual summary of the benefits of the Internet. On the other hand, it reveals a president who saw the tax moratorium as access policy:

> Today I am pleased to sign into law H.R. 1552, which will ensure that the growth of the Internet is not slowed by additional taxation. The Internet is an innovative

force that enables such applications as distance learning and precision farming. Government must do its part to make access to these services affordable. It should not raise costs through additional taxation.

SALES TAXES ON THE INTERNET

While policy on Internet access taxes has been mostly consensual, the question of sales tax on Internet commerce has been controversial from the start. On the surface, Internet sales taxes parallel the Internet access tax debate. The interest of the government is in securing a revenue base. The competing claim is that minimizing the impediment of taxation will produce a greater good of expanded commerce and technological progress. The similarity between access and sales taxes, however, ends there. While access taxes potentially could generate a relatively small amount of money for a variety of governments, the sales tax issue is a high-stakes political battle about a tremendous amount of revenue for state and local government.

State and local governments have a profound interest in how Internet sales are taxed. Although there is much variation, states on average get about one-third of their revenue from sales tax. Internet commerce is a growing part of the economy amounting to billions of dollars annually. States, therefore, are acutely concerned about how Internet commerce is treated for sales tax purposes. In contrast, the federal government has little direct revenue interest in sales taxes. Some legal issues surrounding sales taxes, however, give the federal government an important role in the matter.

The legal framework and accompanying federal role in the political debate over the collection of Internet sales taxes had been set before the Internet was even a factor. In 1992, the Supreme Court ruled that a state could directly collect sales taxes only from companies with a physical presence, or "nexus," in that state.[23] The decision emerged in the context of mail order sales. The decision precluded states from collecting a sales tax directly from out-of-state firms selling products to in-state residents.

The decision did not leave states without an option for collecting sales taxes on mail order purchases, just a bad one. States were denied the right to collect sales taxes directly from the company. They retained the right to collect the sales tax on the out-of-state purchase from the in-state resident. In theory, the amount of sales tax is the same whether it is collected from the business or the resident. In practice, however, the difference is like that between night and day. State governments have had tremendous success in collecting sales taxes from businesses, which are subject to a variety of reporting requirements. Except for big-ticket items like cars, which require registration, states have had little success collecting sales taxes directly from residents. Theoretically, in many sales tax states, residents are supposed to keep an ongoing record of out-of-state mail order purchases. The amount is reported to the state, and a tax is paid on the purchases. One common way to collect this tax is a line for "use tax due on out-of-state purchases" on the annual income tax form. In practice, however, people are not meticulous record keepers; and some states have set a minimum threshold for reporting. The end result is that little sales tax on out-of-state purchases is collected from residents.

The Supreme Court, however, left open one option for collecting sales taxes directly from out-of-state firms. This was if the federal government specifically authorized a system for collecting sales taxes. Enter the federal government, maybe. Politically it was a tough sell to the federal government, which might be accused of raising taxes and had a number of officeholders in states that didn't even have a sales tax. Not surprisingly, the federal government was less than enthusiastic about establishing any system to allow states to collect sales taxes on out-of-state mail order purchases.

As the Internet emerged, the significance of the out-of-state sales tax issue multiplied. Internet purchases immediately were treated as the functional equivalent of mail order purchases. Thus, sales taxes could not be directly collected from out-of-state firms. States were having little success collecting sales taxes directly from consumers. The amount of revenue "lost" to states grew with the expansion of interstate commerce. Legally, the best option for states was to get the federal government to authorize a system for collecting sales taxes.

With a legal framework established in the pre-Internet era, the stage was set for a political struggle. On one side were those who believed the federal government should stay out of the issue. This side included entities directly benefiting from the absence of sales tax collection, such as online merchants and Internet service providers. Politically, it benefited from the fact that members of Congress supporting the measure ran the risk of being portrayed as pro-tax—even though the federal treasury would receive no revenue and a number of members represented states without sales taxes. This side gained philosophical support from those believing that tax collection may burden the growth of the Internet. Spokespeople for this side emphasized that states already had the legal ability to collect use tax from their residents. Ron Wyden, for instance, framed the issue as a lack of political will by the states:

> There is nothing that bars a state or local jurisdiction from going out today and coming up with a better system of collecting and enforcing tax revenue that is currently owed . . . what the debate is about is that they don't want to take the heat.[24]

On the other side, the most prominent advocates were states seeking sales tax revenue. The National Association of Governors, for instance, was a prominent advocate for improved sales tax collection. States were sometimes joined by local businesses, which felt they were at a competitive disadvantage against out-of-state vendors who did not collect sales tax. Politically, this side gained support from the fact that these businesses within the district were constituents while out-of-state vendors were not. This side gained philosophical support from those concerned about the broader struggles of locally owned firms in the new economy.

The first significant event in the politics of sales tax collection was linking the issue to taxes on Internet access. Both sides probably saw some benefit from tying the volatile sales tax issue to the less controversial moratorium on taxing Internet access. Those opposing federal action to facilitate sales tax collection could conflate the two issues into a general position on Internet taxes. Those favoring federal action to facilitate sales tax collection could use the popular access tax moratorium to get a hearing on the more contentious sales tax issue. Whatever the motivation, the issues were quickly linked. Thus, the sales tax issue shares some of the history of access taxes.

As with access taxes, the first major federal forum for the sales tax issue was the consideration of the Internet Tax Freedom Act (ITFA) of 1998. Although states had expressed concern about forgone revenue, there was little support in Congress for raising the issue so early in the development of Internet commerce. Thus, the ITFA was deliberately silent on the issue. The moratorium was written specifically to apply only to special access taxes. It did not preclude the collection of sales taxes on goods purchased over the Internet. The legislation, however, did not take the affirmative step of federal authorization of sales tax collection. States, therefore, had little practical ability to collect sales taxes on out-of-state purchases.

The inaction on sales tax of the ITFA of 1998 represented a strong version of ensuring that taxes would not be a barrier. For practical purposes, Internet products were given preferential status over other goods. The legislation reveals the commitment of policymakers to minimizing the barrier that taxes present to Internet development. One part of this commitment is to promote widespread access. There is also a broader issue about government's role in the economy.

During the initial three-year moratorium, states tried to strengthen their case. The growth in Internet commerce meant that forgone sales tax revenue was already significant. By 2000, estimated sales tax revenue forgone by states from Internet commerce exceeded $25 billion annually.[25] As Congress began to debate the renewal in 2001, the University of Tennessee released a study showing that state and local governments could lose $440 billion over the upcoming decade if nothing was done.[26]

Perhaps the strongest evidence for the states seeking a sales tax on the Internet was a surprising result from a Markle Foundation poll. In early 2000, the Markle Foundation commissioned a poll to solicit public opinion on the issue. The poll asked Americans if "online commerce should be subject to the same sales taxes as other commerce, so that Internet businesses do not have an artificial advantage over other businesses." Although the question wording certainly presented the issue in a way that many Americans had not contemplated, the results were nonetheless comforting to advocates of federal action to facilitate sales tax collection. Only 34 percent of Americans opposed collecting taxes on out-of-state firms. Over 60 percent of Americans supported collecting the sales tax.[27]

Having some public support and mounting evidence of revenue forgone, the states took a more active role in the renewal of the moratorium than it had on the original measure. The House of Representatives, however, passed a moratorium extension under the limited-debate suspension of the rules procedure, with only minor protests about the sales tax issue. The story was different in the Senate. Standing up for those seeking a full debate on the sales tax issue, Senator Dorgan (D–ND) put a hold on the legislation days before the moratorium expired. The moratorium lapsed.

The lapsed moratorium brought with it some heightened rhetoric, a high-profile vote, but ultimately no change in policy. Frustrated with the lapsed moratorium, those favoring an extension of the moratorium criticized opponents for holding up the vote. Barbara Boxer (D–CA) accused sales tax advocates of trying to "look for ways to get more people laid off."[28] Ultimately, advocates for sales tax reform were able to force a procedural vote on whether to consider the sales tax issue, but lost 57–43. The moratorium would be extended. The federal government again acted in a way to ensure that taxation would not impede access and activity on the Internet.

ACCESS TAX MYTH

An excellent indicator of the overall commitment of the government to minimizing the barrier of both access and sales taxes to Internet growth is the politics surrounding a persistent myth about government plans to tax e-mail. Appropriately, the myth is typically circulated by e-mail. In its most common form, the myth goes something to the effect that a Congressman Schnell has introduced a bill in Congress to impose a five-cent tax on every e-mail. The justification for the tax is that the U.S. Postal Service is losing a tremendous amount of revenue from e-mail and needs additional revenue to sustain its operations. After the description of the bill, there is usually a plea to e-mail or telephone your member of Congress to express your concern. Of course, the recipient is also encouraged to forward the "information" to his or her friends.

Like many myths, this story incorporates a small kernel of truth. In this case, the small kernel comes from an obscure report by the United Nations. In July 1997, a development report sponsored by the United Nations concluded with the usual array of pie-in-the-sky proposals. One such proposal was that wealthier nations would provide development aid by paying a tax on e-mail. Unlike its long life in the mythical world, the proposal had a short life in the real world. Shortly after submitting the report, the UN Development Programs responded to criticism by distancing itself from the proposal. Lacking the ability to impose taxes, the United Nations could not have implemented the plan even if it had wanted to do so.[29]

Although the Congressional bill was never real, it has prompted a substantial amount of real-world activity. The origin of this activity is the conventional format of the myth ending with a plea to contact your member of Congress. This plea resulted in a tremendous amount of e-mail being sent to Congress. By early 2000, some members of Congress were frustrated by the tremendous amount of mail being generated on the subject. They contemplated ways to halt the flow of mail.

In May 2000, the U.S. House of Representatives took the unusual step of passing a bill that said Congress was not going to do something. Specifically, the bill said that Congress would not allow any taxes on e-mail. Basically, the House wanted to say that it wasn't even thinking about taxing e-mail. Alas, the Internet Access Charge Prohibition Act failed to gain support in the Senate and did not become law. Perhaps the open confronting of the myth would be enough to dispel the myth once and for all. Or maybe not.

Several months later, the myth had its most prominent airing in a New York Senate debate. The high-profile race between former first lady Hillary Clinton and Rick Lazio drew national attention and live coverage of the debates. As part of the third debate, the moderator, Marcia Kramer, read questions submitted by New York citizens. She addressed Clinton first: "I'd like to ask you how you stand on federal bill 602p." Hillary Clinton responded that she had "no idea" what it was. The moderator elaborated:

> I'm going to tell you what it is. Under the bill that is now before Congress, the U.S. Postal Service would be able to bill e-mail users 5 cents for each e-mail they send even though the Post Office provides no service. They want this to help recoup losses of about $230 million a year because of the proliferation of e-mail, but if you send just 10 e-mails a day that would cost consumers an extra $180 a year. So I'm wondering if you would vote for this bill and do you see the Internet as a source of revenue for the government in the years to come?

Both candidates were given the chance to address the question. Hillary Clinton responded, "It sounds burdensome and not justifiable to me." Rick Lazio was even stronger in his opposition to the bill. He related the tax to broader issues about government: "I am absolutely opposed to this. This is an example of the government's greedy hand in trying to take money from taxpayers that it frankly has no right to."[30]

When candidates are compelled to take strong positions against an imaginary bill, it represents a clear, if awkward, statement about how strong the resolve is not to have taxes impede Internet growth. Legislators had already passed a bill saying that they had not even thought about taxing the Internet. Yet, a member of the House (when the Charge Prohibition Act was approved) called bill 602p an example of "government's greedy hand." The politics of 602p show the enthusiasm of officeholders for taking a strong position against Internet taxes. This eagerness extends to imaginary bills.

CONCLUSION

American policymakers consistently have viewed Internet access as a legitimate interest of government. Having adopted a positive orientation to Internet access, government officials have made a concerted effort to broaden Internet access. Government policy has had two major dimensions. First, public access to the Internet has been secured by providing direct financial assistance to schools and other public facilities to build an Internet infrastructure. Second, home access to the Internet has been favored by government policy that minimizes the extent to which taxes provide a barrier to Internet access. This policy has played a role, albeit a supporting role, in the broadening diffusion of Internet access in the United States.

PART TWO

POLITICAL ADVOCACY ON THE INTERNET

Cybercampaigning

I have been reviewed as the 7th friendliest Web page user and so forth of the 535 members of Congress.

—Frank Murkowski, incumbent candidate for U.S. Senate

History is filled with examples of technology changing how candidates conduct their campaigns. The invention of the telegraph and improved newspaper production techniques enabled campaign speeches to be distributed more widely, but required candidates to consider how the speech would read on paper. The widespread expansion of railroads created the expectation that candidates would travel extensively and communicate with voters in person. The development of radio and television allowed candidates to be seen and heard in the living room of an electorate that may not have sought out the communication. The limited time available in broadcasting, however, meant that the audience increasingly would receive a condensed version of the campaign in which candidate communication was filtered by the media.

The Internet has further changed the nature of campaigns. The change does not necessarily represent a dramatic transformation. After all, the Internet is a computer-enabled assimilation of previous advances in communication. Many of the characteristics of these previous advances are carried over to the Internet. Yet in harnessing these advances to the computer, something important has changed. Internet campaigning is different than other aspects of the campaign. This chapter will explore the fundamental characteristics, distinct eras, and the regulation of Internet campaigning.

KEY FEATURES OF INTERNET CAMPAIGNING

The computer-generated combination of previous advances results in unique features of Internet campaigning. These include low accidental exposure, audience discretion in choosing when and what communication to receive, interactivity on a mass level, and unlimited time and space. Each of these features can be both a blessing and a curse for the candidate.

The lack of accidental exposure sharply distinguishes the Internet from other mass media. Television viewers, for instance, are prone to accidental exposure because they receive signals passively by turning a dial or pressing a remote control. They have little control over the wide array of programming, especially advertising, that they might encounter. Indeed, candidates are attracted to television advertisements because of the opportunity to have an undecided voter, unlikely to seek out information, accidentally be exposed to their material. On the other hand, in order to reach a website a person must actively type in a string of characters or follow a link. The chances of a voter accidentally reaching a campaign website are infinitesimal.

For the candidate, the low incidence of accidental exposure has a positive and negative side. A definite plus is that the candidate knows the site visitor has at least some interest in the campaign. The likelihood of a sustained stay for visitors was documented early in the history of Internet politics. A study by Campaign Solutions of a variety of congressional and gubernatorial sites in 1998 revealed that the average visitor stayed 8½ minutes, far exceeding the amount of time that a television advertisement holds the attention of a viewer.[1] Counting on a sustained viewing, candidates can disseminate more information about themselves and their positions. Further, since the majority of site visitors are likely to be supporters, the campaign site provides the opportunity to raise money and recruit volunteers.

On the negative side, the lack of accidental exposure makes it difficult to reach the undecided voters so important to candidates in close elections. Since undecided voters are statistically the least interested in the campaign, they are extremely unlikely visitors to a campaign site that must be reached through intentional steps. An additional negative is that an important minority of the interested people seeking out the campaign site will be associated with the opposing candidate. Although candidates themselves are unlikely to spend much time at the opposition site, they will no doubt assign staff to search for politically vulnerable material.

A classic example of an opposing candidate using a candidate's website against him occurred in the 1998 Senate race in Alaska. During a televised debate, the candidates were given an opportunity to ask a question of each other. When Republican candidate Frank Murkowski was given the opportunity to ask a question, he chose to base his question on the website of his opponent, Democrat Joe Sonneman. While the syntax of Senator Murkowski's question belies the idea that he himself had ever visited his opponent's site or perhaps had ever been on the World Wide Web, his staff had clearly conducted research and found information that could be used against Sonneman. After receiving the floor from the moderator, Senator Murkowski asked:

> Joe, I've been interested in your interest in . . . the Web page. You've done a lot of work on that and I commend you. I have also been quite a fan of it. . . . I think I have been reviewed as the 7th friendliest Web page user and so forth of the 535 members of Congress. But I was interested in one thing on your Web page, you said, "It's time Alaska had a U.S. Senator as good as Minnesota's Senator Paul Wellstone," who incidentally is a good friend of mine, but I'm wondering if you stand on that statement?[2]

Moving past the contemplation of what exactly would constitute a friendly Web page user, the incident has much to say about Internet politics. It represents the awkward expression of a political figure who knows that it is important to appear technologically up-to-date. It also shows that candidates must be aware that the intentional audience of their website will include the opposition. Finally, it demonstrates that the Internet campaign is not an insulated part of the campaign, but can become a part of the broader campaign whether desired or not.

A second unique feature of the Internet campaign is that the audience has unparalleled discretion in choosing when and what communication to receive. The Web is not like a speech or television advertisement that will be consumed in an order and time chosen by the speaker. The campaign represents the height of convenience for the information seeker. A Web user can visit at 3 a.m. and selectively view a few files or paragraphs. Indeed, when asked the reason for seeking campaign news on the Web, the most common response given is "convenience."[3] By providing this convenience, the campaigner benefits by being able to reach more people than if the time and place were limited. Similarly, the campaigner can take advantage of audience discretion by providing a lot of information that can be selected based on the interests of users.

The flip side of the convenience for the voters is the uncertainty of the candidate about the time and mood in which the audience will receive the communication. Not knowing when or where the audience will see the website, it is almost impossible for the Web campaigner to respond to the audience's mood. Many of the informal trappings of the campaign that can accompany the stump speaker are not present to support the online presentation. It can indeed be a cold page confronting the Web visitor.

A third unique feature of the Internet campaign is the potential for interactivity on a mass level. Candidates have the potential not only to disseminate information to a mass audience but also to receive a message from a mass audience. Hearing from voters can help the candidate understand the desires of the constituency. Further, the audience has the potential to communicate with other members of the audience through chats, listservs, and other forums. This can inspire voters to feel a connection with the campaign. Interactivity can be used to mobilize people for a rally or other campaign event.

The downside of the interactivity of the Internet is that it can raise expectations for two-way communication that the candidate is not able to fulfill. Even before the Internet, candidates and officeholders were having trouble responding to all of their mail and telephone calls. If a candidate is unable to keep up with e-mail, it may leave the dangerous impression that the candidate is not interested in the concerns of the electorate. Of course, typically, the responsibility for handling e-mail is given to the lower echelons of the campaign hierarchy, including interns and volunteers. Even though answering e-mail can be delegated, it still demands scarce resources; many campaigns have been unable to keep up with the volume of e-mail received.[4]

The fourth unique feature of the Internet campaign is the existence of an unlimited amount of time and space for unfiltered communication. Unlike the scarce blocks of expensive time available in the broadcasting medium, and to a lesser extent in newspapers, the Internet offers unlimited time and space. The Internet, therefore, provides an opportunity for in-depth discussion not possible elsewhere. Further, it offers this valuable space with no intermediary between the candidate and the potential voter. The media can be bypassed. Surveys show that the desire to hear directly from candidates without a media filter is the most common reason for visiting a campaign website.[5] This desire of the audience for unfiltered communication fits nicely with the agenda of the advocate, who also wishes to bypass the media. Surveys of candidates with websites reveal that their primary motivation for having a website is to deliver unfiltered information.[6]

As with the interactivity of the Internet, the existence of unlimited time and space for unfiltered communication poses a danger to candidates when expectations are raised beyond what the candidate can deliver. Knowing that a candidate has extensive time to discuss an issue, voters may expect more than the broad generalities that are the limit of a thirty-second advertisement. A candidate, however, may not want to provide further detail. He or she may not have specific ideas about the subject, or may fear that extensive discussion just provides more material for the opponent to take out of context. The opportunity for extensive discussion of issues beyond the major campaign theme may steer the campaign off message.

Using the unique features of the Internet as a backdrop, the remainder of the chapter will consider how candidates have been using the Internet. The major substantive concerns are the effect of resource availability, the balance between negative and positive campaigning, the extent of issue discussion, and the influence of government regulation. These major substantive concerns about Web campaigning will be addressed in the context of distinct historical periods. During the early era of Internet campaigning from 1992–1999, the stakes were fairly low because fewer than half of Americans were online. The modern era began with the election of 2000—one in which the Web had become firmly established as a mass medium.

EARLY ERA OF CYBERCAMPAIGNING (1992–1999)

The early era of Internet campaigning began with the 1992 presidential campaign of Bill Clinton and Al Gore. This was the first presidential election in which the candidates had an Internet presence. At that time, Web browsers did not exist. The online campaign was effectively limited to text-centered applications. The Clinton-Gore campaign took advantage of this modest opportunity by using e-mail and posting press releases, speeches, and position papers on discussion groups and bulletin boards. The campaign also benefited from the independent efforts of supporters, primarily college students, who advocated through e-mail and bulletin boards. The enthusiasm of supporters was seen in the ability of the popular discussion group at alt.politics.Clinton to get approximately eight hundred postings per week during the campaign. In fact, one study found that the Clinton-Gore campaign had difficulty keeping up with the desire of independent supporters to use the Internet: "Several volunteers reported . . . that they volunteered to monitor network discussion lists and to send summaries to Little Rock [campaign headquarters] . . . but that when they heard nothing back, most of them gave up this exercise."[7]

After the Clinton-Gore effort in 1992, the role of the Internet in politics grew slowly. Internet campaigning was rare in the congressional races of 1994. By 1996, the Web had exploded onto the scene with about one-fourth of Americans going online. Thus, 1996 was the first campaign in which the Internet entered general awareness. Use of the Internet continued to grow through the 1998 campaign. The early period ended by 2000, at which time 50 percent of Americans were online.

The early period was an awkward one for candidates. People were just starting to learn about the Internet and its fastest growing component, the World Wide Web. Candidates typically weren't expected to be experts in the new technology. It was, however, important to have a website to show a commitment to new technology. Thus, the goal for many candidates was simply to have a Web page. Little attention was given to the campaign site once it was obtained. This is captured in the lament of U.S. House candidate Rick Sandford: "We are getting one of those pages whatever they are."[8] Low candidate Internet expertise meant that campaign sites were often overseen by volunteers and low-ranking staffers. One of the most technologically sophisticated sites in 1998 was that of U.S. Senate candidate Mark Neumann in Wisconsin. The acknowledgment page made it clear that the campaign site was not a high priority for the candidate: "I am currently going to UW-Milwaukee. Even though I will still update this site regularly, it will probably be only weekends and homework-free weekdays."[9] When the quality of a candidate's Internet campaign is vulnerable to the exam schedules of college professors, there will be awkward moments.

The seminal moment of the early era occurred in the 1996 presidential debate. Before that time, the Web campaign had for the most part existed independently of the main thrust of the campaign and was invisible to the vast majority of the public. During the first presidential debate in Hartford on October 6, 1996, Republican presidential candidate Bob Dole took Internet politics to a new level. When candidates were given two minutes for a closing statement, Bob Dole ended his statement with a reference to his website. His words began a new visibility for Internet campaigning: "And if you really want to get involved, just tap into my home page www.dolekemp96org."[10]

On careful inspection, Dole's statement does more than begin a new visibility for Internet politics. It symbolizes the awkwardness of the early era of Internet campaigning. Dole's lack of expertise with the Internet led to him giving out an incorrect address. Whereas Dole's site was located at www.dolekemp96.org, he gave his address as "www.dolekemp96org". Omitting the final period—a crucial part of the syntax—would be a fatal error to those hoping to visit his site. Fortunately for Dole, many voters were experienced enough to realize his error and added the second period themselves. Unfortunately for Dole, his server was unprepared for the amount of traffic the statement generated. The Dole site crashed, but Internet politics would never be the same.

Effect of Resources

Early in its development, the Web was often described as a level playing field for third-party and poorly funded candidates.[11] The argument was that even the poorest candidate would be able to afford the $70 domain name fee and ask a volunteer to put up a rudimentary site. The Internet wasn't like television, in which large expenditures were required for even small blocks of space. Indeed, it was quickly apparent that low resources were not an absolute barrier to online campaigning. Some poorly funded and third-party candidates were on the Web. The question remained, however, whether the Internet constituted a level playing field.

Systematic data collected on U.S. Senate races during this period reveal that the Web was not a level playing field.[12] The amount of campaign funds clearly influenced whether a candidate ran a Web campaign. Third-party and financially disadvantaged candidates were less likely to have a campaign website than candidates who were not financially disadvantaged. Defining a financially disadvantaged candidate as one who has raised less than half as much as the opponent,[13] 79 percent of 1996 Senate candidates who were not financially disadvantaged had a website compared to 56 percent of major-party candidates who were financially disadvantaged. By 1998, the twenty-three-point gap had shrunk to 10 percent. Similarly, Libertarian candidates were almost 20 percent less likely to have a website than major party candidates in 1996, with the difference declining to less than 10 percent by 1998.

Extending the analysis to consider the substance of the home page, the effect of resources is even stronger. Defining a "substantive" home page as one whose issue section is at least two pages (five hundred words), financially disadvantaged major-party Senate candidates were less than half as likely to have substantive home pages than those who were not disadvantaged in 1996. This gap declined to about 10 percent by 1998. The disadvantage faced by third-party Libertarian candidates was also more pronounced by this measure. Only 10 percent of 1996 Libertarian candidates and 31 percent of 1998 Libertarian candidates had substantive home pages compared to 49 percent and 59 percent for major party candidates in 1996 and 1998, respectively.

Overall, during the early era, poorly funded candidates found themselves at a disadvantage compared to well-funded candidates in running a Web campaign. The claims of a level playing field were ultimately not supported by the evidence from U.S. Senate races. The finding was even stronger in studies that examined campaigns for lower offices.[14] That said, the Internet was certainly closer to a level playing field than other media, particularly expensive television advertising. Further, there was reason to be optimistic about the prospects for a level playing field. Over half of the gap in Senate races had evaporated within two years.

Content

In the early era of Internet campaigning, the content of campaign sites was almost entirely one-directional information dissemination. The sites made little attempt to take advantage of the mobilization potential of the Internet. They typically sought only to more economically distribute information available elsewhere. The most common elements of sites were the official biography, issue positions, and press releases. The lack of originality of most sites drew frequent criticism from those expecting the sites to make greater use of interactivity. In fact, critics of websites spawned a new vocabulary to creatively say that the sites were dull: sites were not just dull, but were "repurposed" or "brochureware."[15]

Despite the criticism of content, campaign sites did provide a useful vehicle for disseminating information about issues. While personality often dominates other parts of the campaign, especially television advertising, it represented only a small part of campaign sites. Perhaps with unlimited space there is a limit to candidates speaking about themselves, and ultimately they must take positions on issues. Regardless of the reason, issue discussion dominated early campaign sites. The amount of issue discussion is impressive, and so is the accessibility of the issue discussion as a result of it being organized into clear topics.

Another important dimension of campaign content is the balance between positive and negative advertising. Experimental evidence suggests that negative advertising alienates voters and reduces turnout.[16] Television advertisements are frequently negative; studies put the negative figure at around 50 percent.[17] The Web may change that balance. In assessing this balance, the longitudinal data on U.S. Senate sites again provides an excellent barometer. *Negative advertising* is defined as a reference to the opponent for the purpose of putting that person in an unfavorable light.

The evidence from U.S. Senate campaigns in the early era shows clearly that the Web was a medium dominated by positive campaigning. Approximately one-third of 1996 candidates and just under one-half of 1998 candidates ever mentioned their opponent in a bad light. The negative campaigning was not prominently featured. Only 16 percent of candidates in 1996 and 38 percent of candidates in 1998 had any negative campaigning or opponent referencing links on their main home page. Where mentioned, the negative campaigning often amounted to a small percentage of the website. Only 8 percent in 1996 and 18 percent in 1998 had as much as a thousand words devoted to negative campaigning.

Beyond the context of U.S. Senate campaigns, scholars were confirming the Senate campaign findings. Looking at 1998 House and Senate candidates, Edward Harpham found that 94 percent of sites discussed at least three major issues, while only 13 percent launched ideological attacks on the opponent.[18] Comparing the television, direct mail, newspaper, and Web campaigns of the same candidates for state and local office in 1998, William Benoit found that the Web campaign was the most positive, with only 2 percent negative content.[19] Studying 1998 gubernatorial candidates from the primary to general election, Greer and LaPointe found that the tendency for positive and issue-oriented campaigning became even stronger as the campaign progressed.[20]

Symbolic of the one-directional information dissemination is the resistance to allow site visitors to share information through an online message board. Internet technology easily allows site visitors and campaign personnel to post and respond to messages in an unfiltered forum. The prospect for this type of discussion had an early appeal to candidates, but the practical reality of losing control reduced interest. President Clinton's website in 1996, for instance, began with the ideal of a free-flowing discussion but edited out messages that weren't favorable.[21] A study following the Web campaign of gubernatorial candidates from the primary through the general election found that three campaigns started with interactive bulletin boards. By the end of the campaign, every candidate had taken the bulletin board off the website.[22] No new discussions were launched. The problems of negative and off-color comments outweighed the benefits of free exchange. By the end of the early era, it was clear that discussion boards would not be part of Web campaigns.

While candidates were eager to use the Web for information dissemination in the early era, they were unlikely to use the campaign site for mobilization. When requests were made for donations or volunteers, the sites typically listed a U.S. postal address or telephone number. In 1996, there was a good reason that campaigns did not collect donations online. Secure credit card technology was in its infancy, and many users were uncomfortable with online transactions. By 1998, the technology had improved. Yet, it was the rare campaign that took advantage of the opportunity. Over two-thirds of 1998 Senate campaigns requesting donations online did not provide online processing, but requested that a check be mailed.[23] Similarly, most efforts to recruit volunteers were introduced online but then referred to traditional contact mechanisms.

Although mobilization was low in the early era, there were some notable efforts to mobilize. In 1996, John Kerry's Senate campaign in Massachusetts had mobilization as a stated goal: "We hope you will use this page as a resource for increasing your political participation." Kerry took advantage of the ability to quickly update the site to display information about the time and location of events. Thus, the Internet was able to increase the attendance and excitement at rallies.[24]

Another early indicator of efforts to mobilize on the Internet was a study conducted by Campaign Solutions in 1998. The consulting firm contracted with the Republican Party to monitor activity on twenty sites of Republican candidates for governor and U.S. senator. Each site had an icon for volunteering to help the campaign. Campaign Solutions surveyed all those who volunteered online. The survey revealed that 90 percent of the volunteers reached on the Web had not previously been in contact with the campaign, while 55 percent were first-time volunteers.[25] Although based on a small sample, the finding was of great interest to campaign managers. The Internet appeared to be bringing in people who had not been effectively recruited by traditional media.

All previous efforts to mobilize, however, paled in comparison to the shock wave created by the Internet campaign of Jesse Ventura in 1998. Running as an independent, Ventura was locked in a three-way race for governor of Minnesota with two well-funded, major-party candidates. The man who didn't "have time to bleed" in the movie *Predator* didn't have time to waste in the campaign. With the election days away and still trailing, Ventura made a final push by traveling the state. Word about rallies and events was distributed on the Internet. Using the Internet to communicate with young voters, Ventura was able to quickly draw large crowds to rallies to demonstrate that he was a viable candidate. This show of support enhanced by the Internet was crucial to a candidate who may not have been taken seriously as a modestly funded third-party candidate with a background in professional wrestling. Young people, who represented a disproportionate share of Internet users, were turned on late in the campaign. This may not have mattered under most circumstances because many potential young voters are not registered. In Minnesota, however, the electoral system allowed for same-day registration. Late mobilization counted, and the Ventura campaign made people aware of how to register. Those registering on the day of the election voted overwhelmingly for Ventura. Although it cannot be definitively proven, the surprise victory of Jesse Ventura is widely heralded as the first election in which the Internet changed the outcome of an election.[26]

While Ventura was showing people how to effectively use the Internet to mobilize, others found that mobilization attempts could backfire. One of the most enduring lessons from the early era about mobilization is how *not* to use the Web for mobilization. While mass e-mails can save much time and expense for disseminating information to supporters, they should not be sent to individuals who have not requested to be on the distribution list. In Internet language, voters don't want to be spammed. The sending of unsolicited mass e-mail, or spam, will not get the result that the candidate wants. The name for unsolicited mass e-mail is not a playful nickname by someone taking a guilty pleasure from the Hormel meat-derived product. Spam is universally detested on the Internet. Not only will spamming not win any votes, a candidate will soon be dealing with a new set of problems. An awkward mass e-mailed apology is unlikely to satisfy angry voters. The candidate may face civil and criminal sanctions.

The first candidate to visibly learn this lesson was Steve Langford, who was running for Governor of Georgia. Mr. Langford was in the middle of a competitive six-way race for the Democratic nomination. Langford calculated that an inexpensive way to get a competitive edge would be to send an unsolicited mass e-mail. The message was sent to over five hundred addresses. Ostensibly concerned that he wouldn't be able to personally answer all the issue-related questions of voters, Langford sent the e-mail from a post-only address, which is able to send but not receive messages. Although Langford had not sought interactivity, his constituents, on the other hand, embraced the interactivity of the Internet. They wanted to respond directly to the candidate, but were frustrated by the post-only source of the message. Indeed, the response rate to his mass mailing—over 6 percent—would make many direct marketers envious. Unfortunately, for Langford, the responses were complaints filed with his service provider.[27] Since spamming violated the terms of his Internet service, the service provider cut off Langford's service. An e-mail address wasn't all Langford would lose. He lost the primary after receiving just under 7 percent of the vote.

MODERN ERA OF CYBERCAMPAIGNING (2000–)

In the modern era of Internet campaigning, the Web exists as a bona fide mass medium. Most Americans have access to the Internet. The Web is a visible part of American life. Yet, a substantial minority of Americans are not regular Internet users. Political use of the Internet remains low. The Internet is a significant component of the political environment, but it remains well in the background behind traditional media. A new era in which the Internet begins to approach traditional media as a vehicle for political life may still occur some time in the future.

The modern era of Internet campaigning began with the 2000 election. Much had changed since the 1998 election. In 1998, the Internet was a medium used regularly by a distinct minority of Americans. Only 41 percent had ever used the Internet. Between the 1998 election and 2000 election, the Internet grew tremendously. By 2000, the modern era began with a majority of Americans having access to the Internet.

For candidates, the modern era brings heightened expectations about the use of the Internet by candidates. There is no credit given just for having a website. What matters is how the site is used. A weak site can reflect poorly on a candidate. Although candidates are getting better at using the technology, there are still awkward moments.

The awkwardness of the modern era is evident in the quirky start to the era in the 2000 elections. On the heels of the Ventura campaign in 1998, there were high expectations about the use of the Internet. The momentum continued when Republican Steve Forbes became the first presidential candidate to announce online. Later in the primaries, the Internet's profile increased with some dramatic demonstrations of online fund-raising capacity. As the national conventions approached, the parties purchased heavy Internet banner advertising. Expectations for the Internet campaign going into the general election were high. These expectations, however, were not met. The money raised online, and Internet advertising, declined after the conventions.[28] The enduring moments of the 2000 Internet campaign were two quirky, unanticipated roles for the Internet.

The first of these unexpected uses was the proliferation of "vote trading" across the country during the latter part of the campaign. The third-party candidacy of Ralph Nader was gaining supporters who in a two-candidate race would have preferred Democrat Al Gore to Republican George Bush. Fearing that votes lost to Nader might be the difference in the election, Gore and Nader supporters devised an interstate vote-trading arrangement that preserved Nader support while benefiting Al Gore. Those who intended to vote for Nader in closely contested states were asked to trade their vote with someone who intended to vote for Al Gore in a state that Gore was certain to lose. As an example, someone who intended to vote for Nader in Florida (close contest) was asked to trade their vote with someone who intended to vote for Gore in Indiana (where Gore was certain to lose). Gore and Nader would each get one vote, just as they would have before the trade. After the trade, however, the votes were distributed to different states in a way beneficial to Al Gore. For the Nader campaign, the state in which the vote was received was unimportant since the campaign's only realistic goal was for a 5 percent national vote, which would guarantee federal funding in 2004.

The mechanism for implementing the vote trade was the Internet. Motivated by the difference between the electoral and popular vote, the trade had to be across states to have any effect. The Internet allowed this far-flung group of people to come into contact with each other. People living in different states who had no previous relationship were brought together for a one-time online transaction. A number of sites, such as nadertrader.org, were set up to coordinate the transactions. Of course, in a secret ballot system, the trades could not be legally binding. As shown on winwincampaign.org, the sites were careful to add a disclaimer to this effect: "There is no way to verify that a person has voted in accordance with their pledge."[29] By Election Day, thousands of voters had agreed to be part of such exchanges.

The sites existed on shaky legal ground. This type of vote trading approached or entered the territory of exchanging your vote for something of value, which is illegal. Thus, the legality of these sites was questioned from the outset. Vote-trading sites themselves were sometimes cautious in advising participants whether the act was legal: "Since this is your own business, please consult your own legal counsel."[30] After being notified by the secretary of state of California that it was engaged in illegal vote brokering, voteswap2000.com shut down and told its clients to "err on the side of caution."[31] Other sites, however, remained in operation, and new ones sprang up during the campaign.

Ultimately the vote-trading scheme did not save Al Gore from the outcome feared by his supporters. In postelection surveys, Nader voters by a 2 to 1 margin indicated that they would have voted for the more ideologically similar candidate Al Gore in a two-candidate race.[32] Had Nader voters in Florida been distributed 2 to 1 in favor of Gore, it would have given Al Gore a victory in Florida and the presidency.

The second of the quirky legacies relates to the role of the Internet in extending the presidential campaign a month beyond Election Day on November 7. After a long evening, the tide appeared to have turned in favor of George Bush. According to network figures, Bush enjoyed a lead of over 1,000 votes in Florida with almost all votes counted. At approximately 2:30 a.m., the three major networks awarded the state to George Bush. When Florida was added to Bush's electoral vote total, it gave him 271 electoral votes, and the networks named him the forty-third president of the United States. Election night, however, was destined not to end.

The dissemination of information on the Internet would play a major role in the continuation of election night. As the apparent losing candidate, Al Gore was en route to giving a concession speech; meanwhile, his campaign aide was monitoring election returns on the state of Florida's website. The aide noticed that Bush's lead on the Florida site was much smaller than the television networks were reporting. In fact, it had shrunk to several hundred votes. With a few precincts and some absentee votes outstanding, the lead was by no means secure. The aide called Gore on his cell phone and told him that the Florida site was showing that the lead had narrowed considerably. Al Gore had the driver turn the car around and returned to his hotel.[33] He would not concede that night. In fact, Gore would not concede until December, after a United States Supreme Court ruling ended a series of legal and political maneuvers that had extended the campaign for over a month.

Effect of Resources

In the modern era, websites are nearly universal in campaigns for higher office. The modern era is distinguished from the previous era by a greater online presence of financially disadvantaged candidates. As shown in table 5.1, financially disadvantaged, major-party candidates actually were more likely to have a campaign website than candidates who were not financially disadvantaged in the 2000 Senate races. The elimination of the gap between candidates of varied resources completed a trend present since the early era of Web campaigning.

The altered landscape of the new era can be further seen in the data on substantive campaigns. In the 1996 Senate campaign, financially disadvantaged, major-party candidates were less than twice as likely to have substantial issue discussion

Table 5.1   Trends in Candidate Resources and Website Characteristics

Characteristic	1996	1998	2000	2002
Candidate Website Existence:				
Financially Disadvantaged Major Party	56	76	96	87
Not Disadvantaged Major Party	79	86	93	96
Total Major Party Candidates	74	82	94	92
Libertarian Party Candidates	45	75	72	86
Substantive Website Existence:				
Financially Disadvantaged Major Party	25	52	77	40
Not Disadvantaged Major Party	56	63	73	90
Total Major Party Candidates	49	59	74	77
Libertarian Party Candidates	10	31	44	62

Notes: Includes all general election U.S. Senate candidates. Financially disadvantaged candidates are those raising less than half as much as their opponent. Substantive websites have an issue section of at least 500 words.

on their site. By 2000, financially disadvantaged candidates had not only eliminated the gap, but had a slight advantage. Although the 2000 election demonstrates that financially disadvantaged candidates can compete online with their better-funded opponents, the 2002 election demonstrates that parity is not guaranteed and candidates must choose to run a substantive Web campaign. Any broader meaning to the 2002 reversion is unlikely since the pool of financially disadvantaged candidates was smaller than in previous years and included several campaigns with little activity, online or otherwise.

Libertarian candidates have made consistent gains over the life of the Internet. The number of Libertarian candidates with home pages increased from 45 percent in 1996 to 86 percent in 2002. More impressive is the fact that Libertarian candidates with substantive home pages doubled from 31 percent in 1998 to 62 percent in 2002. The significant gains by Libertarian candidates in 2002 left little room for future growth in website adoption.

Overall, the evidence suggests that a lack of resources is not a barrier to Web campaigning. Financially disadvantaged candidates have shown the ability to match their better-funded counterparts in having substantive home pages. Indeed, there is no theoretical reason to believe that when countless Americans are routinely buying domain names for $10 and maintaining them for marginally more, money is stopping candidates from outlining their issue positions on the Web. On the other hand, financial resources better enable a campaign site to incorporate the latest technological bells and whistles. Even this advantage of resources, however, should not be exaggerated, since the gap between financially disadvantaged 2002 Senate candidates and those who were not was greater for having a substantive issue section (40%–90%) than for having video files accessible from the website (40%–62%). Although technologically sophisticated sites may be more attention grabbing, they do not necessarily impress voters. Surveys continue to show that voters want more than anything to receive substantive issue information from campaign sites.[34]

Content

In the modern era, information dissemination remains the major function of campaign sites. As in the early era, it is mostly a one-directional transmission of information available in other parts of the campaign. Candidates regularly disseminate biographical and voter registration information. Above all, however, issues continue to dominate campaign sites.

One important content characteristic for which consistent data are available over time is the balance between negative and positive campaigning. In the early era, the Internet was disproportionately a venue for positive campaigning. In Senate races, most candidates never discussed their opponent with the intent of placing that individual in a bad light. As the early era progressed, a trend toward more negative campaigning became apparent. As the modern era began, many questioned whether the trend would continue or if the appeal of a positive outlet would appeal to candidates often criticized for negativity.

As shown in table 5.2, negative campaigning has become an accepted part of campaign websites in the modern era. From 1996 to 2002, the percentage of Senate candidates using some negative campaigning doubled from 34 percent to 68 percent. Further, the prominence and amount of negative campaigning also increased dramatically. Approximately two-thirds of candidates now have some negative campaigning on the main page. The number of Senate candidates with extensive negative campaigning of over one thousand words quadrupled between 1996 and 2002.

While information dissemination continues to flourish, it is increasingly being accompanied by efforts to use the Internet to mobilize. The disproportionately young Internet audience provides an attractive pool for recruiting campaign volunteers. In private, many candidates cite raising money as the primary motivation for an Internet presence. Compared to direct mail, which can often cost more than it raises, the price of raising money on the Web is low. It is estimated that for each campaign dollar raised on the Web, the cost is about 10 cents. This represents a dramatic savings over direct mail, in which 50–90 cents is often spent for each dollar raised.[35] The low costs have motivated candidates to try raising money online. In 2002, for example, every single Senate campaign site requested a contribution, with 85 percent of the candidates capable of online credit card processing and 15 percent asking visitors to mail a check.

Whether a significant amount of money is actually raised is another question. Certainly the modern era represents a dramatic improvement over the early era in receiving donations. Secure credit card technology has wide acceptance, although many are still nervous about online transactions. Yet, the aggregate amount of money raised on the Internet has been quite low. The modern era began with es-

Table 5.2   Trends in Negative Campaigning on Campaign Websites

Characteristic	1996	1998	2000	2002
Some Negative Campaigning	34	48	63	68
Negative Campaigning on Main Page	16	38	55	65
Extensive Negative Campaigning	8	18	31	35

Notes: Includes all Republican and Democratic general election U.S. Senate candidates. *Extensive negative campaigning* is defined as devoting over 1,000 words to placing the opponent in a bad light.

timates that about 2 percent of all money raised in the 2000 federal elections was raised on the Internet.[36] Many candidates, especially those running for lower offices, continue to have difficulty raising any money online. In campaigns for higher offices, however, a growing number of candidates are using the Internet for significant fund-raising.

The seminal event in the history of raising campaign money on the Internet was the 2000 primaries. Before that time, donations had trickled into campaigns in unimpressive amounts. In a 1998 U.S. Senate race in California, for example, Barbara Boxer's online fund-raising amounted to $25,000, which was one-tenth of 1 percent of her total contributions.[37] The 2000 primary season proved that online fund-raising could add up to a significant amount. Specifically, the experience of two candidates—Bill Bradley and John McCain—announced the arrival of the Internet as a way to raise substantial campaign dollars.

The first indicator of the potential for online fund-raising was the success of Bill Bradley in the Democratic presidential primary. Less successful with the wealthy contributors than his opponent Al Gore, Bradley had to find innovative ways to raise money. He promoted his campaign website and emphasized his ability to receive online donations. By October 1999, he had raised a reported $770,000 on the Internet. This was more than five times greater than the amount raised online by either of the favored candidates Al Gore or George W. Bush.[38]

If Bradley's early success created a ripple, the big splash in online fund-raising was made later in the Republican primary by John McCain. After a quiet start, McCain had been making steady progress in his struggle against his heavily favored and well-funded opponent George W. Bush. In February 2000, McCain pulled off a surprise victory in the New Hampshire primary. With his funds running low, McCain saw the potential to benefit from Internet speed in fund-raising. And he did. McCain shattered all previous online fund-raising efforts by raising a reported $3 million online in the ten days following his victory in New Hampshire. The political fund-raising world was taken completely by surprise with the speed at which significant sums of money could be raised online.[39]

Building on the efforts of Bradley and McCain, presidential candidates in 2004 emphasized Internet fund-raising early in the campaign. Well ahead of Bill Bradley's 2000 pace, Democrat Howard Dean became the first candidate to pass the $1 million mark in online fund-raising in spring 2003. More significant was the relative importance of online fund-raising. While Bradley ultimately raised only about 6.5 percent of his money online, in some months Dean's online contributions represented about half of his total receipts.[40] Dean's high proportion of Internet fundraising, however, remains the exception.

REGULATION OF INTERNET CAMPAIGNING

Like any federal campaign activity, campaigning on the Internet is subject to regulation by the Federal Election Commission (FEC). The FEC administers a complex set of rules governing the activity of campaigns, especially the receipt and disbursement of funds. Disclosure has been a bedrock principle of the campaign finance system for decades. There are also restrictions placed on who can contribute to candidates and how much can be collected. Corporations and labor unions, for instance, may not make direct contributions to a campaign. These and other regulations are enforced by requiring the return of certain contributions, by the imposition of fines, or in rare cases by criminal prosecution. Seeking to avoid the punishment phase, the FEC gives advisory opinions to campaigns asking for clarifications and interpretations of the law.

The overall approach of the FEC to regulating campaign activity on the Internet can be divided into eras that parallel the eras of campaigning more broadly. This is not entirely coincidental. The advisory opinions of the FEC have the effect of encouraging or discouraging certain behavior by campaigns. In the early era of Internet campaigning from 1992 to 1999, the FEC did little to encourage Internet campaigning and may have slightly slowed its development. As Internet campaigning matured into a new era, the FEC shifted to a position more encouraging of Internet campaigning.

In the early era, both the action and inaction of the FEC seemed to discourage Internet electioneering. On the action side, the FEC took a tough stance against independent individuals and organizations who wanted to distribute opinion and information about the election online. In the 1998 Leo Smith advisory opinion, the FEC considered the reporting obligations of an ordinary citizen using a personal website to advocate for a candidate. Leo Smith, a self-described "Independent voter," used part of his website to support a congressional candidate. He urged visitors to vote for Charlotte Koskoff for Congress and provided a link to her campaign site. There was no evidence that Koskoff had coordinated activity with Leo Smith, although she did make a friendly request that his site correct the spelling of her name. The FEC classified independent sites as "general public political advertising" required to identify the sponsor. Further, the FEC advised that the website constituted "something of value under the Act because it expressly advocates the election of a federal candidate, and the defeat of another federal candidate." Thus, its costs fell under the requirement that those spending over $250 must file disclosure reports.[41] Although an enforcement mechanism was never created, the concern was voiced that countless Americans might be required to report their use of personal websites for taking sides in elections.

In another case, the FEC issued an advisory opinion prohibiting an online service provider from giving free websites to political candidates. In 1996, the online service provider CompuServe proposed to provide a website free of charge to all candidates for state and federal office. The FEC advised that giving candidates a free website would violate the law that prohibits corporations from contributing anything of value to a candidate. According to the law, the value of a contribution is "the difference between the amount actually charged and the usual and normal charge." Since the normal charge was $9.95 for basic membership plus incremental costs, the use of an Internet account did have value and constituted a prohibited contribution.[42] In drawing this conclusion, the FEC refused to include online service providers in the exemption that allows traditional media editorial discretion to give blocks of free time to election competitors. The CompuServe advisory opinion was perhaps the hallmark of a tough stance on Internet campaigning: not only was the Internet subject to reporting requirements of traditional media, but it lacked some of the privileges of traditional media.

The tough stance of the FEC in the early era also can be seen in its inaction on the eligibility of credit card donations for matching funds. Funded by the income tax checkoff, the matching program allows presidential candidates meeting donation requirements to receive matching funds. During that period, the FEC continued to exclude credit card donations from the matching program for violating the rule that an eligible contribution "means a gift of money made by a written instrument." With the Internet having greatly expanded credit card transactions, the significance of the FEC inaction on credit cards grew. This inaction, combined with the two key advisory opinions, began to raise concerns in the Internet community about how the FEC was approaching the Internet.

To the relief of its critics, the new era of Internet campaigning in the 2000 election saw a more encouraging approach from the FEC. The first important matter in the new election cycle was a request by the Bill Bradley for President campaign to revisit the issue of credit card donations. In its Bill Bradley advisory opinion, the FEC noted that the Internet was well established as evidenced by the increase in electronic commerce and the approximately 50 percent of Americans who had Internet access. The FEC considered whether this critical mass of Internet activity had parallels in the non-Internet world. Finding that it did, the FEC adopted phrases such as "the functional equivalent of a written instrument." The last step for the FEC was to overrule its own precedent: "Under the current regulatory regime, your proposal appears contrary to the regulations. . . . [but] the Commission has approved revisions to the above cited regulations that would allow federal matching payments for credit card contributions."[43]

Following this decision, the FEC sent a strong signal that it was considering much broader change in Internet campaign regulation by making a general request for suggestions. The response of the public and interest groups was unusually unified. Estimates showed that 99 percent of comments warned the FEC against too much regulation.[44] The public and interest groups were especially concerned about the 1998 Leo Smith advisory opinion, which seemed to discourage political participation on the Internet by requiring extensive reporting. As expressed by FEC Commissioner David Mason, the public response would be difficult to ignore: "[I]f there's a broad social consensus that the Internet should be relatively free of regulation, certainly we should take that into account."[45]

Shortly after requesting comments, the FEC showed a willingness to reconsider the issue of independent participation in campaigns. The opinion was requested by the Bush campaign, which suggested that ambiguity about FEC regulations was forcing it to discourage Internet activity by independent supporters. The Bush campaign advisory opinion backed away from the strict reporting requirements implied by the earlier question involving Leo Smith. The decision characterized most independent Internet activity on behalf of a candidate as falling under a reporting exception for volunteers acting from their home. Not only is there no requirement for the volunteer to report, but there is no requirement for the candidate: "[The Bush campaign] does not have an obligation to search the Web to discover the existence of pro-Bush activity."[46]

The FEC also proved willing to ease restrictions on providing free time to candidates. In its Democracy Network (DNet) advisory opinion, the FEC approved a proposal to provide an online forum for candidates. As part of the proposal, the nonprofit DNet would give candidates an ID and password so they can load online biographies, taped statements, and issue positions onto the DNet site. The FEC ruled that the forum could fall under a "nonpartisan activity designed to encourage individuals to vote or to register to vote" exception for campaign contributions.[47] In a June 2000 opinion, the FEC also ruled that the exception also applied to the Ampex Corporation plan to provide online video coverage of the party conventions. The FEC drew a parallel between the Ampex iNEXTV site and traditional media: "The website is viewable by the general public and akin to a periodical or news program distributed to the general public."[48]

In subsequent decisions, the FEC has continued to craft a regulatory framework that allows candidates and interested independent citizens to take advantage of the Internet's capacity to disseminate information and mobilize in political campaigns. In August 2000, for example, the FEC ruled that the young persons' advocacy group Third Millennium would not violate its tax-exempt status by conducting a study in which potential voters would be shown online ads for candidates. Working with the Internet service provider Juno, Third Millennium showed potential voters pop-up ads from zero, one, or two candidates and sought to determine if the ads had any impact on the decision to vote.[49] In 2001, Third Millennium reported that undecided voters who saw online pop-up ads were more likely to vote.[50]

One thing that the FEC has been unable and unwilling to do in any era is to protect political candidates from the often harsh realities of the domain name system. Under the first-come, first-served domain name assignment process, candidates are not guaranteed their most preferred domain name. In fact, when applying for a domain name, candidates may find that their preferred domain name is already held by the opponent. It is estimated that of the 37 most logical domain names pertaining to the George Bush campaign, the only two registered first by the Bush campaign were Bush2000.org and GeorgeWBush.com.[51] Many of the other permutations, including GeorgeBush2000.com, were held by people who intended to use the site to criticize George Bush (except presumably if the Bush campaign offered a large sum for the domain name).

Frustrated by his domain name difficulties, George Bush lamented that "there ought to be limits to freedom"[52] and embarked on a number of strategies, which failed to varying degrees. One strategy that largely failed was moving in late and buying the domain names of sites that potentially could be used against him. This did not solve his larger problem; it only added to the environment of misleading domain names by having visitors to Bushsucks.com greeted with a warm welcome and a lovely fireplace photo of George and Laura Bush. The biggest failure was publicly criticizing gwbush.com, which gave the site ridiculing Bush as a cocaine addict enough publicity to convert a modest audience into 500,000 monthly visitors.[53] Bush also asked the FEC to investigate the site. In April 2000, the FEC found that gwbush.com did not violate any laws. Further, the FEC implied that the matter bordered on the trivial: "[The] matter is less significant relative to other matters pending before the Commission."[54] The FEC sent a clear message to future candidates. The critical first step of a Web campaign is to secure the most logical domain names.

CONCLUSION

The Internet is now an established part of political campaigns. During the early era of Internet campaigning from 1992 to 1999, candidates awkwardly embraced the new medium. By 2000, the modern era of Web campaigning began, with higher stakes because most Americans were then online. While the FEC seemed to discourage Internet campaigning in the early era, it has been more supportive in the modern era. Indeed, candidates have flocked to the Web to take advantage of a unique forum of low accidental exposure, audience discretion in when and what communication to receive, interactivity on a mass level, and unlimited time and space for communication. Essential to democracy, the dissemination of political information and mobilization are facilitated by the Internet campaign. These opportunities are available to far more candidates on the Internet than through any other mass medium. Over time, candidates will continue to find better ways to take advantage of the technology. At minimum, voters can expect fewer candidates to describe themselves as friendly Web page users and more candidates to offer user-friendly Web pages.

6

Party and Group Advocacy on the Internet

Advocacy on the Internet is not limited to candidates. Interest groups and political parties take advantage of the Internet's capacity for information dissemination and mobilization to further their organizational goals. In a brief period of time, the Internet has become central to the lives of many of these advocates. In some cases, the Internet constitutes the only organizational life. The use of the Internet by political parties and interest groups will be examined in this chapter. The first consideration will be the extent to which advocates of varying resource levels have adopted the medium. Measures of the prominence of interest groups and political parties in cyberspace will be compared to prominence in the nonvirtual world. A consideration of the effect of resources on Internet advocacy is followed by an exploration of the nature of information dissemination and mobilization by interest groups and political parties. Key techniques are identified and illustrated with noteworthy examples.

INTEREST GROUPS

The importance of the medium of communication used by interest groups has long been recognized. In a book that some view as beginning modern political science, David Truman argued that politics could be broken down into the essential element of interest groups. He believed that groups make a crucial choice about how to communicate: "The success of the interest group propagandist depends in no small measure on his skill in selecting the appropriate media and channels for his efforts at communication."[1] In the modern era, almost every interest group finds the Internet to be an appropriate medium for advocacy. What's not to like about disseminating information and mobilizing at a fraction of the cost of other techniques of communication? Indeed, groups of all beliefs and resource levels have taken to the Internet.

The viewpoints expressed by groups online range from the mainstream to the highly unconventional. Of course, the most prominent interest groups are well established on the Internet. They are joined by numerous other mainstream groups that are not as well known or well funded. The World Wide Web is also home to many groups that are well outside the mainstream. The beliefs articulated by these groups span the range of human thought. For many groups, the Internet provides the only evidence of their existence.

Perhaps the most notorious example of a non-mainstream group for whom the Web constituted its only public visibility was the California-based cult known as Heaven's Gate. In March 1997, the nation was left looking for answers after thirty-nine people were found dead in bunk beds, lying beside their packed suitcases in a rented home. It became apparent that the deceased were members of a small cult known as Heaven's Gate. Since the reclusive group had little contact with the outside world, there was little insight into what may have prompted the mass suicide. The major breakthrough in learning about the group came from the discovery of its website, which documented the teachings of leader Marshall Applewhite and suggested that the suicide victims were seeking salvation on the Hale-Bopp Comet. In the days following the discovery, the site went from obscurity to being one of the most visited sites on the Web.

One type of non-mainstream group that has gained attention for online activity is the group that promotes hatred of others based on socio-ethnic characteristics. The proliferation of online hate groups prompted a matter-of-fact statement by fictional president turned Internet historian Josiah "Jeb" Bartlett on the TV show *The West Wing:* "The Internet has been a phenomenal tool for hate groups."[2] A milestone in awareness of online hate groups was the release of an interactive CD-ROM by the Simon Wiesenthal Center in 1997. Reporting a 300 percent increase over the previous year, the Center compiled data on over six hundred hate groups on the Web. The Center distributed the information with the express purpose of trying to bring public pressure on Internet service providers to discontinue service to listed hate groups.[3] By 2002, the Wiesenthal Center was monitoring 25,000 sites every month and issued an updated CD-ROM that highlighted two hundred groups that promote terror.[4]

The Internet is also home to a wide range of informal discussion groups. Through a variety of Web-based discussion areas, Usenet groups, and chat rooms, people informally come together to communicate about politics. Such groups are the focus of one of the most significant early studies of online political behavior. In *Cyberpolitics,* Kevin Hill and John Hughes systematically examined 1,525 discussion threads in political Usenet groups and the America Online (AOL) "cloak room" over a several-month period. They found that 40 percent of threads began and ended with one participant. In the other threads, an informal group emerged to discuss politics. Although reinforcement of beliefs was a common purpose, about one-third of the threads did lead to a debate in which both sides of a position were expressed. Symbolic of these groups existing in cyberspace, Hill and Hughes found that in only 16 percent of the threads was there any effort to recruit for activity beyond cyberspace. Although groups covered the political spectrum, the authors found that discussion threads were three times more likely to emphasize the ideological Right than the Left.[5]

Not only can advocates of all beliefs be found on the Internet, but advocates of all resource levels. The Internet is home to interest groups ranging from the very rich to the very poor. Since a primitive site is possible for no more than a few hundred dollars, resources are seldom an obstacle for a group wishing to establish an Internet presence. Using volunteer labor and a standard e-mail account costing less than $100, activists have been able to get online petitions signed by hundreds of thousands of people.[6] With such a minimal investment required, it is not surprising that a Web presence is almost universal for interest groups. In the cases where a group does not have a website, it is unlikely that the inability to raise $100 is the reason.

While it is difficult to find evidence of resource bias in the existence of a group website, the Internet does not completely eliminate differences between groups based on resource level. Groups with greater resources typically have more sophisticated sites. Although the benefits from having the latest technical bells and whistles are limited by the presence of end users with less advanced equipment, more sophisticated sites generally have more to attract and retain the site visitor. Resource level also affects the ability to promote a website in other media. The persistence of these resource-based differences in group advocacy on the Internet, however, does not detract from the larger picture of a medium in which low resources do not preclude effective advocacy.

In fact, compared to other media, the Internet is a medium in which low-resource groups are profoundly more competitive. In many cases, other media are not even an option. Only the wealthiest groups can afford a television advertisement. Social scientists have long known that traditional media focus their limited news coverage on resource-wealthy groups.[7] In contrast, the Web offers the potential to reach an unlimited audience at virtually no cost. Although the competition for attention is intense, groups are using the Internet to attain a visibility all but impossible in other media.

While maintaining the promise of heightened visibility, resource-poor groups may also benefit from the more mundane advantages of Internet use. These resource-poor groups, which often struggle to survive, may benefit from the cost savings of transferring administrative functions to the Internet. The efficiency gains in organizational maintenance are more important for resource-poor groups than for well-funded groups. In particular, the Internet allows groups to disseminate information without incurring expensive printing costs. Instead of fulfilling requests for copies of group reports, interest groups can refer interested parties to their website.

The quantity of information distributed can be tremendous. Unlike the expensive space in other media, the Internet provides virtually unlimited space at marginal costs (approaching zero). Groups need not select a few reports to actively distribute, but can provide comprehensive access to group materials including archived historical materials. All of this material can reach a potentially unlimited audience on the Internet. Information dissemination can be further enhanced when groups work together to create a unified resource. The information provided can perform a real service to group members and to the public.

One example of the important information dissemination undertaken by groups is the campaign finance data provided by the Center for Responsive Politics. In 2002, the Center's opensecrets.org became the first two-time winner of the prestigious International Academy of Digital Arts and Sciences (IADAS) Webby Award for Best Political Site.[8] Compiling Federal Election Commission data into a user-friendly format, opensecrets.org is an outstanding resource for anyone interested in how campaigns are funded. One long-standing feature of the site is a search that allows the user to type in a zip code and immediately learn the amount, recipient, and source of all campaign contributions from that zip code. The site also offers more conventional ways of accessing data by candidate or contributor.

An early milestone in groups coordinating the dissemination of information was the creation of townhall.com. A joint project of the Heritage Foundation and *National Review*, townhall.com was designed as a central destination for conservatism on the Web. The site was launched with tremendous fanfare at a ceremony attended by Speaker of the House Newt Gingrich and Senate Majority Leader Robert Dole. When a Benjamin Franklin impersonator announced, "On this the 29th day of June in the year of our Lord one thousand nine hundred and ninety-five, we open the doors of Town Hall in a spirit of experiment and good will to preserve liberty and prevent tyranny," it was the cue for Gingrich and Dole to call up the townhall.com website.[9] Expanding beyond the twelve conservative interest groups attending the launch, the site now has more than one hundred members.

Interest groups also benefit from the effectiveness of the Internet in mobilization. The Internet allows groups to channel the participation of supporters into activities that the group views as politically effective. Serving as an intermediary between citizens and public officials, an interest group is constantly challenged by how to encourage its members to communicate with public officials on behalf of the group. In confronting the challenge, groups benefit from the interactivity of the Internet. Interest groups routinely provide e-mail links to public officials in their material distributed over the Internet. The response rate to these links has been impressive. The Chamber of Commerce, for instance, reported that the percentage of chief executives following up on a Chamber request to contact public officials rose from 5 to 50 percent after e-mail links to public officials replaced traditional techniques.[10]

The Internet dramatically increases the speed of group mobilization. The use of e-mail distribution lists means that in the time it takes to click on a "send" icon, the entire membership can be sent a request for mobilization. By combining a website with e-mail, interest groups can quickly coordinate the actions of group members and supporters. Rapid online mobilization in support of a specific policy issue is known as a flash campaign.

The classic flash campaign is the moveon.org mobilization against the impeachment of President Clinton in 1998. The effort was started by a married couple in their basement, using a standard Internet account. Wes Boyd and Joan Blades supported censuring the president for his misbehavior and then trying to "move on." They hoped to demonstrate support for this course of action by circulating a petition opposing impeachment. Working outside of existing political channels, they began mobilizing with an e-mail to friends. The e-mail included a request to visit the moveon.org website and sign the petition. There was also a request to forward the e-mail to additional friends. Within a short period, the site accumulated a list of 500,000 signatures and e-mails. The site also solicited contributions for candidates running against pro-impeachment incumbents in Congress. With an average contribution of $37, moveon.org broke online political fund-raising records by taking in $250,000 in a five-day period and getting pledges for $13 million overall in 1999.[11] Although the effort did not prevent the impeachment of President Clinton by the House of Representatives, it was a dramatic demonstration of Internet mobilization.

Online mobilization can be enhanced when groups work together. The global nature of the Internet opens the possibility for coordinating groups in different countries. The most dramatic examples of Internet mobilization have been on global trade issues. In 1998, the government of France specifically credited Internet communication across borders by nongovernmental organizations as leading to the downfall of the Multilateral Agreement on Investment.[12] At the 1999 World Trade Organization meeting, Seattle police admit being unprepared for the level of Internet-enhanced coordination of 45,000 protesters, who delayed events by preventing delegates from entering meeting places and became part of a violent environment that ultimately resulted in more than five hundred arrests, $17 million in damages, and the resignation of the police chief.[13] Examining the use of the Internet by opponents of the Free Trade Agreement of the Americas to disseminate information, convey strategy, and directly pressure decision makers, Jeffrey Ayres argues that the Internet has made activism on trade issues somewhat more egalitarian and open to those in poorer nations.[14] A broadened base of activism is also apparent from the successful use of the Internet to coordinate the activities of AIDS activists in poor countries.[15]

Earning a Nobel Prize for its efforts, the International Campaign to Ban Landmines can make a strong case for having the most successful use of the Internet to mobilize groups throughout the world. The organization was founded in 1992 by Jody Williams, who became concerned about the damage inflicted by landmines while visiting Nicaragua in the 1980s. She began advocacy against landmines on a small scale with educational and humanitarian projects. Finding her ultimate goal of an international treaty to ban landmines seemingly far away, she wanted to increase the pressure on public officials. Since many anti-landmine organizations were already in existence, the key was to coordinate their efforts. Working out of her rural Vermont home and relying on the phone, fax, and Internet, Jody Williams was instrumental in coordinating more than seven hundred groups into a unified effort for an international treaty.[16] Her efforts reached fruition with the signing of the 1997 Mine Ban Treaty. In 1997, Jody Williams and the International Campaign to Ban Landmines won the Nobel Peace Prize.

POLITICAL PARTIES

Like interest groups, political parties are intermediaries that link citizens to the government. In their capacity as intermediaries, political parties also benefit significantly from the Internet. The fundamental capabilities of the Internet to disseminate information and mobilize are useful to parties, which must aggregate enough people to be able to compete in elections. With similar needs to those of interest groups, political parties—not surprisingly—have used the Internet in similar ways. Many differences are a matter of scale. It is also true, however, that the landscape of political parties and the Internet is not nearly as filled with dramatic mobilizations from scratch. For major parties, such dramatic mobilizations are simply not necessary. Political parties are established institutions consisting of an extensive network of national, state, and local organizations.

One major similarity between the use of the Internet by interest groups and political parties is that organizations of all resource levels and political persuasions are online. Of course, the major political parties have an elaborate presence on the Web. They are joined online by many minor parties. Although their sites may not be as sophisticated as major parties, minor parties do have websites. These sites are being used to inform and mobilize. Often having limited resources, minor parties benefit from a rare opportunity to reach a broad audience at low cost.

In fact, the Internet appears to be a venue particularly favorable to minor parties. The difference with other media is profound. Minor parties are lucky to run any television advertisements. This applies even to better-known candidates, like Ralph Nader in 2000. Nader, who ran ads in a limited number of markets, was able to secure broad awareness for his ads only after provoking a lawsuit from MasterCard for adopting its "priceless" motif. While minor political parties can afford less than 1 percent of the television advertisements of major parties, they effectively have 100 percent of the websites of the major parties—each party has one primary site.

Since the Web began, the evidence has consistently shown that minor parties face a far more favorable political landscape in cyberspace than they do outside of cyberspace. In 1996, Harry Browne announced that he had "cyberwhipped" Bill Clinton and Bob Dole after winning a number of Internet presidential polls.[17] In

1999, political scientists Michael Margolis and David Resnick offered dramatic evidence of how much friendlier the cyberworld is for minor parties than the noncyberworld. They found that not only did all minor parties have a website, but also that the Libertarian, Communist, and Natural Law parties had more pages than the Democratic site. Extending their analysis of the prominence of minor parties in cyberspace, Margolis and Resnick measured "backpointers," which represent the number of external websites that link to a specific page. They documented a cyberworld in which the Libertarian, Communist, Green, Reform, and Natural Law parties had 78, 45, 31, 26, and 21 percent, respectively, of the backpointers of major parties. Although less than parity, these percentages compared favorably to the less than 10 percent of newspaper and television stories that the minor parties typically received.[18] The results are more dramatic if another measure is added to their study—the percentage vote in the 2000 presidential election. The Libertarian, Communist, Green, Reform, and Natural Law parties received 0.4, 0.0, 2.4, 0.3, and 0.1 percent of the vote, respectively.[19] Comparing the average of these five minor parties to the average of the two major parties, they have 100 percent of the websites and 41 percent of the backpointers in the cyberworld, compared to 1 percent of the votes in the non-cyberworld. Cyberspace is, indeed, an environment that is distorted in favor of minor parties.

Political parties are using the Internet to disseminate information. Recognizing an unparalleled opportunity to disseminate large quantities of information at low cost, parties quickly began disseminating information online. By 1998, the Republican, Democratic, Libertarian, Communist, Reform, and Natural Law parties had websites consisting of more than one hundred pages.[20] In 2000, the Republican Party crossed the 10 percent threshold for the percentage of its staff devoted to the online effort.[21]

A good indicator of how the Internet has developed as an information disseminator is to examine its use during the party convention. The most visible activity of American political parties, the national convention brings together the party organization, party-in-government, and party-in-electorate every four years. Parties want the public to learn about their convention. This task has become more difficult in an era in which the major television networks have dramatically curtailed convention coverage. Helping to fill the void, the Internet is an effective way to inform people about the convention. With each succeeding convention, the political parties have implemented more elaborate strategies for disseminating information online.

The 1996 Republican National Convention represented an elaborate first venture into cyberspace. Audio and video access to floor proceedings was supplemented with exclusive online discussions. Some of the most prominent party members participated in these discussions. One Republican chat room at the convention, for instance, included General Colin Powell asking, "Who is out there?" and getting a reply from then–Missouri Senator John Ashcroft. Opportunities were available for ordinary citizens to ask questions of prominent party members. The site archived transcripts of speeches delivered at the convention. An estimated

700,000 people took part in the online convention experience. Although its coverage was less interactive, the Democratic Party followed up the Republicans by using the Web for the first time in 1996 to disseminate convention information.[22]

The 2000 online conventions stand out for having a huge promotional buildup followed by virtual silence. In preparation for the 2000 conventions, both parties devoted significant resources to promoting the party through banner advertisements. This was an important development for online party activity because banner ads cost money and represent an effort to draw people to the party site from other websites. Estimates were that the parties purchased over 3.5 million banner ads during the week of their convention, primarily on media sites. With the big promotional buildup, it is not surprising that both parties undertook significant efforts to disseminate information about the 2000 convention over the Internet. Following the convention, however, the parties were unable to sustain the momentum for an increased online presence. Once the convention ended, the political parties devoted no new expenditures to banner advertising in the year 2000.[23]

Political parties also use the Internet to mobilize. Mobilization is nearly universal on state and national party sites, which emphasize asking supporters to volunteer time, donate money, and attend party functions.[24] Combining the website with e-mail further enhances mobilization. E-mail distribution lists are well suited for coordinating communication within the highly decentralized American political parties. Even minor parties can wage impressive mobilization efforts online. In March 1999, for instance, a Federal Deposit Insurance Corporation (FDIC) rule was repealed after Libertarian Party members mobilized over the Internet. The individualized e-mail responses of Libertarian Party members constituted an estimated 67 percent of the 250,000 responses to the banking rule. The chair of the FDIC made it clear that the mobilization played a key role in the repeal: "When customers can get excited about an esoteric bank regulation, we have to pay attention."[25]

A minor party was also the source of a landmark event in mobilizing people to vote online. While the websites of major parties were explaining how to vote in the non-cyberworld, the Reform Party became the first party to allow online voting in its presidential primary in 1996. Those formally registered were able to cast an online ballot any time over several weeks. Online votes were equivalent to those cast by other means. In the end, over two thousand Reform Party voters cast their ballots online in a primary ultimately won by Ross Perot.[26] In 2000, the Reform Party again allowed Internet voting; the number of online ballots cast rose to 5,437, which was 7 percent of all ballots cast. Interestingly, online voters behaved diametrically opposite to paper voters in the two-way contest between Patrick Buchanan and John Hagelin: Hagelin received 64 percent of the online votes, while Buchanan received 65 percent of the paper votes.[27]

A political party hoping to combine mobilization and information dissemination may try to become an Internet service provider (ISP). The size, resources, and visibility of political parties make this a viable option. If successful, the party would have an effective way to communicate with a large number of party identifiers. If unsuccessful, few resources would be lost. The choice to enter the ISP market seems to be an easy one. History, however, has shown that political parties have a difficult time competing in the ISP market.

The first significant party foray into the ISP market was short-lived. In 1996, the Democratic Party started an ISP called freeDem.com. The price of the service was comparable to other services—about $20 per month. Subscribers received updated information about Democratic activities and news. After the presidential election, what little enthusiasm there was for the service declined. The Democrats soon abandoned the ISP market.

Not to be deterred, the Republican Party introduced its own ISP service in November 1999. Subscribers to Gopnet.com received Internet service for approximately $20 each month. When introduced, the service was hailed as a way to appeal to the young: "This is not your Father's Republican Party anymore."[28] ISP subscribers received access to updated news from the Republican Party. The ISP marketed itself as a family-friendly environment free of pornographic images. The venture was short-lived.

Reentering the ISP field, the Democratic Party went in a new direction. This time the service would be free. In June 2000, freeDem.com began with revenues dependent on selling targeted advertising. The Democratic Party framed the service as symbolic of its broader commitment to reducing the digital divide. As in the first effort, subscribers received updated news and events from the Democratic Party. Again in 2000, the end of the campaign was closely followed by the end of the service. Days after the election, the free Web access firm used by the Democrats ceased operations. Subscribers got a message that the service was suspended.

CONCLUSION

The Internet is a vital component of the advocacy of interest groups and political parties. It offers tremendous advantages in information dissemination and mobilization. It is a medium that is open to advocates of all resource levels. The Internet has no rivals for disseminating information inexpensively. While enjoying the benefits of the Internet, advocates should not forget that it provides these opportunities to everybody—even opponents. Indeed, the Internet can be a dynamic environment of trying to one-up the opponent.

The unique capacity for confronting opponents online is seen in the action of advocates opposed to hate groups. Opponents have not been content just to monitor the expanding universe of hate groups on the Web. Using the technology to their advantage, the Southern Poverty Law Center has purchased banner advertising on the Yahoo! search engine. The organization created a number of ads including ones that say, "Bias doesn't just happen" and "What are you teaching your kids?" The advertisements, however, are not used for all searches. Rather, they are triggered by the use of specific search terms. Thus, when a person types *neo-Nazi* into the search engine, a banner ad might ask the unsuspecting person: "What are you teaching your kids?"[29]

PART THREE

GOVERNMENT AND MEDIA
USE OF THE INTERNET

7

E-Government

Government has been an early adopter of the Internet. The Department of Defense and the National Science Foundation were instrumental in the development and expansion of the network. Two of the watershed events in the transition of the World Wide Web into a mass medium involved government websites. The 1997 Mars Pathfinder mission prompted an unprecedented 47 million hits in one day on the NASA website, which at the time represented two times more traffic than any other event in Web history.[1] In 1998, the Internet release of the report of the Independent Counsel on the misbehavior of President Clinton shattered previous traffic records and transformed a government source document into an instantaneous cultural phenomenon. These high-profile government Web events have been accompanied by the less dramatic but ultimately more important phenomenon of the everyday use of the Internet to increase the openness and efficiency of government.

INTERNET USE BY GOVERNMENT

E-government, which refers broadly to the use of the Internet by government, increases openness and efficiency. The original goal for the Internet was to increase the efficiency of the Defense Department by facilitating contact with regular clients. It continues to be used for this purpose. The most visible manifestation of this is in contracting. The Internet offers a variety of advantages to government acting as a purchaser. Paper requirements can be short-circuited. Bids, revisions, and other parts of the process can be streamlined, especially on smaller projects.

By putting specifications online, firms that are not necessarily large government contractors can offer competitive bids.

Extending well beyond the Defense Department, Internet use has allowed government to become more efficient in communication and information management. Three decades after the Internet began, the breadth of the efficiency gains were seen in a nationwide survey finding that over 80 percent of government officials believe e-government has had a positive effect on government operations, and only 1 percent believe the federal government is doing a "poor job" in "using the Internet to improve the efficiency" of government.[2]

Adding to the original goal of efficiency, use of the Internet has also resulted in government becoming more open. Quite simply, the Internet represents a tremendous leap forward in the amount of freely available information from government. Much information technically had been public for some time, but it was often difficult to obtain. Information that previously required digging is now wide open.

Indeed, for some it may be too open. Data ranging from property assessments to bankruptcy creditor information, which had been difficult to access, is now open to even the mildly curious. Mild wasn't the extent of the irritation of many farmers when a website began identifying farmers by name and the amount of federal subsidies received in early 2002. In its first forty days, over 10 million searches were conducted on a government data set of subsidy recipients. One subsidy recipient publicly complained that open wasn't necessarily better: "To see my subsidies on that site was just like being naked at a school reunion . . . something has to be done about that site."[3] In this case, technically, the information wasn't on a government site, but on the site of a nonprofit group posting the government data. Thus, even if political pressure may lead an agency not to publish information, other entities are free to publish government information that has no copyright protection.

In using the Internet, government occupies its own domain. Private and educational entities share a variety of domains, most commonly .com, .org, .edu, or .net. The .gov extension, on the other hand, is used exclusively by government. This domain has been managed differently than the others. While other domains were at one time managed by Network Solutions and are now open to competition, the government has overseen its own domain. Since 1997, the Center for Electronic Messaging Technologies, located within the General Services Administration, has been responsible for the .gov domain.

The popularity of government websites is mixed. Some high-profile events on government websites have brought in extraordinary numbers of visitors. These events include the 1997 Mars Pathfinder mission, the 1998 Mars Polar Lander mission (which doubled Pathfinder traffic and was destined to be the largest Web event ever until the landing failed),[4] John Glenn's space shuttle mission, and the Starr Report. Although special events may propel a government site into the upper echelons of popularity, the day-to-day traffic at government websites does not compete with the major entertainment sites. This is not to say, however, that routine traffic is not substantial. Over half of Internet users had already visited a government website as early as the year 2000.[5] A number of government websites will routinely exceed a million unique visitors per month. One annual, albeit despised, routine that draws many people to online government is filing tax returns. During its peak months, the Internal Revenue Service (IRS) site has come in one spot ahead of two formidable Internet cities—porncity.net and travelocity.com—and well ahead of nytimes.com.[6]

FEDERAL GOVERNMENT AND THE INTERNET

All the major components of the federal government have a substantial Web presence. Responsibility is decentralized, with each agency operating its own site. Federal sites can thus look very different from each other. They also can change dramatically from one administration to another. Typically, government domain names are attached to the institution. When a new administration takes over, the site of the old administration is replaced by new material.

The highly visible presidential website (www.whitehouse.gov) has been maintained by every president since Bill Clinton. While President Bush made no effort to establish a website before leaving office in January 1993, President Clinton set up a Gopher site in his first month in office. Moving its speeches and documents from Gopher, the Clinton administration launched whitehouse.gov in October 1994.[7] As structured, the website emphasized information:

> *Welcome to the White House* has four principal functions. First our service allows users to link to all online resources made available by U.S. government agencies . . . provides an enhanced interface for sending electronic mail to the President . . . provides indexing of all White House publications so that finding and retrieving documents is made easier. . . . Finally, our service lets people view White House photographs and listen to the President's Saturday radio addresses and other audio segments.[8]

Another goal of the Clinton site was to add a light touch to politics through features such as a White House tour for children and a series of cartoons depicting Al Gore. Socks, the Clinton cat, had his own website by 1996. The evolution of President Clinton's website is archived by the National Archives and Records Administration at clinton.nara.gov.

The first presidential Web transition was an awkward one. Within hours of taking office, the Bush administration put up a new version of whitehouse.gov. Starting from scratch, the new administration's site drew widespread criticism for its lack of information and glitches. The home page would periodically reveal the phrase "Insert Something Meaningful Here." Web design expert Jakob Nielsen found fault with the kids' section of the site: "They have a site for kids which is nice but it's completely empty—that's going to be really disappointing for little kids."[9] Acknowledging the shortcomings of the site, the administration relaunched the site in August 2001 with great fanfare. Over time the site made substantial improvements, particularly in using its fast server to implement a variety of audio and video formats.

Despite having websites, neither President Bush nor President Clinton were themselves frequent Internet users. In eight years in office, President Clinton sent only two e-mails. He e-mailed John Glenn in space and sent a Christmas message to a military ship.[10] President Bush was an avid e-mailer before taking office. Fearing that any e-mail he sent might potentially be considered a public record, President Bush abandoned e-mailing when he took office. Upon taking office, President Bush sent one final e-mail to his regular contacts: "I will miss your ideas and encouragement. So perhaps we will talk by phone . . . sadly I sign off."[11] Thus, well into the era of majority use of the Internet, the president of the United States was only a nominal user.

The most-visited federal sites are those of the major federal agencies. The amount of information on these sites is staggering. A survey of the sites that routinely get the most traffic suggests that people are searching for general information more than political process information.[12] The U.S. Post Office site (www.usps.gov), for example, gives customers "no lines" in conducting postal business such as buying stamps and checking on the status of mail. In addition to high-profile missions, the NASA website (www.nasa.gov) provides basic information about the space program. The National Institutes of Health site (www.nih.gov) provides the results of clinical trials and other information to health care providers and consumers. National Weather Service information is found on the National Oceanic and Atmospheric Administration site (www.noaa.gov). For selected months, no government site can compete with the IRS (www.irs.gov) for traffic. Compiling all major tax documents, the IRS website shows the advantage of the Internet for open and efficient government. There is simply no comparison between the ease of obtaining special tax forms and publications through the Internet compared to previous methods of telephoning or visiting field offices. For those seeking a statistical profile of the United States, there is also no comparison between the ease of accessing data at the Census Bureau (www.census.gov) and earlier trips to government document sections of libraries.

While executive department sites are often focused on practical and often nonpolitical information, congressional sites are more political. Each chamber has its own website. The websites of the House of Representatives (www.house.gov) and the Senate (www.senate.gov) provide information about members, legislation, and the leadership. Much information is consolidated into Thomas—Legislative Information on the Internet (thomas.loc.gov). This service of the Library of Congress facilitates searches for legislation, members, floor schedules, and the *Congressional Record*.

Of all the branches of government, the judiciary has the least sophisticated websites. The thirteen judicial websites included in a prominent study of the services and information offered on about sixty federal websites constituted the thirteen lowest-rated sites.[13] The judicial branch was also the slowest to go online. In 1999, a *Los Angeles Times* editorial put the absence of a U.S. Supreme Court site in perspective: "While the Supreme Court of Mongolia has its own official website, the U.S. Supreme Court doesn't."[14] The editorial's plea remained unanswered for almost another year. Finally, in April 2000, the U.S. Supreme Court went online (www.supremecourtus.gov). The site now includes the full text of court opinions and oral arguments. Where voids have existed in judiciary sites, they have long been filled by a variety of legal research sites that post court rulings.

FEDERAL GATEWAY ODYSSEY

Symbolic of the tremendous amount of federal information available online is the odyssey to create a gateway for accessing federal resources. Having one place to search all federal records would give average citizens, who are often unfamiliar with the jurisdiction of specific federal agencies, the opportunity to conveniently access resources from several agencies having responsibility in a policy area. Implementing a unified federal resource, however, proved to be difficult. The history of establishing a federal gateway is a cycle of enthusiasm and frustration.

The first effort to create a central federal resource was the Government Information Locator Service (GILS). A successor to the failed Federal Information Locator Service (FILS), GILS began at the behest of the Office of Management and Budget in 1994. The goal was to encourage government agencies to standardize their information for eventual incorporation into a unified resource. The explosion of the Web, however, minimized the potential gains from the project, which was originally envisioned as being accessible from various sources including toll-free phone numbers and CD-ROMs. In 1997, the official evaluation of GILS implementation found little awareness of GILS. The report clearly suggested that the problem wasn't exclusively with nonusers: "[Users] find it hard to use at best and inexplicable and frustrating at worst."[15] GILS would never become a widely used gateway.

Another attempt at a unified search was made by the Department of Commerce working with the private firm Northern Light. They created a new search function at usgovsearch.com that compiled independent federal sites. The service began with high expectations in May 1999. The Commerce Department promoted usgovsearch.com as a major advancement: "Govsearch is a breakthrough in the reinvention of government that Vice President Gore is continually trying to achieve."[16] There was one problem, however. The new site charged for the service. Fees were announced at $15 for a one-day pass or $30 for a monthly subscription. As the launch date approached, criticism of the fee structure grew. Within hours after the site was introduced, the fees were lifted by extending the free trial period.[17] One month later when the project converted to a fee-based service, the Department of Commerce abandoned usgovsearch.[18]

Another effort at a gateway never made it off the ground. Slowed by technical troubles, efforts to create WebGov were given momentum by President Clinton's endorsement in December 1999. President Clinton praised its conception of locating information "by the type of service or information that people may be seeking."[19] A director with the White House's National Partnership for Reinventing Government characterized it as having the potential to be "the mother of all gateways."[20] Technical problems continued, and the operation was harmed by someone else having purchased webgov.com.[21] WebGov would not become a major gateway.

President Clinton made a dramatic kickoff of the next major effort at a federal gateway. On September 22, 2000, the first live Web-only presidential address was given. In it, President Clinton announced that firstgov.gov was officially online. The administration made sure to learn from the past. The service would be free.

The project, however, may have taken a good thing too far. In this case, not only was the service free to citizens, but it was free to the government as well. The major components of the service, in fact, had been donated to the government. This unusual occurrence came from a lack of funding for the project. After President Clinton's June 2000 challenge to the General Services Administration (GSA) to have a gateway running within 90 days, estimates were obtained. The GSA estimated that it would cost $7.5 million to build. While GSA requested $7.5 million, it received only $4.5 million.[22] Believing that it could not be done for the reduced amount, GSA found the offer of FedSearch—to donate the search capacity for three years—too good to refuse.

Despite the high-profile presidential launch, the first incarnation of firstgov.gov was destined not to become a major gateway. The search function was not as effective as originally hoped. Citizens were not flocking to the new service. After over six months, firstgov.gov still struggled to get visitors. It ranked 82nd not among all websites, but among all government websites.[23] By July 2001, the government announced that it was ending its relationship with FedSearch after only the first of the three years outlined in the contract. Administration officials expressed frustration as it came to light that under the contract FedSearch would be able to keep the database of federal websites after the contract expired.[24] Putting in a request for a new vendor, GSA continued to aim high. Its bid requested the capability of 17 million visits by 2006.[25]

STATE AND LOCAL GOVERNMENT ON THE WEB

State and local governments are also online. All states have a website. Local government sites are common. Although about half as likely as federal sites to offer online services,[26] the websites of state and local governments can be elaborate and attract a large audience. The first state website to attract the nation's attention was the site of the Florida secretary of state. On election night 2000, the site was featured prominently on the television networks and served as the information source prompting Al Gore's famous retracted concession. On a more routine basis, California's website (www.ca.gov) has millions of monthly visitors and often joins the major federal agencies on the list of most-visited government sites.[27]

The late 1990s was a period of exceptional growth for state and local government in establishing an Internet presence. Although exact figures are difficult to verify, the year 2000 was probably the year in which the halfway point was reached in relation to county governments being on the Web.[28] Cities without websites by 1999 were already being seen as behind the times, as shown by the assessment of county administrator Thomas Iler: "People doing research on possible locations for a new business expect to be able to do it on the Internet. If your county is not on the Internet, you probably won't be considered."[29]

The growth in the absolute number of state and local websites was accompanied by growth in the functions of existing websites. Early websites seldom aspired to more than one-way information dissemination. Over time, websites broadened the content of the website and added interactivity. The sites of state bureaucracies, although typically less sophisticated and popular, now provide the same types of information as their federal counterparts. For instance, tax forms and publications are available. Other unique state and local prerogatives have been moved to the Web. For instance, information about automobile registration, drivers licenses, and property taxes is increasingly found on the Internet, as is the capacity for actual transactions.

The opportunity to complete transactions online can minimize some of the inconveniences of a federal system. The complexity of complying with various state regulations can be eased significantly when one doesn't have to be physically present in the state. Taxpayers, for example, benefit by being able to conveniently access tax forms from any number of states with which they have tax obligations. In some cases, out-of-state residents constitute the heaviest users of online transactions. In Nebraska, for instance, most of those obtaining hunting licenses online are out-of-state residents.[30]

One leader in e-government is the state of Washington. Placed in shopping malls in 1994, Washington Information Network kiosks within three years were providing over 200,000 people annually the capacity for instant government services such as online job and property searches.[31] Washington became the first state to compute and receive business taxes online in 1997[32] and to receive a digitally signed contract bid in 1998.[33] These efforts contributed to Washington finishing first out of the fifty states every year from 1997 to 2000 in the Progress and Freedom Foundation's annual "Digital State" survey. Already recognized as a national leader, the state of Washington overhauled its website in 1998 to add a search function and to rearrange the site by subject matter instead of the specific agency. In the first month of operation, the overhauled site increased the 5 million hits of the previous site to 20 million.[34] Washington was able to preserve its lead until the year 2001, when Illinois became the first state other than Washington to finish first in the Digital State survey.

Over time, states and localities have steadily introduced new online functions. Some examples can help illustrate the diversity of e-government initiatives. In 1999, Texas introduced a website with photographs of children available for adoption, which subsequently increased the adoption rate and drew praise from then-Governor George W. Bush.[35] Refreshing every five seconds, a live webcam on the website of the Alaska Division of Motor Vehicles (DMV) was created in 2000 to give people the opportunity to observe how fast the lines at the DMV are moving without physically being there. In February 2002, New York launched a website compiling profiles of nearly 50,000 physicians, including their location, training, board certification, hospital privileges, disciplinary actions, and insurance participation.[36] In 2003, state websites were given the go-ahead by the Supreme Court to include a registry of convicted sex offenders. This Web component of Megan's Laws, which are laws that provide information to the public about convicted sex offenders, was found not to violate due process even if a hearing is not held on the current danger posed by the offender.[37] While Megan's Laws focus on providing information about released criminals, states have also created websites profiling current prison inmates. Over time, the profiles have become increasingly sophisticated. In 1995, Florida posted a spreadsheet of inmate names. By the year 2000, the most elaborate inmate profiles were available on the Death Row site in Texas. It had profiles of offenders, last meal requests, last words, witness lists, and myriad statistics about death row. Adopting the infelicitous acronym KOOL, the Kentucky Offender Online Lookup, Kentucky promoted its new inmate profile service as particularly helpful to reporters on the crime beat. Besides reducing media requests for information, another common justification for the sites is for victims and inmate families to keep up with an inmate, albeit for different reasons.

INDIVIDUAL OFFICEHOLDERS

Websites are established not only in the name of governmental institutions but also by the individuals working within them. An Internet account on the government server is a well-established perk of holding office. In Congress, for example, the adoption of websites was concentrated between 1995 and 1998. The number of individual sites in the House of Representatives went from 2 percent of members in mid-1995 to 65 percent in mid-1997 to over 95 percent by 1999.[38]

Criticizing the content of Congress members' sites has long been fashionable. The pursuit even drew the attention of a prominent presidential candidate. Ralph Nader co-authored a *Los Angeles Times* article in 1999 characterizing the websites of members of Congress as dominated by fluff and lacking voting records.[39] The anecdotal criticism finds some support in systematic content studies. A study of House member sites by Richard Davis found that a member biography was three times more common than discussion of recent legislation.[40] Stated broadly, the criticism is that officeholder sites emphasize promotion over providing legislative information.

Although officeholder sites have failed to live up to the ideal of focusing on legislative matters, the systematic findings of scholars show that officeholder sites can be a valuable source of information. Alongside promotional material, there is substantive information. The information function has been apparent since the first systematic study of congressional sites found that they were primarily devoted to providing information and downplaying credit claiming. In comparing one hundred sites to a sample of print newsletters, John Messmer found that information on websites was more national in scope and less likely to involve position taking.[41] Another early finding that has been subsequently confirmed is the widespread provision of information about the casework assistance available to constituents.[42]

Further, officeholder sites promote constituent interaction. By routinely having an e-mail icon, these sites constitute an additional way to communicate with elected officials. It is a very convenient way. It is so convenient that the amount of e-mail directed to individual officeholders is extremely high. Its convenience was seen clearly in September 2001; at that time, even though an anthrax scare was slowing the U.S. Postal Service, the amount of e-mail sent to Congress increased by 20 percent.[43] In fact, it is not unusual for e-mail to exceed all other communication (mail, telephone, fax) combined. The issue is not whether these sites allow citizen input into politics. It is clear that they do. Rather, the issue is whether the volume of citizen input makes it difficult for officeholders to respond. A landmark study in 2001 by the Congress Online Project revealed that Congress was not able to keep up with its e-mail. Mass e-mails from groups were particularly troubling to members who simply don't have the staff to handle the over 80 million e-mails received annually.[44] This is despite an improved infrastructure for receiving e-mail. By January 2002, all members of the U.S. House of Representatives had BlackBerry handheld e-mail equipment.[45] That members of Congress came quickly to enjoy the fruits of their $6 million wireless investment is evident from a congressional administrator's unusual plea in early 2003 for the parties in a BlackBerry technology patent dispute to resolve their differences without placing the House's "critical communications" at risk.[46]

One important influence on the content of officeholder sites is regulation. The sites are prohibited from communication that explicitly seeks political support. As explained by Darrell West, the prohibition is applied narrowly: "If they are just saying I'm a great person for these reasons that is perfectly reasonable."[47] The Senate has an additional rule that members are not allowed to change their sites within sixty days of an election. This regulation is based on the assumption that communication near an election is likely to constitute an indirect solicitation of political support. Both the regulation of the substance and timing of Web communication represent a direct application of a regulatory framework established in the context of the congressional franking privilege of sending mail to constituents at public expense. In fact, in 1996, the Senate applied the same rule and literally the same time period to Web communication as to franked mail.

EVALUATING E-GOVERNMENT

Looking beyond anecdotes, scholars have undertaken systematic studies to assess e-government. The results of these systematic studies are mixed. The consensus is that e-government is not living up to its potential, especially as it relates to inter-activity. The Internet has not fundamentally changed how people interact with government. While not living up to the ideal of a widespread, fully integrated, on-line citizenry, e-government does advance the cause of openness and efficiency. Perhaps the strongest confirmation of this improvement comes from the positive responses of citizens to e-government.

Systematic studies clearly demonstrate the tremendous amount of information disseminated on government websites. Many basic government functions are uni-versal on federal and state websites. In some cases, the shift to the Web was rapid. The availability of tax forms online, for instance, went from 56 percent of states in 1998[48] to over 95 percent of states providing both forms and the opportunity to actually file online by 2001.[49]

While the amount of information dissemination on government sites is impres-sive, sites are less focused on actually delivering services online. Summarizing a sys-tematic study of the content of about 2000 federal and state sites, Darrell West highlighted the difference between information dissemination and service deliv-ery: "Government websites tend to offer more basic information than features that make their websites interactive."[50] Although often not the primary focus of sites, service delivery represents a significant and increasing percentage of sites. With a high standard of service delivery, requiring that the entire transaction be com-pleted online, over 20 percent of government sites are providing at least one on-line service. One factor holding down service delivery is that only 10 percent of government sites accept credit cards.[51]

Despite, or perhaps because of, the emphasis on information provision, gov-ernment websites generally appear to have found favor with the public. This is clear from the landmark study of public opinion on e-government conducted by Hart and Teeter for the Council for Excellence in Government. When the pub-lic is asked to choose from a list of e-government services, the most popular choice of getting medical information far exceeds filing taxes or renewing drivers licenses. When asked to "rate the quality of the government websites that you have vis-ited," 71 percent chose "excellent" or "good" instead of "just fair" or "poor." Not surprisingly, then, the public sees an overall improvement from e-government.[52]

The positive ratings suggest that academics and government officials may be holding government sites up to an ideal of interactivity and online consummation that is not necessarily shared by average citizens. Citizens generally do not want the Internet to initiate a new virtual world of interaction with government, but want to interact more effectively in the existing world. They seem happy with conveniently obtaining a form online and then submitting it by regular mail. Cit-izens are not demanding that e-government be an end-all. They also are not demanding rapid implementation of e-government. When asked whether the United States should proceed "slowly" or "quickly" with e-government, government officials by a nearly 2 to 1 margin select "quickly." In contrast, the public by a greater than 2 to 1 margin selects "slowly."[53] Citizens seem happy with steady, incremental improvement in their interactions with government. Indeed, e-government may be fulfilling the vision of Bill Gates as articulated in his June 1999 remarks to the Joint Economic Committee: "As government increasingly incorporates technology into its operations it will make information flow even more open and efficient."[54]

ONLINE VOTING

One highly visible dimension of e-government is voting online. The source of its visibility is clear. Voting is the most fundamental act in a democracy. It is also a frequent act in the American system of federalism. While renewing a drivers license online would save a trip to the license branch about every five years, voting online would facilitate a far greater number of transactions. With primaries and general elections taking place for local, state, and federal elections, a person can select officeholders at least twice a year. Further, the potential frequency of voting on specific issues is unlimited. Online voting or any other technique that can facilitate this significant and frequent activity will naturally draw great attention.

Online voting demonstrates the challenges in moving from information dissemination to actual service delivery. Information dissemination about voting has been widespread on the Internet for many years. The number of sources for information about voting procedures is common not only on government sites, but also on candidate, party, media, and interest group sites. The information has focused on how to register to vote, and in some locations the opportunity to register online is provided. While informing people about how to vote poses no logistical challenges, actually providing the service of online voting is more demanding. It requires providing the actual mechanics for the vote and ensuring the validity of the vote. It also must meet these challenges in an accessible way.

A milestone in online voting occurred in Arizona in March 2000, when Internet voting was used for the first time in a binding statewide election. One option for voters in the Democratic primary was to vote by remote over a four-day period at election.com. Voters could also mail in ballots or vote at a polling booth on Election Day. The online option proved to be popular; 41 percent of all votes were cast by remote Internet voting. The figure is even higher for 18- to 24-year-old voters, who chose the online option an estimated 75 percent of the time.[55]

Later in the same year, the federal government encountered difficulties in a pilot program for online voting. The program was designed to facilitate voting by overseas military personnel. The Defense Department spent $6.2 million to establish the hardware and software for allowing votes to be counted online. On

Election Day, overseas military personnel with legal residencies in participating counties in five states were able to cast their ballots online. There would be no delays caused by waiting for military ballots in the mail. Despite the opportunity, few military personnel voted online. In the end, only eighty-four votes were cast online. The final estimate: $74,000 for each vote to be tabulated. Officially, the Pentagon described the program as a success.[56]

A major study of online voting was released in 2001 by the National Science Foundation. Commissioned by President Clinton in 1999, the study was critical of any online voting system that included voting at nonpublic terminals. The study found much to be done to address the security concerns associated with remote online voting. On the other hand, Internet terminals were viewed as an effective replacement for traditional voting models as the nation updated its voting infrastructure. The study's overall skepticism toward online voting is shown in its warnings against putting even the initial voter registration process online.[57]

REGULATION OF GOVERNMENT INTERNET USE

Private and public sector entities face different regulatory environments on the Internet. On one hand, private sector communicators generally can say or not say whatever they want online. They have tremendous latitude in providing good or bad content. If so inclined, companies can freely divulge their trade secrets on their Web page. They might also choose to set up a lousy page, fail to update it, and then provide inadequate server capacity to allow people to view their lousy, outdated site. In fact, they don't have to set up a website at all.

In contrast, governmental use of the Internet is subject to extensive regulation. Legislation passed by Congress establishes rules for federal governmental websites. The Office of Management and Budget (OMB), which is given substantial responsibility for overseeing the governmental Internet infrastructure, issues numerous guidelines on what governmental websites can and cannot do. Yet other rules are imposed by agencies such as the Department of Justice and National Archives and Records Administration. Sometimes these guidelines specify language, images, and links. The myriad regulations have prompted an agency webmaster to complain about overregulation: "Changing an agency home page may someday literally take an act of Congress."[58]

The regulation of e-government is further secured by the 1993 case *Armstrong* v. *Executive Office of the President,* which made it clear that e-mail is subject to the same reporting requirements as traditional documents. Under the Federal Records Act, agencies must get the approval of the archivist before disposing of substantive documents and correspondence. The case considered whether agencies had an obligation for e-mail record keeping beyond printing a paper copy. In ruling that paper copies did not absolve officials from maintaining e-mail records, the District of Columbia Court of Appeals referred to paper versions of e-mails as "amputated paper printouts" and "dismembered documents" that often omit critical information about addresses and distribution lists. The court condensed the issue into a metaphor about the proximity of cousins:

> [T]he mere existence of the paper printouts does not affect the record status of the electronic materials unless the paper versions include all significant material contained in the electronic records. Otherwise, the two documents cannot accurately be termed "copies"—identical twins—but are, at most, "kissing cousins." Since the record shows that the two versions of the documents may frequently be only cousins—perhaps distant ones at that—the electronic documents retain their status as federal records after the creation of the paper printouts.[59]

Although burdensome at times, regulation does deserve some of the credit for the gains in openness and efficiency of government outlined in this chapter. Technology itself, of course, has provided much of the impetus for increased openness and efficiency. The gains from the Internet, however, are not realized if government resists change and fails to use the technology. To some extent, regulation has forced government to use the Internet. It has done so expressly to promote openness and efficiency.

There are many eloquent defenders of the idea of requiring government to be open. The desirability of an open approach to knowledge in general has drawn the attention of J. Robert Oppenheimer (1963), the director of the lab that prepared the first atomic weapon. He argued that openness becomes more important with technological advancement:

> This open access to knowledge, these unlocked doors and signs of welcome, are a mark of a freedom as fundamental as any. . . . The open society, the unrestricted access to knowledge, the unplanned and uninhibited association of man for its furtherance—these are what may make a vast, complex, ever-growing, ever-changing, ever more specialized and expert technological world nevertheless a world of human community.[60]

An open society must be led by an open government. Within certain bounds, people expect to have access to knowledge collected by the government at public expense.

The technological characteristics of the Internet are well suited to increase openness. All computers are connected through an open infrastructure. Information posted publicly on one computer can be seen by any other computer in the network. The potential for information sharing on the Internet is infinite. Thus, advocates for open government have focused their attention on the Web. Ari Schwartz, a policy analyst at the Center for Democracy and Technology, believes that government is obligated to use technology to promote openness: "Information should be available by the means most accessible to the average citizen and right now we think [that means] the Web."[61] So long as the Internet remains the most accessible medium, the pressure to release more information through the Web will not subside.

There is also pressure to make the documents as inexpensive as possible. Historically, most government documents have been available through the Government Printing Office (GPO), which often imposes a fee to offset expenses. The Internet, however, neutralizes two of the primary reasons to charge for government documents: printing and mailing costs. Printing costs are not incurred by the government when a document is put online. If citizens wish to have a paper copy of a Web document, they use their own printer and paper. The Web has often been referred to as the world's largest photocopier, and it is one in which costs are passed on to the consumer. There may be no need to print the document at all if a citizen can simply view the desired material on a monitor. There clearly is no need to mail any documents, since they can be downloaded by the citizen. Any residual justification for charging for online government documents depends on collection costs. The desire to pass on these costs, however, runs up against the ethos that government information is already paid for by taxpayers and should be free. There is also an ethos against government sites making up for lost revenue in other ways. Systematic studies show that less than one-half of 1 percent of government sites have commercial advertisements, and only 2 percent impose user fees.[62]

The Internet does not, however, remove barriers to openness based on concerns about privacy and security. In fact, these concerns are probably heightened. Information that was public but arduous to obtain seems even more public now that it is easy to obtain. Information that previously was geographically localized is now located on an open network and may be less secure against outside efforts to infiltrate the system.

Legislation guides federal use of the Internet in promoting openness without breaching privacy and security. This legislation represents not a new Internet-specific framework, but rather an extension of existing frameworks to the Internet. In fact, much of the major legislation on the subject was passed well before the World Wide Web was created. In recent years, the legislation has been modified to bring the Internet into the existing framework.

The major legislation on openness of government information is the Freedom of Information Act (FOIA), which became law in 1966. As described by the Department of Justice, this act "established for the first time an effective statutory right of access to government information."[63] The most used part of the law allows an individual to fill out a FOIA request for an agency to furnish a particular piece of information. The agency, however, is not required to meet any request. The FOIA set up twelve categories of exemptions to account for factors such as privacy and law enforcement needs. Over time, Congress has adjusted these exemptions based on the political climate of the day. Thus, the backlash to Watergate led to substantial amendments in 1974 that promoted openness by narrowing exemptions for national security and law enforcement. The pendulum had swung back by 1986, when the Freedom of Information Reform Act was passed to expand the exemptions for law enforcement.

Although records are not always provided quickly and some agencies liberally apply exemptions, the act is still seen as an important step in making government more open. Looking back on its three decades, former President Clinton praised the FOIA: "Openness in government is essential to accountability and the Act has become an integral part of that process."[64] The FOIA has served as the framework for requesting public information for three decades. New laws have been named amendments or reform of the Freedom of Information Act and have not sought to establish a new paradigm. Thus, it is not surprising that when the Internet came into existence, it was incorporated into the FOIA.

The legislation known as the Electronic Freedom of Information Act (EFOIA) was enacted in 1996. The intent of the legislation was to preserve the spirit of the FOIA in a new environment. It extends the definition of records to include electronic data. The law mandates that agencies provide data, if possible, in the form (electronic or paper) that is requested. These provisions are important because previous court decisions had reached the opposite conclusions.[65] The legislation also required agencies to provide electronic access to a list of the records that it has provided in response to EFOIA requests. Further, agencies were instructed to facilitate access to the most popular documents.

The increased emphasis on providing the most "popular" documents has received mixed reviews. Clearly, this emphasis enables large numbers of people to be satisfied. On the other hand, the widespread availability of a document is viewed by some as reducing its value, or at least its novelty. *Dayton Daily News* reporter Russell Carollo denigrates agency information on the Web: "Someone tells me something is on the Web—I don't want it. I want the stuff that no one has ever asked for."[66]

Openness can also be enhanced when the government publishes information that is already collected in user-friendly formats. The Environmental Protection Agency (EPA), for instance, began a project in 1995 in which specific information about corporate polluters was incorporated into a broader report to be placed on the agency's website. This action was challenged on the basis that an agency should not alter the purpose of data. In *Tozzi* v. *EPA,* however, this argument was rejected by the U.S. District Court for the District of Columbia. Judge Hogan dismissed the injunction and affirmed the ability of the government to publish previously collected information in different and perhaps unanticipated ways.[67]

In addition to the regulation concerning the openness of federal records, federal government use of the Internet must comply with regulations related to privacy. The Privacy Act of 1974 provides the basic framework for privacy protection. The law limits the extent to which personal information can be collected. It gives people additional rights in ascertaining what information has been collected about them. There are also strict limits placed on how much personal information can be disclosed by the government. Specific Web issues have been treated in various memoranda issued by either the Office of Management and Budget or the Department of Justice, which are the primary overseers of the federal Web presence.

In general, Internet policy has preserved the Privacy Act framework in a new environment. For instance, privacy considerations have been extended to include graphics and other formats supported by the Internet.

Agencies must also comply with regulations designed to preserve security. The most relevant security legislation is the Computer Security Act passed in 1988. The National Institute of Standards and Technology assists agencies in carrying out the act's requirement for meeting a threshold of security protection. This legislation sets only minimum standards, and obviously an agency like the Department of Defense far exceeds them. With many hacker attacks each year, the Department of Defense is continually upgrading its technology and divides its network into security levels.

Security concerns arise not only from unauthorized use, but from authorized use. The Defense Department, for instance, believes that it voluntarily gave away too much information in the early days of the Web. Part of the reason for this is that the responsibility for defense websites was originally placed in the hands of public relations departments. Arthur Money, a Defense Department official, argued that the public relations mentality was too enthusiastic in putting material on the websites: "It's not a declared competition, but clearly within the military there is a drive to see who's got the sexiest home page. The problem is we're giving away too much information."[68] His thoughts were echoed by another military official, Philip Loranger, who argued that the Defense Department was being too open: "In our zealousness to share information, we are disclosing targeting information [useful to an enemy]."[69] In 1998, concern about the use of information by adversaries led to an order restricting websites. Departments were ordered to remove information about lessons learned and military asset movement where such information might jeopardize "sensitive" operations. Personal information about military personnel, including their social security numbers, home addresses, and information about family members, was banned from websites.

After September 11, 2001, the focus on security shifted to agencies besides the Department of Defense. This was due to the changed nature of the threat leading to a broader conception of what type of information might prove damaging to security. Information about potential targets like power plants and water facilities suddenly took on security dimensions. The FBI issued an alert that al-Qaida terrorists were possibly using the Web to learn about civilian targets.[70] In the immediate aftermath of the attack, agencies overseeing potential targets such as the Energy Department removed potentially damaging information. After scrutiny, much of the material was returned to the Web. Symbolic of these efforts is the Geographic Information Systems Data on the Bureau of Transportation Statistics site, which was removed on September 25 but reinstated by November 8. In trying to pull data from the Web, agencies run into the difficulty that once something is on the Web, it is hard to remove completely. Lacking copyright protection, government data can be freely copied and republished in other places. Thus, when a Toxic Substance and Disease Registry report was pulled, it could still be found on the sites of several nonprofits.[71] Despite the challenges and the eventual return of much pulled data, there is certainly a new era of caution about posting information on the Web. Brookings Institution Director Paul Light summed up the post–September 11 environment: "We're in a period where the secondary goal will be access and the primary goal will be security, and that's a significant change."[72]

Federal use of the Internet is also subject to regulations designed to promote efficiency. People are naturally sympathetic to Harry Truman's well-known remark about the dangers of too much efficiency: "Wherever you have an efficient government you have a dictatorship." Most, however, see little imminent danger of government becoming too efficient and desire to make it more efficient. Over time, many reform efforts have been aimed at making the bureaucracy more efficient. These efforts include such well-established laws as the Pendleton Act of 1883, which set up a merit-based system of government employment.

Recent reform has emphasized the use of computers in general and the Internet in particular. Computers reduce reliance on costly and time-consuming paper transactions. To realize efficiency gains from Internet use, regulations are imposed on government agencies to mandate the use of electronic data. Information technology becomes central to the mission of government agencies. As stated in Executive Order 13011, these regulations require agencies to "effectively use information technology to improve mission performance and service to the public."[73]

A variety of recent reforms ensures that things are done electronically. The Government Performance Results Act mandates that agency budgets are contingent on an annual performance plan that outlines how information technology is used to enhance performance and service. The Information Technology Reform Act, commonly known as Clinger-Cohen, sets up a management structure for overseeing government use of technology headed by OMB. The law makes a chief information officer within each agency responsible for ensuring that information technology is used to further the agency's mission. Another reform track is a series of laws that seek to reduce government reliance on paper by facilitating electronic transactions. The title of the acts became increasingly ambitious, moving from the 1995 Paper Reduction Act to the Government Paperwork Elimination Act of 1998. Combined, the reforms increase the extent to which government business is conducted electronically, thereby increasing the amount of information that is available for Internet applications.

Overall, e-government is enhanced by regulations aimed at openness and efficiency. As efficiency reforms require more data to be in electronic form and openness regulation promotes the public's right to know, government websites can be a tremendous resource. While provision of information by nongovernmental entities may ultimately end up following pay-per-view, advertising, or subscriber models, government websites should remain a reliable source of free information. Legislation gives the public rights to taxpayer-funded data. Though enforcement mechanisms can be lax, government websites are in a sense required to be good.

CONCLUSION

E-government promotes openness and efficiency. The Internet has dramatically increased the amount of government information that is easily accessible to citizens. It has facilitated communication within government and between citizens and government. In using the Internet, citizens are not necessarily looking to inhabit a new world modeled after the optimistically titled Paperwork Elimination Act. They seem content to use e-government opportunities to make targeted improvements in conventional ways of dealing with government.

8

Journalism and the Internet

The release of the Starr Report narrating the misbehavior of President Clinton was a watershed event in online journalism. It showed in profound ways the Internet challenge to old media. Prominent national television reporters were made to look foolish while on camera at their computer terminal, scrolling down and reading the report word for word to the audience. People could just as easily have read the document themselves at their own terminal. On this occasion, people didn't need journalists. They could get the document for themselves, and they did as millions downloaded the Starr Report, causing many servers to overload.

This chapter will explore how political journalism has been affected by the Internet. It will look at how traditional news organizations have responded to the Internet challenge. In many cases, these organizations have used the World Wide Web to offer content that is not available through other media. The Web is also home to a number of nontraditional news disseminators. This combination leads to a substantial amount of original political information on the Internet. Normative cases about the impact of this new medium on journalism are outlined.

In exploring these issues, insight will be gained from a unique study of the leading state newspaper sites. Specifically, the website of the daily newspaper with the largest subscription base in each of the fifty states will be analyzed. By including one site from each state, the study offers a national view of Web-based media. It maintains geographic balance in the context of significant newspapers. The largest paper in a state often receives statewide attention for news or practical features such as centralized job listings. Daily circulation of the papers ranges from 32,000 subscribers of the *Casper Star Tribune* in Wyoming to the over 1 million subscribers of the *New York Times* and *Los Angeles Times*. Unlike other studies, which usually analyze a convenience sample of local or prestige papers, this study is national in scope and chosen for systematic reasons.[1]

TRADITIONAL JOURNALISM EXPANDS TO THE WEB

Websites are almost universal for traditional news organizations. Any large news organization will have a website. The highest-circulation newspaper in each of the fifty states, for instance, has a corresponding website. Smaller news organizations also have established a Web presence. A website is now understood to be part of the overall news product.

The expansion of traditional news organizations to the Web was a rapid phenomenon, completed some time ago. As early as the fall of 1998, an era of universality was imminent. A 1998 survey by Middleberg Associates showed that over 90 percent of newspapers and magazines were online or had plans to go online.[2] This represented a significant increase in a short period of time. The largest single-year increase occurred when the number of print publications with websites grew from 25 percent in 1995 to almost 50 percent in 1996.[3]

The motivation behind the expansion of traditional media to the Web is the same as it is for most other activities: it can help them make money. On some level the benefits of having a website exceed the costs. In some cases, media organizations quickly turned a profit on websites. By 1999, one out of four online newspapers sites including *USA Today* and the *New York Times* were reporting a profit.[4] For other news sites, the websites technically may not turn a profit. The often slow road to profitability should not be a huge surprise. After all, it took a number of years for many radio broadcasters to become profitable. Even when not profitable on its own, the website may be making contributions to the overall organization by promoting traditional moneymakers. It may also be laying the groundwork for future profitability.

For news organizations, the critical part of the profitability equation is low costs. With a news organization already in place, the initial investment required to move to the Web is extremely low. Operating costs are also low. Internet publication avoids the high cost of paper, ink, and delivery. The news organization does not incur additional costs for content when stories generated for the traditional format are shared with the website. The website can reproduce stories appearing in another medium or run "new" stories that did not make the cut for the limited space available in the traditional product. In some cases, traditional organizations have further reduced the costs of Web publication by sharing them with other organizations.

These partnerships can be difficult to maintain, as illustrated by the case of PoliticsNow. This was not a minor collaboration. PoliticsNow was a joint partnership between ABC News, *National Journal,* and the *Washington Post* to provide online political news. In the 1996 election, PoliticsNow was the second most popular Internet-exclusive source of campaign news behind CNN/Time All Politics; it was visited by 16 percent of all those seeking election news online.[5] Despite its high profile, PoliticsNow simply disappeared. On March 4, 1997, the site posted a brief message announcing that it was ceasing operations immediately. The sudden decision came as a surprise to employees who moments before had been promoting an online chat for later in the week. Stating that the site "fulfilled the special needs of an election year," the partners explained that they were focusing efforts on their own products.[6]

To translate low costs into profitability, revenue must be generated in excess of costs, albeit minimal, that are incurred. The two main ways for news organizations to get revenue are to charge for advertising and to charge for content. Both revenue-making techniques have posed significant challenges. Despite the challenges, successful models do exist.

Advertising has become an increasingly viable way to make money from a news website. The value of advertising space is dependent on the number of people that will view it. In the early era of the Internet, website operators could not charge much for space that few visitors would encounter. As the user base expanded, the value of advertising space grew. As with traditional media, the largest share of revenue from most news websites now comes from advertising.

The most compelling advantage of advertising online is the ability to target. It is easy to program a news website to continuously update and refine advertisements based on the content accessed by the audience. One pioneer was the *New York Times,* which used its free registration system to compile data to present advertisers with a picture of online behavior tied to broad demographic factors. Although this type of targeting is present in other media, it is far more efficient on the Web. The technology of the Web also allows for new strategies of advertising. Some of these blur the line between content and advertising. Book and other consumer product reviews in the news media, for instance, are often linked to a vendor that compensates the news organization if a click-through leads to a purchase.

The position of advertisements on news websites also offers an advantage over advertisements in print publications. By convention, newspapers rarely have advertising on the front page. As the Web has developed, this same convention has not applied to Web publications. Indeed, one of the most common forms of Internet advertising is the banner advertisement. The banner is a narrow advertisement that stretches across the entire screen. It typically offers room for brief text, an icon, and an opportunity to click through to the advertiser's site. News sites have frequently sold banner advertising space as well as other space on the front page. Looking at the leading state newspaper sites, 78 percent of sites sell space in the initial page view. For the sites with ads in the initial page view, about 13 percent is devoted to advertising.

Another lucrative part of the advertising market is the online classifieds. The online format is an efficient way to present this material. Electronic searching techniques can quickly identify advertisements meeting certain criteria. In fact, a number of other enterprises have tried to make inroads into this market on the

Web. Solidifying their hold on this lucrative market is an incentive that has convinced newspapers to get online.

The other major alternative for revenue is to charge for content. The classic way to charge for content is the subscriber model. Access to the website could be password protected. Subscribers could receive an access code that allows them to receive the content. Rather than a blanket subscription model, there could be charges for specified content. Either revenue strategy runs into the ethos that information wants to be free on the Internet.

The vast majority of news websites resist charging for subscriptions. None of the major broadcasting networks have adopted a subscription model. This is not surprising, since television broadcasters are used to relying entirely on advertising. More surprising, perhaps, is that print publications, which have a subscription model well ingrained in their business, also have been reluctant to adopt a subscription model. Only a few newspapers limit access to paid subscribers. This is clear from the websites of the leading state newspapers. Only two of the fifty, *Albuquerque Journal* and *Little Rock Gazette,* deny access to nonsubscribers. All other sites offer access to at least some of the news content for free.

So far, the benefits of free content seem to outweigh the benefits of charging. Obviously, a free product avoids the infrastructure requirements of a subscription model. By far, however, the greatest benefit of a free site is the ability to attract more visitors. When sites begin charging for content, their audience drops dramatically. The *St. Paul* (Minnesota) *Pioneer Press* website quickly lost its online lead in the local market once it adopted a subscriber-based model.[7] The website of the Idaho Falls *Post Register* experienced a 75 percent decline in visitors when it imposed a fee on nonsubscribers.[8] When these visitors leave, they may find other alternatives on the Web. They may never come back, even if the site were to become free again. Losing visitors comes with a huge price in regard to advertising. There is a trade-off between getting subscription and advertising revenue.

Recognition of the trade-off has led to notable instances of backtracking on a subscription model. An early visible example was the national newspaper *USA Today.* In April 1995, USAToday.com instituted a subscriber-based service for $15 per month. By August 1995, the subscriber model was abandoned.[9] It is not just high-profile papers that have backtracked, but smaller papers such as the *San Jose Mercury News, Colorado Springs Gazette,* and the *Hays* [Kansas] *Daily News.*[10]

Although subscription models have been resisted, there are important exceptions. The most notable exception is the specialized news publication. In particular, business publications have fared well on the Internet. At some level, people seem willing to spend money to make money. Other specialized news publishers such as *National Journal* for politics and the *Chronicle of Higher Education* for higher education have a long history of charging for content.

The strongest model for a subscriber base of daily news is the *Wall Street Journal,* which was one of the earliest newspapers to adopt a subscription model. In 1996, the *Wall Street Journal* began charging for content. By 2000, the site had $50 million in annual revenue with 40 percent from circulation and 60 percent from advertising. It has effectively used the marketing technique of giving a brief free trial subscription and then offering the opportunity to purchase. Customers insert credit card and other information in order to receive the paper on a free trial basis. It is reported that over 90 percent of those taking advantage of the trial subscription become regular subscribers.[11] Despite the early success of the *Wall Street Journal,* few daily newspapers followed its example.

The practice of not selling subscriptions, however, is not set in stone. The calculation of costs and benefits may change in the future. This might occur if traditional organizations begin to believe that their website is taking business away from the more lucrative traditional format. No doubt, traditional organizations become a little nervous when they hear former television reporter Christopher Harper counsel people that the Web version makes a paper version obsolete: "I have canceled my subscription to the *New York Times* because I can receive all the articles I want from the Internet edition."[12]

If a news organization doesn't want to charge for content on a blanket subscription model, it can charge for specified content. Parts of the current site may limit access to subscribers. An increasing number of organizations use variations of paying per page viewed. This possibility has been enabled by advances in micropay technology, which is capable of small repeated transactions and better online commerce technology generally.

The most common type of specialized content that is sold is archived stories. This content builds on a well-established infrastructure of charging libraries and others for the use of archival databases. It is not surprising that charging for archives is now the norm on news websites. Looking at the fifty leading state newspaper sites, forty-one provide archives of at least thirty days or more. Eighty-three percent of these companies charge for use of the archives. The median fee is $2.50 per story.

As the Internet has been incorporated into the product of traditional news organizations, it also has been incorporated into the lives of their journalists. The Internet has enhanced the ability of journalists to complete their fundamental tasks. Journalists increasingly use e-mail as a way to contact their sources. The adoption of e-mail by journalists was rapid. A Middleberg survey found that Internet use by journalists increased from 50 percent in 1996 to over 98 percent by 2000.[13] The convenience and speed of e-mail makes it the most preferred method for journalists to contact regular sources. It has held this status for some time. Middleberg Associates found that in 1998, for the first time e-mail edged out in-person and telephone contact as the most preferred way of contacting regular sources.[14] By 2002, e-mail had become the most preferred way for contacting new or unknown sources.[15]

Journalists also frequently use the Internet for research. While Lexis-Nexis and other article databases effectively compile published material, the Web fills a niche for finding material that has not been published. It can be useful for obtaining background information about organizations and individuals. The website of one type of person, the political candidate, has drawn special interest from journalists. Biographical information, position papers, and press releases are consolidated in one convenient location.

Looking at the overall transition of traditional media organizations and journalists to the Web, it is clear that most have adjusted quickly. In some ways, the field is well suited for the transition. Traditional news organizations provide information, which is central to the Web. They also have a tradition of low prices for content, which melds with the way people have thought about the Internet. The Web allows traditional news organizations to attractively package their excess material. Newspaper journalists are well trained to deal with time pressure and are unlikely to be fazed by the speed at which life proceeds online.

NONTRADITIONAL JOURNALISM ON THE WEB

In addition to the sites of traditional media organizations, news can be obtained on the Web through a variety of nontraditional sources. Typically, these are low-budget operations with few, if any, paid personnel. Often, the news is reported by those without formal training in journalism. In the words of Matt Drudge, anybody can be a reporter: "Now, with a modem, anyone can follow the world and report on the world—no middle man, no big brother."[16] Posted on the Web, this reporting has a potentially unlimited audience.

The viability of nontraditional sources of news is increased by broad disillusionment with the mainstream media. The mainstream media are widely perceived as being too powerful. Harris Interactive regularly asks Americans whether the media has "too much," "too little," or "about the right" amount of power. About three-fourths of Americans respond "too much."[17] In recent years, approval ratings for the media have been well below 50 percent. A Fox News poll found that only 14 percent of Americans have "a great deal of confidence in the news media"; this finding placed the media behind nearly every other institution, including the 16 percent who have a great deal of confidence in the Internal Revenue Service.[18] The disillusionment with the media was articulated in a prominent *Atlantic Monthly* article, "Why Americans Hate the Media," by James Fallows. The indictment of the media by Fallows included ethical shortcomings, excessive predictions, and a general lack of reporting.[19] Written in 1996, his article implied the potential for new outlets of news. Beginning its explosive growth at the time, the Web presented itself to this untapped market.

This untapped market, to whatever extent it exists, has proved challenging for nontraditional organizations to capture. It is true that many nontraditional organizations have set up sites. In reality, however, most of the sites have few visitors. They routinely lose the competition with large, traditional news organizations. Yet, some nontraditional organizations have found a way to be competitive for at least some of the market. These nontraditional organizations have mostly pursued a specialized market, but in a few cases have reached a general audience.

Typically, a nontraditional organization provides specialized information. Because of the low costs incurred by a website, a large market is not necessary. Fulfilling niches that are uncovered by traditional organizations has become the most common way to secure an audience, albeit a smaller one than captured by general news organizations. Most specialized news is on popular subjects like sports and entertainment. There are, however, a number of nontraditional news organizations that provide political news. This news can be found in various Internet newsgroups and on the Web. It is common for specialized political sites to focus on a specific policy domain or part of the government.

If a general audience is pursued, the focus tends to be on commentary. The site frequently offers a consistent viewpoint. It has been suggested that the Web is sparking a modest revival of the partisan press of the nineteenth century, which integrated advocacy and news.[20] Cultural and media criticism sites have found an audience. Political commentary is also prevalent. In this way, nontraditional websites compete primarily in news interpretation and not news gathering.

Occasionally, nontraditional organizations are thrust into the limelight. The first three nontraditional news organizations to receive a high public profile were the *Drudge Report, Salon,* and *Slate.* These websites embody many of the characteristics of the typical nontraditional news provider on the Web. Thus, they serve as useful models of how nontraditional organizations operate on the Web, with the caveat that their prominence makes them unusual.

The *Drudge Report* found itself at the center of the President Clinton–Monica Lewinsky story. The website run by Matt Drudge, an independent writer working out of his home, had slowly gained a reputation for supplying gossip about famous people, including a key *Seinfeld* scoop.[21] Drudge presented information that he got from tips or that he had culled from other publications. In 1998, Drudge was given a tip: *Newsweek* was sitting on a story written by Michael Isikoff that detailed an improper sexual relationship between President Clinton and a former White House intern. It was not the first time that Drudge had received a tip about a future story by Isikoff. A year earlier, Drudge claimed that he received a tip from another *Newsweek* employee that Isikoff was writing a story about a woman named Katherine Willey, who claimed that she had been sexually harassed by President Clinton. In both cases Drudge ran with the tip, beating Isikoff to his own story and setting off a chain of events that ended with impeachment hearings.

The *Drudge Report* highlights the irony that the first major story broken by a nontraditional news organization was prematurely divulging the contents of a story in the traditional media. The nontraditional site gained credibility because it, in fact, was telling a traditional media story. The *Drudge Report* is also tied to the mainstream media in that much of the site consists of links to traditional media organizations. A further manifestation of the not-so-arm's-length relationship between traditional and nontraditional sources was that Drudge used his notoriety to secure a position in the traditional news media—a television show on Fox and a talk show on ABC Radio.

The online magazine *Salon* has received numerous awards for being the best independent news site. It was founded by disgruntled former employees of the *San Francisco Chronicle*. The site emphasizes political, cultural, and entertainment commentary and has a number of guest contributors who offer occasional articles. *Salon* also has an openly acknowledged political perspective in support of liberal policies. Considering its political perspective, it is not surprising that *Salon* reached a previously unknown level of prominence by running a decades-old story about the marital infidelity of Henry Hyde, the man who was leading the House investigation of President Clinton. The story was acknowledged by Hyde, who characterized the affair that occurred when he was 41 years old as a "youthful indiscretion." Its awards and prominence were not enough to save *Salon* from losing approximately $68 million its first six years in business. Frustrated with the losses, *Salon* switched to a subscriber model in April 2001.[22]

Ironically, it is the Microsoft-affiliated *Slate* whose difficulties in making money have been most publicized. The concern with finances arises because Microsoft has insisted that the online publication not be subsidized. Its efforts to stand on its own, in turn, have garnered publicity primarily for wavering on a subscription model. It began as a free site and grew to over one hundred thousand weekly visitors. In late 1997, founding editor Michael Kinsley announced that the publication soon would be available only to subscribers. Shortly after, Microsoft reversed itself. As expressed succinctly by Kinsley, *Slate* recognized the problems with selling political news: "Even in our headiest moments, we couldn't convince ourselves that people lust for political and cultural commentary the way they lust for sex and money."[23] *Slate,* however, did not recognize the problems for long. The next year, *Slate* again announced that it would become subscriber based effective March 1998. Microsoft hoped that its readership would decline no more than from 150,000 to 20,000.[24] In February 1999, *Slate* again reversed itself, abandoning the $20 annual subscription price. In a letter to readers, Kinsley reflected on the decision: "The spreadsheet wizards figure that ad revenue from the increased traffic will more than compensate for the lost subscriptions."[25] In 2002, Kinsley's odyssey at *Slate* ended with his resignation.

BLOGS

One new format that has emerged online from both traditional and nontraditional news organizations is the blog. A *blog* is an online journal in which the most recent entries are added to the top of a document. The name has emerged as an abbreviated version of the term *Web log* and the name of a software program for presenting online journals. Blog authors, or bloggers, can write on any subject matter. A number of people outside traditional journalism have created blogs that emphasize news, especially commentary. Although typically associated with nontraditional journalism, the blog has made inroads into traditional organizations. In 2002, for example, MSNBC introduced a new feature to its website called Weblog Central. In announcing the feature, MSNBC suggested that the format was an important development in journalism: "These interactive diaries promise to transform and democratize the media landscape."[26]

The audience for blogs can be unpredictable. Personal blogs usually have a minimal audience that may not extend much beyond the author's relatives and lawyers for those regularly lampooned in the blog. In other cases, a personal blog may obtain a broader following. Perhaps the first prominent example of a news story influenced by blogs was the birthday-party speech by Trent Lott, praising the 1948 presidential candidacy of Strom Thurmond. The story began quietly in the mainstream media, but received substantial attention in blogs. In a *New York Times* article, Paul Krugman described blog-author Joshua Marshall as more responsible than anyone else for raising the profile of the story, which ultimately led to Lott's resignation as Senate majority leader.[27]

Blogs reached a new level of prominence during Operation Iraqi Freedom in 2003. During the war, the blogosphere was filled with observation and opinion from military personnel, journalists, dissidents, and others communicating some sense of how they were experiencing the war. War blogging also produced a vivid example of the uneasy mix of traditional and nontraditional media. Aptly named for the Internet age, Kevin Sites supplemented his reporting for CNN with an independent blog of personal observations about the war. Suggesting that the blog was a distraction from his "full-time job," CNN asked Sites to cease publication of his independent blog.[28]

OBTAIN NEWS WITHOUT JOURNALISTS

On some occasions, the Internet means that people don't need journalists at all—traditional or nontraditional. The Internet increases the ability of people to obtain primary documents that they previously relied on journalists to interpret. The classic example is the Starr Report, which people were able to retrieve themselves. Although many people obtained the Starr Report from the sites of traditional news organizations, the event demonstrated the weakened position of journalists to the extent that people did not have to rely on journalists to interpret the document for them. They could read and understand it for themselves. The same thing can be true for any variety of documents that routinely are made available on the Web by governmental entities. People can easily access the primary documents of Congress, the president, and the Supreme Court. They can also access many primary documents from nongovernmental organizations, such as position papers on campaign websites.

Symbolic of the weakened position of journalists on the Web is the way in which the public can access documents previously available exclusively to the press. Perhaps most important is that the public can get direct access to wire stories. Another example is the press release. A substantial majority of journalists report using the Web to obtain press releases.[29] People can easily get the press releases themselves from the originating website. In the context of the Web, the term *press release* is a virtual misnomer. Posted on the Web, the original announcement is not something that is released only to the press, but is available to the public.

ONLINE NEWS CONTENT

In an early article on the Internet in the *Columbia Journalism Review,* Jon Pavlik establishes a three-phase typology for the originality of the websites of traditional media organizations. In the first phase, the website merely reproduces on the Internet the stories that appear in the newspaper or on a television show. In the second phase, some of the potential of the Web emerges in the form of original content, hyperlinks, some interactivity, and customized menus. In an ambiguously defined third phase, the website becomes an interactive medium allowing live entrance and participation in actual events.[30]

Most news sites are well into the second phase of using Web features to generate original content. When Pavlik introduced his framework, most organizations were in the first phase. In 1996, for instance, it was estimated that only 17 percent of magazines and newspapers provided as much as 20 percent original content on their website. At that time, only one-third of news organizations ever allowed the website to run a story before the print publication. Most experts consider that it was not until February 28, 1997, that the first big story was broken online.[31] On that day, the *Dallas Morning News* broke news of Timothy McVeigh's confession to the Oklahoma City bombing in its online version. This decision set the tone for a rapid shift to original content. In 1998, the number of news sites with at least 20 percent original content reached 50 percent.[32] By 2000, most news organizations expressed a willingness to allow the website to run a story before the print publication.[33]

The use of Web-enabled features in the second stage is evident from the content of the leading state newspaper sites. One common Web-enabled feature is the site search engine, which appears on over 90 percent of the leading state newspaper sites. Another Web-enabled feature, indeed the defining characteristic of the Web, is the opportunity to use links to move from one document to another. A systematic study of the major stories on the leading state newspaper sites reveals that links are present for 35 percent of the stories. All of the links are outside the story, either at the end or off to the side. The most common link is to other stories related to the topic. The second most common link is to an opportunity to post a comment or add to a discussion board. Fewer than 5 percent of the stories have links to comprehensive poll results, audio or video files, and background research.[34] Solidly in the second stage of being an original medium, news organizations generally have not begun to approach the third stage of being an avenue to live involvement in actual events.

Whether or not news organizations are taking full advantage of the technology, it is clear that online content represents a staggering increase in the quality of easily accessible news. While traditional journalism is limited to narrow broadcast spots and available print space, the Internet provides virtually unlimited space to a news organization. Traditional organizations have used the space to increase their number of stories. Further, nontraditional news providers and direct access to primary documents have brought content that previously was not available to the public.

There is not only more news, but different news. The different substance of Internet news has been regularly demonstrated through content analysis. One important early study was conducted by Jennifer Greer and Donica Mensing. In some ways, the design of their study seemed likely to produce high similarity between Internet news and other news. The researchers compared the content of a newspaper to its corresponding website. Even with the same organization producing the product, Greer and Mensing identified substantial differences in content. They found that the lead story in the print publication matched the lead story in the noon online version of the same organization only 15 percent of the time. Further, they found systematic differences in the types of stories that were featured in the online and print versions. Specifically, international and crime stories were more common online than in print.[35]

Indeed, the comparatively high opportunity for receiving international news online is well documented. Greer and Mensing suggest that the overnight hours, when little is happening in America, provide an opportunity for international news to become the story of the moment. More than a function of time differences, the substantial increase in international news is multifaceted. Across other American media, it has been estimated that international news accounts for about 5 percent of all stories.[36] On the other hand, international news is never far away in the online world. People have an unparalleled ability to go directly to international sources to get a foreign perspective on the news of the day. The accessibility of wire services results in huge opportunities for international news. The extra space available online allows the routine posting of stories from overseas that generally are rejected for the limited space on television or in newspapers. The tremendous array of opportunities for international news on the Web prompted the *National Journal,* well before the World Trade Center attacks, to proclaim that foreign news was making a comeback on the Web: "[F]oreign news is in the midst of a major renaissance in the new-media outlets frequented by middle-class Americans online."[37]

The potential for receiving different news is further increased by the capacity for online news to be customized. Websites and e-mails can be customized to deliver news based on the expressed preferences or previous behavior of consumers. For all its advantages, customizing content took off slowly among news organizations. A key turning point in the acceleration of customized content was the May 2002 announcements by the *Los Angeles Times* and *Washington Post* that they were increasing customization with an emphasis on differentiating content between local and nonlocal site visitors.

News delivery online is also faster than through traditional media. Journalism has always been a profession based on speed, but the Internet sets the clock even faster. While the product of traditional journalism is deadline-centered on a particular time for broadcast or publication, online journalism is perpetually a work in progress. If organizations want to be the first to break a story, they may no longer be able to wait to publish it in the next edition or next broadcast. The story may have to be broken in the perpetual work in progress, the online edition.

The key, then, is to have the online and traditional products working together. By working together, the organization improves its chance of breaking the story first. Beyond speed, integrating the online and traditional products can result in greater depth of stories. For example, a print version may provide results to a couple of survey questions, while the Web version may provide the results in their entirety. In this way, the various dimensions of news organizations can work together to provide a more thorough news product.

Indeed, integration is an important goal for news organizations. Despite the appeal of integration, many organizations started out with the ideal of having an independently operated online product. Web operations were frequently established as separate entities. This was in the days of dot-com euphoria, when Internet-only ventures had a novelty attraction with customers and markets. Over time, however, many organizations realized that the website would have more value if it were integrated with other products. By 1998, print and Web operations had been integrated in over half of the newsrooms.[38] The trend toward consolidation was cemented with the early 2001 announcements by CNN, Fox, and CBS that separate Web entities were being folded into broader news operations.[39]

A milestone in integrating the website with traditional products occurred in the context of a nonpolitical program, although the program did include a fair amount of voting. The television show *Survivor* was the first major demonstration of the success of the integrated product. People were able to get subsidiary information about the show and its contestants on the website. On one occasion, the manner in which the website was assembled sparked a widespread rumor (ultimately false) about the outcome of the contest. The website helped fuel interest in the traditional format. CBS Vice President David Katz describes *Survivor* as the turning point for integrating media: "[*Survivor*] was our first foray into having an integrated entertainment Web experience. . . . We learned a lot, were extremely successful and realized that this was the model we needed to follow for all of our shows."[40]

ONLINE NEWS CONSUMPTION

The Internet is an important source of news for many Americans. Presently about half of Americans receive at least some news online. People, in turn, use the news they get online. In the 2000 presidential election, nearly half of those receiving news online said that online information affected their vote.[41] By the year 2000, active stock traders were citing the Internet over television and newspapers by about a 2 to 1 margin as their main news source for deciding how to invest their money.[42]

Internet news consumption has grown dramatically. The number of daily consumers of online news went from less than 1 percent in 1995 to about 16 percent in 2002. Milestones for the percentage going online for news at least once a week include 10 percent of Americans in 1996, 20 percent in 1998, and 33 percent in 2000.[43] The growth can also be seen in relation to where people have obtained news about election campaigns. The percentage of Americans going online for presidential election news rose from 4 percent in 1996 to 18 percent in 2000.[44] The percentage of Americans going online for midterm election news rose from 6 percent in 1998 to 13 percent in 2002.[45]

This growth has enabled the Internet to join television, newspapers, and radio as one of the four major sources of news for Americans. As shown in table 8.1, the Internet has been growing as a news source when other media have been struggling to maintain an audience. The 35 percent of weekly online news consumers in 2002 was slightly higher than the approximately 32 percent of Americans who "regularly" watched the nightly network news. Weekly Internet news consumers also exceed the "regular" news audience for NPR, talk radio, and news magazines.

The primary source for online news is the website of a traditional news organization. The single most common source for online news is CNN.[46] For local news, the most common source is the website of the local newspaper.[47] By far, the most common Internet-specific source of news is the Internet service provider.

Table 8.1   Trends in Sources for News

News Source	1993	1996	1998	2000	2002
Newspapers	75	71	68	63	63
Local Television News	77	65	64	56	57
Online News	n/a	4	20	33	35
Nightly Network News	60	42	38	30	32
CNN	35	26	23	21	25
Network TV News Magazines	52	36	37	31	24
Network Morning Shows	n/a	n/a	23	20	22
Fox Cable News	n/a	n/a	17	17	22
Political Talk Radio	23	13	13	14	17
National Public Radio	15	13	15	15	16
Weekly Print News Magazines	24	15	15	12	13
Public Television News Hour	10	4	4	5	5

Source: Pew Biennial Media Consumption Surveys.
Notes: Q: "For each that I read, tell me if you watch or listen to it regularly, sometimes, hardly ever, or never." Percentages are for "regularly." A similar but not identical question is asked for online news: "How frequently do you go online to get news . . . every day, 3–5 days per week, 1 or 2 days per week, once every few weeks, or less often?" Percentages are for at least 1 or 2 days per week. Data for 1996 and later are for April of the given year, except Internet data for April 1996 are unavailable so June 1995 data are used. Data for 1993 are from May except talk radio from April 1993 and newspapers from June 1992.

The home page of ISPs such as America Online (AOL) has become a major addition to where Americans get their news. Although nontraditional, the ISP shares much with traditional sources including an emphasis on wire service news. Besides ISPs, Internet-specific news sites cannot compete with traditional organizations for the mass audience.

People have a variety of motivations for receiving news online. Surveys show that the single largest reason for getting news online is convenience. This has not always been the case. In 1996, the 53 percent of Americans who cited the inability to get all they want from "traditional news sources" was greater than the 45 percent who cited convenience as a reason for going online for election news. By 2000, convenience had not just passed the inadequacy of traditional news sources as a reason for getting online news, but overwhelmed it by 56 to 29 percent.[48]

Another important dimension of online news consumption is that the people who receive news online do not represent a typical social and demographic cross section of Americans. The receipt of online news varies with socioeconomic factors. Both use of the Internet and consumption of news generally increase with education. It is, therefore, not surprising that those receiving news online are generally better educated than the average American.

Consumers of online news are also younger than the average American. The percentage of 18- to 29-year-olds going online for news weekly is nearly five times that of those over the age of 65. The age gap is a long-standing phenomenon. From 2000 to 2002, the percentage of adults under 30 going online for news held steady at around 45 percent, with adults over 65 at around 10 percent.[49] While other Americans tend to use the Internet as a supplement to other media, the Internet is emerging as the primary source of news for young Americans.

The use of the Internet for news by young Americans is a major development. Young Americans have historically had the least knowledge and interest in the news. While 68 percent of those over 65 enjoy keeping up with the news, only 33 percent of those 18–29 enjoy keeping up with the news.[50] Receiving less enjoyment from keeping up with the news, young Americans seem unlikely to exert much effort to obtain news. The convenience of the Internet, then, becomes critical to the ability of young Americans to receive news.

Thus, the Internet is the one medium where young people get more news than the elderly. The most extreme example of the usual situation is the nightly network television news. Young Americans have largely abandoned the nightly network news. Those in the 18–29 age group are only about one-third as likely to watch the nightly network news as those over 65 years of age. Setting aside the perennial debate of whether the chicken or the egg came first, young Americans do not have to sit through too many Viagra ads to understand that the nightly network news is not for them. Young Americans have also largely abandoned the practice of reading newspapers every day. Only 26 percent of Americans ages 18–29 regularly read a newspaper, which is less than half the percentage of those over 65.[51] These trends cannot be blamed on the Internet and, in fact, were well in place before the Internet. What the Internet has done is to act as a counterbalance to these long-standing trends. This is an important development for a democracy that depends on citizens receiving information about public affairs.

Despite the increasing prominence of the Internet, the United States is still a television nation. Surveys consistently show that television is the major source of news for Americans. Television is cited about twice as often as any other source for news. In particular, cable television has experienced significant growth and is now the source most widely seen as doing the best job of covering the news.[52]

One way to measure what medium is central to life is to observe where people turn during a crisis. In a crisis, Americans continue to look to television as the major source of news. This was readily apparent in the events surrounding the September 11, 2001, attacks on America. Despite assertions that the Internet was becoming the key source of news, the Internet was destined to take a back seat in the crisis. Approximately four days after the attacks, Americans were asked about their major source of news about the war on terrorism. They were allowed to name up to two different sources. No medium came close to television. Television was cited by 90 percent of survey respondents, far exceeding the 14 percent and 11 percent citing radio and newspapers, respectively. The Internet, named by 5 percent of Americans, was a distant fourth.[53]

This role of television in a crisis actually was predicted months before the events of September 11, 2001. In 2000, the Pew Center asked Americans where they would turn in a crisis. The wording of the poll was eerily similar to facts about the actual attacks: "If you heard that there had been a major terrorist attack on a large U.S. city, where would you go first for more information about this . . . ?" In 2000, 66 percent of Americans responded that they would turn on the television. The Internet and radio were tied for second at 10 percent.[54] When—tragically—this scenario occurred one year later, people acted as they said in polls. They turned to television. As the immediate crisis eased and normal activities resumed, the Internet returned to its significant and growing role in how Americans get their news.

The United States is not yet an Internet nation for news. Television will continue to be the major source of news for the foreseeable future. The Internet, however, is an important source of news for many Americans. With continued growth, it may not be long before it passes newspapers and radio to become the second most utilized source for news. With so many Americans receiving news online, the question arises whether the Internet has implications for the accuracy of news.

IMPLICATIONS OF THE INTERNET FOR THE ACCURACY AND AVAILABILITY OF NEWS

Clearly, the widespread availability of new journalistic content has implications. There is, however, a substantial amount of disagreement about what they are. Part of the disagreement results from the fact that it is early in the life of Internet journalism and the future is uncertain. Another part of the disagreement is a more fundamental issue about the value placed on getting it out and getting it right. At this stage in the development of Internet journalism, two normative cases about the implications of the Internet for journalism have emerged. Proponents of these cases have surprisingly little disagreement over the main premise. All agree that the Internet has led to more news being provided by more sources faster and more directly. The disagreement lies in whether Internet journalism strikes an acceptable or unacceptable balance between getting it out and getting it right—between availability and accuracy.

Acceptable Balance

While Internet journalism results in more and faster news, it is able to maintain an acceptable balance between availability and accuracy. This case has been stated with varying degrees of confidence—from a cautious optimism to the bold assertion of Matt Drudge that "the Internet is going to save the news business."[55] The case for a positive effect of the Internet on journalism often starts by pointing out that mistakes are frequently made in traditional journalistic formats. Any marginal reduction in online accuracy is seen as more than offset by tremendous gains in availability. In short, the balance between accuracy and availability is not lost by news coming more rapidly from more sources.

The availability of more sources does not raise fundamental questions for accuracy. The market has long sorted out news providers in other media and can do so on the Internet. Where nontraditional organizations prove to be unreliable, people will tune out. After the market clears, what remains are some nontraditional news providers that can make a contribution to the news environment. These nontraditional sources can be a valuable complement to the coverage provided by traditional media organizations, which have increasingly drawn the ire of the American public. Media consultant Roger Ailes describes how traditional media are perceived by many: "If you look at the polls on journalists, they tend to rank about the same as used car salesmen, politicians, and hookers."[56] Thus, nontraditional organizations may provide a welcome new viewpoint on major news stories. They may also deliver original news accurately. As described by Matt Drudge, this ability is not limited to traditional organizations:

> We have entered an era vibrating with the din of small voices. Every citizen can be a reporter, can take on the powers that be. . . . And you would be amazed what the ordinary guy knows. From a little corner in my Hollywood apartment, in the company of nothing more than my 486 computer and my six-toed cat, I have consistently been able to break big stories, thanks to this network of ordinary guys.[57]

The speed of news on the Internet need not be a substantial detriment to accuracy. The currency of journalism has always been speed, and the profession is well prepared to manage in a world moving ahead at Internet speed. Frequent updates are not new phenomena. In the early twentieth century, a large city newspaper might issue ten different editions per day. Broadcasters have long had the capability of going live to an event, as well as routinely updating the news. In fact, speed may be an advantage to accuracy. While mistakes in a newspaper have to wait twenty-four hours to be corrected, a mistake on a website can be corrected instantly.

Unacceptable Balance

News provided faster from more sources has upset the balance between availability and accuracy. While acknowledging substantial increases in availability, advocates of this perspective believe that increased availability has come at too high a price. This case is summarized in strong terms by the most prominent newscaster in the history of television, Walter Cronkite, who has described the implications of the Internet on the news industry as a "frightful danger to all of us."[58] Even a pioneer in Internet journalism, Michael Kinsley of *Slate,* says that in order to receive accurate news he sticks to an old medium: "Today, if I hear about a major breaking news story, I'll turn on my TV. I may be missing some cutting-edge insights, but at least I'm getting trustworthy information."[59]

The presence of nontraditional sources raises serious problems for accuracy. Many of the stories from nontraditional sources are filed by reporters who lack formal training and do not adhere to professional journalistic norms. This may result in stories that are more likely to be inaccurate or inappropriate. Since they are often low in the pecking order of receiving stories, these reporters may be given the choice to run a story that has been rejected by traditional organizations for failing to meet journalistic norms. Even the well-respected online publication *Salon,* which is authored by professionally trained reporters, received its first huge wave of publicity for running a story on a "youthful" affair by Henry Hyde that had circulated to traditional organizations for $7^1/_2$ months.[60]

The increase in inaccurate stories is exacerbated because it can be difficult to assess the credibility of a source on the Internet. Even those in the journalistic profession who have been trained professionally to deal with these issues have had problems. As articulated by Brant Hudson, Executive Director of Investigative Reporters & Editors, it is difficult to say why journalists have trouble gauging online sources: "Journalists for whatever reason are more gullible when something is on a computer screen."[61]

The best-known incident of a journalist being misled by online sources involved Pierre Salinger in 1997. An unreliable document had been circulating on the Web for some time, suggesting that the U.S. Navy had accidentally shot down TWA Flight 800 in 1996. Salinger, a former ABC News correspondent, saw the document and reported that he had evidence that a missile caused the airline disaster, which government investigators had already determined was caused by mechanical problems. The prestige of Salinger gave instant credibility to the missile theory. The Salinger "evidence" received significant attention in the global media before being discredited. Salinger's mistake in assessing credibility is notable because of his background. He had substantial experience in the media working as presidential press secretary to John F. Kennedy and Lyndon Johnson and working about forty years as a journalist for prestigious outlets such as the *San Francisco Chronicle* and ABC News. His career had culminated with a five-year ABC investigation of the bombing of Pan Am Flight 103 in 1988. Although Salinger prefaced his reflections on the Pan Am 103 investigation in his biography as "I did my homework,"[62] libraries throughout the nation have compiled brochures to dissuade students from the Internet homework techniques used by Salinger on his TWA Flight 800 research.

Making sure a story is accurate in its detail takes time—time that is not allowed on the Internet. Tom Rosenstiel of the Project for Excellence in Journalism sees an inherent weakness in online journalism compared to traditional forms: "The reason newspapers tend to be more accurate than electronic media is that newspapers have a news cycle of about 12 hours, where a group of editors can paw over stories and second-guess them."[63] The speed of Internet journalism also seems to make mistakes less costly: mistaken information can be quickly removed—as if it never happened.

There are a number of examples where the Internet news product has sacrificed accuracy. In January 1998, the websites of both the *Wall Street Journal* and the *Dallas Morning News* reported that White House service personnel had seen Bill Clinton and Monica Lewinsky in a compromising position. After the sources did not check out, the only compromising positions were those maintained by the news organizations having to correct their stories. In other cases, inaccurate information has been spread in the guise of a credible news organization. It is easy to copy images and create documents that look like they are from a reputable source. In October 2001, for instance, a mischief maker from Michigan was able to exploit a bug in CNN.com's system to enable his hoax about Britney Spears being killed in a car accident to be listed as the most popular story on CNN.com.[64]

Reconciliation of Cases

The competing cases are unlikely to be reconciled soon. There is no reason to expect people to fundamentally change how they value accuracy and availability. The Internet is still a young medium, and its development will be unpredictable. The use of any medium depends on the quality of the people who use it. Thus, the balance between availability and accuracy will continue to be a tenuous one. Some will see it as acceptable, others will not.

There are, however, some possibilities for reconciliation. It is possible that the market eventually will weed out sources that fail to provide valuable news. These organizations will simply disappear, and there is no easier place to disappear than on a worldwide network of millions of sites. To some extent, this possibility is dependent on educating the public to better assess credibility. Fraught with challenges, such education would be an ambitious undertaking.

The best chance for reconciling the two cases appears to be that people will get their online news from traditional organizations. These organizations have a great incentive to ensure that their Web product does not sacrifice accuracy. The credibility of the broader news organization is at stake. The public knows this. In surveys, less than 10 percent of the online public disagrees with the statement that "If a source is credible offline, it is likely to be credible online."[65] The public, therefore, trusts that a news organization will apply the same standards of accuracy to the online product as its other products. Breaking this trust could jeopardize the credibility of both the online and traditional product of the organization. Traditional organizations are left with the simple solution of applying a high standard to the online product.

CONCLUSION

The Internet, of course, cannot force people to be interested in the news. According to Pew Research, only 50 percent of Americans say that they enjoy keeping up with the news.[66] The availability of news in a different medium is unlikely to alter fundamental interest in the news. What it can do, however, is to provide a diversity of opinion and subject matter that can increase the likelihood of tapping into the news interests that people do have.

Where there is some interest, the online news opportunities are staggering. Consider the case of an environmentally interested immigrant from Britain who initially moved to Boston and now lives in Indianapolis. Prior to the Internet, finding news about Britain, Boston, or the environment might have entailed time-delayed, prohibitively expensive mail subscriptions and ad hoc publications. The individual in question may now read British papers online before most British are awake, scan same-day Boston media sites online, and choose from any number of specialized environmental news sites compiling environmental stories from around the world.

While most citizens have been content to receive online news from traditional media organizations, some online news arises from new sources. Indeed, the prospects for preserving ordinary voices are higher on the Internet than in other high-cost media. Nontraditional organizations often find that the Internet is the only available forum for their news. Newsgroups have made editors of ordinary citizens. While news distributors in other media are often overwhelmed by the need to pay bills, Internet communicators face less financial pressure because costs are so low. With minimal resources, nontraditional sources can compile and comment on news. With more resources, nontraditional organizations have been able to provide specialized original reporting. In either case, nontraditional organizations may provide a valuable alternative to mainstream media.

The presence of new voices on the Web provides a sharp contrast to greater consolidation of ownership in the traditional media. Competition in the daily newspaper market, which had been the norm, is now the exception. For the vast majority of subscribers, their daily newspaper is not independently owned, but part of a chain. The Top 25 television groups now own nearly half of all commercial television stations in the United States.[67] Summarizing the increased concentration of ownership, Ben Bagdikian estimates that six companies control over half of what Americans read and watch in the media.[68]

The emergence of new sources poses enough of a threat to make established media organizations nervous. It is not surprising that established media organizations and individuals are among the harshest critics of online journalism. Daniel Schorr, legendary television and radio broadcaster at NPR, CNN, and CBS, cites the use of computer-generated images to suggest the lack of a minimal standard of professionalism for online journalists: "Indeed, on the Internet, a journalist doesn't have to be human at all."[69] On his Fox television show, Bill O'Reilly advised the publisher of worldnetdaily.com to avoid the usual shortcomings of Internet-only news organizations: "Just be accurate, 'cause I've had a lot of trouble, not with worldnet, but with a lot of other Internet sites, because they just put whatever they want, you know."[70] Surveys of media personnel reveal a suspicion of online news. Less than one-third of media workers, for instance, believe that "online news sites currently meet the same standards as other more traditional sources."[71]

In fact, there is a huge gulf between the established media and citizen perceptions of online news. The gulf persisted even after the Internet had become a majority medium. This is clear from a survey comparing media personnel with the online news public. While 77 percent of media elites said that the public was less comfortable with the reliability of online news, only 28 percent of the online public said that it was. While only 27 percent of the online public agrees that "there is too much news on the Internet to sort through and make sense of it all," over half of media elites said that "there is too much news on the Internet for the public to sort through and make sense of it all."[72]

In summary, citizens feel empowered while media elites are somewhat threatened by political journalism on the Internet. It seems likely that America's founding fathers would be comforted by the Internet's influence on political journalism. Early American newspapers were often partisan and sometimes wrong. A long-standing faith in public judgment and the free press is seen in the words of Thomas Jefferson: "Our citizens may be deceived for a while, and have been deceived, but as long as the presses can be protected, we may trust them for light."[73] In modern life, the light may come from a glowing monitor.

PART FOUR

LEGAL AND REGULATORY FRAMEWORK

9

Fundamentals of Cyberlaw

The Internet communication described throughout this book occurs in the context of cyberlaw. Embodying how the legal system addresses Internet-specific issues, cyberlaw offers constraints and opportunities to Internet communicators. It has strong implications for the effectiveness of Internet communication. Advantages go to those Internet communicators who understand cyberlaw; disadvantages go to those who do not. Cyberlaw frames Internet communication whether someone is sending a personal e-mail or offering a public website. Although it is a new field, cyberlaw draws on long-standing principles.

As the field of cyberlaw began, there was a possibility that a new legal paradigm would be established. Cyberlaw, after all, regulates a new virtual world. The virtual world differs significantly from the physical world. The virtual world moves at a pace much faster than the physical world, thereby prompting the expression "Internet time." The virtual world is characterized by an uncertainty about identity and location. These characteristics pose fundamental challenges to existing legal frameworks.

The establishment of a new legal paradigm for cyberspace, however, has not been realized. Instead, the fundamental principle of cyberlaw is that it is a product of applying legal frameworks established prior to the Internet. Although the rejection of an Internet-specific paradigm appears solid, a fundamental caveat for any consideration of cyberlaw is that it is still early in the development of the field. By outlining the fundamental challenges, principle, and caveat of cyberlaw, this chapter provides a strong intuition for contemplating the development of more specific questions of cyberlaw.

FUNDAMENTAL CHALLENGES OF CYBERLAW

One fundamental challenge of cyberlaw is that technology moves faster than the law. Technology races forward as the legal process drags on. This is a reality faced by all decision makers who seek to control the Internet. Wrestling openly with this fact during oral argument in the landmark case *Reno v. ACLU,* Justice Anton Scalia poses the dilemma of assessing the constitutionality of a constantly moving subject: "Is it possible that this statute is unconstitutional today, or was unconstitutional 2 years ago when it was examined on the basis of a record done about 2 years ago, but will be constitutional next week?"[1]

Technology is fast. In 1965, Gordon Moore suggested that computing power would double every 18 months. The success of his prediction has led to it becoming known as Moore's Law. Although not precisely following Moore's Law, the power and speed of the Internet have increased tremendously. User-friendly programs have made websites and other Internet communication accessible to millions.

In contrast, the law is slow. The Framers of the Constitution wanted it that way. In designing a system of checks and balances, they wanted to ensure that the law would not move too quickly. Alexander Hamilton, writing as Publius in 1788, supported the Constitution for its protections against hasty lawmakers: "They will consider every institution calculated to restrain the excess of law-making, and to keep things in the same state in which they happen to be at any given period, as much more likely to do good than harm, because it is favorable to greater stability in the system of legislation."[2]

On a personal level, major lawmakers have been slow to understand and adopt new technologies. Although computers had been on the desktops of workers across America for many years, members of Congress were slow to adopt computers. The Senate authors of the Telecommunications Act of 1996 had reportedly never used a computer.[3] The legal profession has been notoriously slow in adopting new technology, as can be attested to by anyone who has ever waited for the triplicate copy of a legal document to arrive by mail. Writing in *Texas Lawyer,* Mark Grossman notes that the legal profession has trailed business in adopting the memory typewriter, word processors, Windows, and e-mail. He suggests that sending an e-mail attachment to most lawyers means that "you'd better expect to become their tech support."[4] The resistance to new technology is out of line with other professions. While people have been reducing their dependence on professional services by using software to aid in filing taxes and getting medical information, the legal profession has used its power to resist this development. In January 1999, for instance, a judge interpreted a general "practice of law" statute to mean that legal aid software was illegal in the state of Texas. Judge Barefoot Sanders rejected the idea that technology could help the average person better understand the law and ironically suggested that his decision was a necessary response to the computer age:

In other words, QFL [Quicken Family Lawyer] is a "cyber-lawyer." . . . Absent the regulation, as it is being applied in this case, the State's ability to combat the unauthorized practice of law in the computer age would be hindered. The State possesses an interest in protecting the uninformed and unwary from overly-simplistic legal advice.[5]

One of the implications of technology being faster than the law is that technological solutions may ultimately trump legal solutions. Waiting for government to respond may not be a feasible alternative for solving Internet-related problems. It is quite possible that by the time the lawmaking process has played itself out, technological change may have rendered a law moot or inappropriate. Writing laws that are flexible to technology does not necessarily solve the problem and may, in fact, add to the confusion. Where the law is written in flexible terms, such as requiring speech limitations to employ the "least restrictive" means of pursuing a governmental interest, constantly improving technology may literally mean that the demands of the law are constantly changing.

The second fundamental challenge of cyberlaw is the uncertainty about identity and location inherent in Internet communication. No concept has been more fundamental to asserting legal accountability than determining that a specific person did something in a specific location. Uncertainty about identity on the Internet makes it difficult to assign legal responsibility. Internet communicators, to a large extent, have the technical ability to remain anonymous. People are not bound by their legal names in creating an Internet identity. This identity, or "handle," can be unknown to the closest of real-world acquaintances, such as the use of the handle "Shopgirl" in an early Internet-themed film *You've Got Mail*. Even assigning responsibility to an Internet identity is difficult since the log files of visitors seldom reveal more than a general domain. There is no caller ID. If an additional guarantee of anonymity is desired, users can employ a variety of anonymizing software packages. Users can also hide what they say through encryption.

Uncertainty about location has the potential to make existing law a nonstarter: laws are applicable only in places where a governing authority has jurisdiction. People have a reasonable expectation under due process to "structure their primary conduct with some assurance as to where the conduct will and will not render them liable to suit."[6] To some extent, this expectation is undermined by technological change. On the Internet, there is often great uncertainty about where communication occurs.

POTENTIAL FOR A NEW PARADIGM

Responding to these fundamental challenges, some scholars saw the potential for a new paradigm for cyberlaw. As suggested in the *Cornell International Law Journal*, earlier models may simply be inadequate for cyberspace: "Despite the availability of several regulatory tools, no previously used methods are suited for regulating the Internet."[7] If the challenges of cyberspace did prove too difficult for existing frameworks, a new paradigm was possible. A number of scholars hinted at some possible contours of a new legal paradigm.

The most prominent argument for a new model is a 1996 article in the *Stanford Law Review*. David Johnson and David Post make the case for cyberlaw to develop as a "distinct" doctrine. The challenge of uncertain location is foremost in their minds:

> Global electronic communications have created new spaces in which distinct rule sets will evolve. We can reconcile the new law created in this space with current territorially based legal systems by treating it as a distinct doctrine, applicable to a clearly demarcated sphere, created primarily by legitimate, self-regulatory processes, and entitled to appropriate deference—but also subject to limitations when it oversteps its appropriate sphere. The law of any given place must take into account the special characteristics of the space it regulates and the types of persons, places, and things found there. Just as a country's jurisprudence reflects its unique historical experience and culture, the law of Cyberspace will reflect its special character, which differs markedly from anything found in the physical world.[8]

FUNDAMENTAL PRINCIPLE OF CYBERLAW

Despite the possibility that cyberspace would inspire the creation of a unique regulatory regime, it has not happened. The fundamental principle of cyberlaw is that it is a product of applying established legal frameworks. Lawmakers have resisted seeing the Internet as something altogether new. This is consistent with the way institutions are established and the way that people think. The primary doctrine of the legal profession—precedent—is predicated on finding parallels in the past. Cognitively, people assimilate new information into their long-standing orientation to the world. Ultimately, most people don't want to inhabit a new virtual world, they want to communicate more effectively in the real world. Lawmakers, therefore, try to make the virtual world more like the real world. In doing so, cyberlaw scholar Lawrence Lessig believes that they are likely to find support from the courts: "For good or bad, laws that make cyberspace just like home will not be found to be unconstitutional."[9]

As a means of communication, the Internet is fertile ground for a vast range of existing law. People communicate online about the entire wealth of human experience. Law already concerns itself with much in the realm of human experience. A change in the mode of communication does not change the underlying character of the activity. Marketing a product over the Internet, for example, does not make the action any less commercial. Business is still business. Business law has been applied to transactions facilitated by the Internet. Similarly, criminal and other bodies of law have been applied to Internet communication.

The breadth of law available for application to the Internet has frequently been used to reject the creation of new, Internet-specific law. Historically, policy review committees seldom conclude their work with a call for government to simply apply current law. Yet a number of Internet committees have done just that. A 1998 directive from the Office of Management and Budget (OMB), for example, issued no new regulations. OMB officials told government agencies to follow existing rules: "Do paper rules apply? You bet."[10] Applying existing law was at the forefront as Al Gore announced an eleven-agency effort to combat crime facilitated by the Internet: "The working group will help to make the Internet a safe place for all Americans by examining the extent to which existing federal law and technological tools are effective in combating crime on the Internet."[11]

One way that existing law can be brought to bear on a new phenomenon is through analogy. Some aspect of the new phenomenon is said to be the functional equivalent of an earlier phenomenon. Finding analogies to previous communication devices is a time-honored method of approaching a new means of communication. The telephone was named to reflect the idea of a telegraph that transmits sound. The result of adding sound to movies did not create a new phenomenon, but a "talking picture."

The tendency to find analogies to previous means of communication is readily apparent in early Internet cases. Since the Internet represents a combination of earlier methods of communication, there are many analogies from which to choose. During oral argument in the first landmark Internet case, the telephone analogy was most on the minds of the Supreme Court. Justice Breyer asked whether restrictions on frank sexual discussion would be constitutional in analogous contexts: "My concern is whether, analogizing this to the telephone, it would suddenly make large numbers of high school students across the country guilty of federal crimes as they try to communicate to each other either singly or in groups?" Later in oral argument, the questioning of Deputy Solicitor General Waxman drifted seamlessly from talking about the telephone to talking about the Internet:

> *Breyer:* We are—might be talking about telephones, which was the point of my example with the children. Can Congress suddenly decide that all private telephone conversations will be monitored to see if there is indecent material going across the telephone that children will knowingly pick up? That was my concern.
>
> *Waxman:* I think the answer is no.
>
> *Breyer:* If the answer is no, then how does this differ, because the Internet after all is, in addition to being a little bit like a common, is very much like a telephone?
>
> *Waxman:* The difference—the regime you've hypothesized is one in which all telephone calls between all people in the United States would be monitored.
>
> *Breyer:* No, what you'd have is an analogous statute that applied to the telephone so that when the high school students get on the phone and talk about their experiences, suddenly that all becomes a crime, and it suddenly looks a little bit worse from a First Amendment point of view.
>
> *Waxman:* It does—
>
> *Breyer:* —If what you're talking about is the telephone.
>
> *Waxman:* It does.
>
> *Breyer:* The Internet is rather like the telephone.[12]

More than a cognitive device, analogy solves legal problems. There is precedent to apply. The analogy makes an entire legal framework available for application. The analogies used have placed the Internet within a wide body of communications law. Legal rulings and frameworks from the treatment of the newspaper, telegraph, telephone, radio, and television are all available to be applied to the Internet.

An example of how adopting an analogy solves legal problems is seen in the issue of whether an Internet service provider (ISP) should be liable for the communication of its customers. Ultimately, ISPs have been analogized to the telephone company as a common carrier with enhanced discretion. In an early case, however, an ISP was found liable for the communication of its customers when a judge viewed it as going beyond a common carrier role into publishing. Ostensibly aware of the legal complications of his decision, the judge invited Congress to pass legislation: "Whether a new exemption should be carried out for online service providers is to be resolved by Congress, not the courts."[13] Congress, in fact, did respond to these rulings with a statute adopting a telephone company analogy for ISPs. Thus, a judge in 1998 took the new law into account: "While Congress could have made a different policy choice, it opted not to hold interactive computer services liable for their failure to edit, withhold or restrict access to offensive material disseminated through their medium."[14]

The use of analogy and the application of existing law often include confronting head-on the challenges of the Internet environment. Policymakers have no choice but to make decisions regardless of how fast technology is moving. Judges must resolve cases. The need to make a decision despite challenges was well expressed by the Second Circuit Court of Appeals: "Although we realize that attempting to apply established trademark law in the fast-developing world of the Internet is somewhat like trying to board a moving bus, we believe that well-established doctrines of personal jurisdiction law support the result."[15]

Policymakers have tried to facilitate making identity known on the Internet. They have been aided by technological change in ascertaining identity. In fact, the change has prompted Jonathan Zittrain, Executive Director of the Berkman Center for Internet and Society at Harvard, to advise members of Congress that an increased difficulty of maintaining anonymity should be a key calculation as they confront the future Internet environment.[16] In the current era, the most significant efforts to ascertain identity have been to obtain information from ISPs about their customers.

Legally, the most attention has been devoted to confronting the fundamental challenge of location uncertainty. Recognizing that communicators are in a place, lawmakers have continued to assign jurisdiction. The potential for ascertaining jurisdiction is apparent even as scholars David Post and David Johnson articulate a theory of the unique nature of location on the Internet. The distinctiveness of the virtual world is as tenuous as literally hitting the print button: "In contrast, the approach that treats the global network as a separate place would consider any allegedly defamatory message to have been published only 'on the Net' (or in some distinct subsidiary area thereof)—at least until such time as distribution on paper occurs."[17]

Jurisdiction cases primarily apply the long-standing legal framework of determining if sufficient contacts occurred within that jurisdiction. One early guideline for assessing jurisdiction is that the mere ability to access a website from a particular place does not constitute sufficient contact to warrant jurisdiction. In the straightforward early case *Cybersell AZ* v. *Cybersell FL* (1997), the judge did not grant Arizona jurisdiction over Cybersell of Florida, partly because "No Arizonan except for Cybersell AZ 'hit' Cybersell FL's website."[18]

Typically, the determination of sufficient contacts with a jurisdiction is based on interaction generated by the site. When interactivity includes non-Internet contacts, the case for jurisdiction is especially strong. This principle was expressed in a defamation case involving Matt Drudge. Running a website out of his California apartment, Matt Drudge allegedly defamed presidential aide Sydney Blumenthal by suggesting that he had a history of wife beating. The question for the court was whether Drudge could be sued in Washington, D.C., where Blumenthal lived. The Washington court accepted jurisdiction after finding sufficient non-Internet contacts in the form of some personal visits and telephone calls.[19]

The subtlety of the legal response in dealing with the uncertain location of Internet activity can be seen in a dispute between Tampa and Voyeur Dorm. There was little subtle about the services offered by Voyeur Dorm. The Internet business put cameras in every room of a house occupied by six young women. The city of Tampa, Florida, tried to shut down Voyeur Dorm as running an adult business in violation of zoning requirements. With over three thousand paid subscribers, the popularity of the service apparently extended beyond professors making sure that students were completing their homework. There was little doubt that adult entertainment was being offered, since Voyeur Dorm promised subscribers the "most intimate acts of youthful indiscretion." The question before the court was where the adult entertainment service was being offered. Even though the women were physically present in Tampa, the Eleventh Circuit Court of Appeals ruled that Voyeur Dorm did not violate the zoning ordinance because "the public offering occurs over the Internet in virtual space."[20]

Uncertainty of location also complicates the question of which law applies in cases where there are competing governing authorities. Policymakers are resolving disputes in favor of the traditional framework of the sovereign nation-state. In *Yahoo!* v. *LICRA*, for instance, a U.S. district court judge ruled that Yahoo!'s First Amendment rights in the United States precluded a French court from requiring it to remove Nazi-related items from its auction site.[21] Within the United States, there appears to be a strong movement toward using the commerce clause to overturn state laws regulating the Internet. The first major articulation of this theory was *ALA* v. *Pataki* (1997), in which a New York statute was ruled to unconstitutionally infringe on the ability of Congress to regulate interstate commerce.[22] The trend continued as federal courts used the commerce clause to overturn other state-level Internet regulations in Michigan and New Mexico.[23]

FUNDAMENTAL CAVEAT OF CYBERLAW

A fundamental caveat of cyberlaw is that little is set in stone in this young field. There are few landmark laws and court cases. As the Internet becomes part of everyday life, the number and complexity of potential legal issues rises. Law cannot keep up with technology, although it may try. The effort of lawmakers to keep up with technology has drawn the attention of Jeffrey Eisenach, president of the Progress & Freedom Foundation: "The only thing growing faster than the Internet is the number of bills in Congress dealing with the Internet."[24] Judges will be called on to resolve disputes concerning the application of these laws. The laws of today might be altered by the laws or technology of tomorrow.

CONCLUSION

Lawmakers have rejected the creation of a distinct doctrine of cyberlaw. The fundamental principle of cyberlaw is that it is a product of applying legal frameworks established prior to the creation of the Internet. It has been well documented that when approaching a problem, legislators usually make changes at the margins. Judges preside in a system based on precedent and will look to previous laws for ways to think about the case. Long-standing legal frameworks will continue to resonate.

In the next three chapters, analogy and traditional legal frameworks will be central to understanding key areas of cyberlaw. The printed page analogy has proved compelling to courts assessing the First Amendment protection of Internet communication. In regulating where Internet communication occurs, domain name law draws heavily on the well-established concept of trademark. Coping with the challenges of Internet piracy and privacy, lawmakers have contemplated various analogies including the telephone wiretap and the VCR.

10

Content Regulation

The most fundamental question in cyberlaw or media law generally is the extent to which government controls content. Guaranteed by the First Amendment, freedom of speech has been long cherished. Yet, free speech has never been absolute. Government, for instance, can censor when national security is seriously endangered. The Constitution does not protect communication that meets the legal standard of "obscenity." Government can also place reasonable limitations on the time, place, and manner of communication. In determining the level of regulation permitted, the Supreme Court has stated unequivocally that the medium of communication matters: "Differences in the characteristics of a new media justify differences in the First Amendment standards applied to them."[1]

This chapter will consider the compelling legal issues related to Internet content regulation. First, the regulation of pornography will be considered. This area of content regulation has drawn the most attention from government and is the context in which most broad legal issues have been addressed by the courts. While sexual content receives much attention, there are other areas of content regulation that merit attention. One Internet-specific content issue is whether the First Amendment confers the right to distribute unsolicited mass mailings, or spam. Another content-related concern is how the criminal justice system treats Internet content that facilitates the committing of crimes. Lastly, it will be important to consider regulation of content by entities other than government. Specifically, the obligations of employers to their employees will be considered.

PORNOGRAPHY

In regulating pornography on the Internet, government can employ one of two basic approaches. First, government can target the transmitters. It can seek to ban transmitting certain types of material to all or some of the population. Civil and criminal penalties may be imposed for the production of content meeting certain criteria. On the other hand, government can seek to regulate the receivers. Obligations might be imposed on manufacturers of receiving units, such as the 1996 law requiring new televisions to include a V-Chip that allows parents to block programs based on their rating.[2] Receivers might be required to place filters or other screening devices on a product. Since these two approaches typically represent distinct legal paths, they will be considered separately.

The first significant attempt to regulate the transmission of indecent communication over the Internet was the Communications Decency Act (CDA). The legislation was crafted in a climate of concern about the direction of content in the early days of the World Wide Web. In 1995, Pew Research Center surveyed people to learn whether they would "favor or oppose a law that would make it illegal for a computer network to carry pornographic or adult material." Americans favored such legislation by a 52 to 41 percent margin, with 7 percent not responding.[3] As introduced, the CDA did not include the general prohibition suggested in the Pew poll, but focused on transmitting indecent material to children. The legislation received little formal debate in Congress. There was no committee fact finding. Never passed on its own, the CDA was attached to the wide-ranging Telecommunications Act of 1996 in the late stages of that legislation. Other issues related to broader telecommunications dominated final debate. On February 8, 1996, President Clinton signed the Telecommunications Act and the CDA became law.[4]

As passed, the CDA imposed civil and criminal penalties for transmitting indecent communication to children over the Internet. The penalties applied to those that transmitted, either knowingly or unknowingly, such communication to children. The CDA applied to the Internet broadly, including e-mail, newsgroups, and the Web. The legislation did not specifically define *indecent,* but did refer generally to "patently offensive" depictions of "sexual or excretory activities." Violators faced civil damages and up to two years in prison.

Legal action was taken quickly to prevent the law from going into effect. The American Civil Liberties Union (ACLU) became the lead plaintiff challenging the law and was joined by a variety of other organizations. The law was challenged as an infringement of the First Amendment right to free speech. Ruling in favor of the ACLU, the district court judge issued a preliminary injunction preventing the law from taking effect.[5] The United States government, nominally represented by Attorney General Janet Reno, appealed. Since a U.S. law was declared unconstitutional by a lower court, the likelihood of the Supreme Court hearing the case was high. Accepting the case, the Court heard oral argument in

March 1997. The decision of the Supreme Court in the first cyberlaw case was eagerly anticipated.

On June 26, 1997, the Supreme Court announced its landmark decision in *Reno* v. *ACLU.* The Supreme Court unanimously struck down the CDA. The statute was ruled to be a violation of the First Amendment right to free speech. As a content-specific restriction, the legislation was subject to the strict scrutiny standard of being narrowly tailored as the least restrictive means for achieving a compelling objective. The Court agreed that protecting children was a compelling objective. The Court, however, ruled that the legislation fell short of the requirement to be a narrowly tailored measure that does not unnecessarily restrict legitimate free speech. It would effectively burden a large amount of speech for adults. The Court emphasized that Congress had provided little evidence that the regulation was the least restrictive approach: "Particularly in the light of the absence of any detailed findings by the Congress, or even hearings addressing the special problems of the CDA, we are persuaded that the CDA is not narrowly tailored if that requirement has any meaning at all."[6]

In failing to meet the standard of narrow tailoring, the Supreme Court emphasized two aspects of the legislation that were too broad. First, the nature of prohibited communication was not narrowly tailored. As documented by the Court, the CDA varied the language of the prohibited communication from "indecent" to "patently offensive" and did not formally define either term. Thus, the language in the CDA was ambiguous and broad when the Court required it to be clear and narrowly tailored. Second, the scope of regulated activity was broad. The legislation prohibited indecent communication on the "Internet" without any limitations. The Internet, of course, includes a broad array of activity from e-mail to bulletin boards to the Web. In its decision, the Court all but suggested a less restrictive option: "The arguments in this Court have referred to possible alternatives such as . . . regulating some portions of the Internet—such as commercial websites—differently than others, such as chat rooms."[7]

In its decision, the Supreme Court demonstrated that instead of choosing a new framework for the Internet, it was applying existing frameworks as well as it could. Specifically, the Supreme Court discussed its outcome in terms of the print and broadcasting models. For indecent communication, the key characteristic justifying different treatment of media was the likelihood of accidental exposure by children. The Supreme Court focused on whether the Internet was more similar to the print model of extensive First Amendment protection or to the broadcasting model of more limited First Amendment protection. Examining the incidence of accidental exposure on the Internet, the Supreme Court found that it was more like print than broadcasting: "Unlike communication received by radio or television, the receipt of information on the Internet requires a series of affirmative steps more deliberate and directed than merely turning a dial."[8]

Although its application to indecent communication was most central, the ruling in *Reno* v. *ACLU* has implications for cyberlaw more generally. It was the first landmark Internet decision. It was unanimous. The language of the Court often extended beyond the context of indecent communication. In fact, the language of the Court suggested an adoption of the print model of greater First Amendment freedom well beyond the context of indecent communication. The Court spoke of the rationale beyond accidental exposure for allowing greater regulation of broadcasting. It noted, in particular, the limited bandwidth in broadcasting that prompted a strong historical role for government in maintaining order. Contemplating whether this characteristic justifying regulation in broadcasting applied to the Internet, the Supreme Court found that the Internet had "relatively unlimited, low cost capacity for communication." Finding that the Internet lacked both characteristics justifying higher regulation in the past, *Reno* v. *ACLU* laid the groundwork for broad First Amendment rights for the new medium.

With its original attempt to regulate sexual content on the Internet overturned by *Reno* v. *ACLU,* Congress tried again in 1998 with the Child Online Protection Act (COPA). Introduced by Michael Oxley (D-OH), COPA imposed civil and criminal penalties on commercial websites providing material that was harmful to minors. Similar to its predecessor, COPA did not get sustained attention from Congress. The measure received little committee attention and initially cleared the House through a voice vote. Seemingly stalled in the Senate, the measure found new life when it was added to an omnibus appropriations bill in the waning days of the 1998 Congress. The omnibus bill was a must-pass bill consolidating the funding of several appropriations bills into a $500 billion package. With half a trillion dollars in the remainder of the bill, COPA was not the subject of much discussion. After clearing Congress, the omnibus appropriations bill containing COPA was signed by President Clinton on October 21, 1998.[9]

As passed, COPA focused on protecting children from getting access to pornography on the Web. Penalties were established for allowing those under age 17 to receive material that was "harmful to minors." As judged by "contemporary community standards," communication that was harmful to minors was sexually explicit material that lacked any educational value for minors. The legislation applied only to "commercial websites." If a website made a good-faith effort by establishing some form of adult password verification, it would have a defense against the penalties should a child receive the communication. Violators could face up to six months in jail and a fine of $50,000.

As structured, COPA was designed to minimize the breadth of the CDA, which had run afoul of the requirement to be narrowly tailored. First, the "indecent" standard was replaced by a "harmful to minors" standard. The harmful-to-minors standard had a stronger legal history behind it and had been upheld in the context of state-level restrictions on communication. Second, instead of targeting the entire Internet, COPA focused on one aspect. Seemingly taking up the invitation of the Supreme Court, the language adopted the exact phrase "commercial websites" that the Supreme Court suggested as a possible alternative to the breadth of the

CDA. By incorporating these two narrowing features, supporters of the legislation hoped that it would meet the narrowly tailored requirement. Supporters argued that they had created a cyberspace equivalent to obtaining adult material in other media. Committee Chair Thomas Bliley (R-VA) suggested that the limitations on Internet communication did not exceed limitations on other media: "HR3783 [COPA] merely requires adults to purchase adult material in cyberspace the same way that they do in the real world."[10]

Within twenty-four hours of passage, COPA was challenged as a violation of the First Amendment. Again the lead plaintiff, the ACLU was joined by a variety of organizations including a website for the sexual health of disabled individuals, the online newspaper *Salon,* and a condom distributor. Opponents derided the legislation as CDA2 and were confident that the legislation had the same, albeit modified, flaws of the CDA. The first legal issue for the district court judge was whether to grant an injunction to prevent the law from taking effect. In his ruling, Judge Lowell Reed Jr. lamented the proliferation of pornography on the Internet and the inability of Congress to address it. Despite misgivings, he granted the injunction based on the likely finding that it violated the First Amendment by not being narrowly tailored enough to minimize the adult speech that would be burdened.[11] The Third Circuit Court of Appeals upheld the injunction, on the basis that the community standards criterion in the legislation was too broad. In the unique Internet context, the community standards guideline would allow the least tolerant community to set the standards for the entire nation.[12]

The case next went to the Supreme Court. The tone of the questioning in oral argument gave supporters reason to hope for a different outcome. ACLU attorney Ann Beeson was placed on the defensive when she was challenged by the justices to suggest a less restrictive alternative to pursue the compelling interest of protecting children:

> [T]here is a genuine problem that Congress is trying to address, and if your position is you just forget about it, that you've got to live with the problem, that's quite a different position than if you think, well, there's a less restrictive alternative that would accomplish what the Congress is trying to do, and you're suggesting to me there isn't a less restrictive alternative.[13]

Subsequently, the Supreme Court sent the case back to the Third Circuit with instructions to explore other issues besides the community standards criteria.[14] On remand, the Third Circuit again ruled that COPA violated the First Amendment. Beyond reinforcing its finding that the community standards criteria was too broad, the court found that COPA's modifications of the Communications Decency Act were not enough to meet the strict scrutiny standard of being narrowly tailored as the least restrictive means of achieving a compelling objective. In making this assessment, the court emphasized that the legislation was not narrowly tailored in that it burdened some speech that is protected for adults and older minors and suggested that parental use of filtering software is a less restrictive way to protect children from Internet pornography.[15]

Having had its broad regulation of pornography transmission overturned, Congress has turned to a more focused effort on regulating pornographers who use domain names that appeal to children. While the April 2003 "Amber Alert" legislation is best known for promoting a rapid response to a child abduction, it also had an Internet pornography provision. Specifically, it drew on the doctrine of false advertising to make it a crime to use a "misleading domain name" to transmit pornography to children.[16] Although the legislation does not affect most pornographers, it offers a legal tool for pursuing a few high-visibility pornography websites.

Rather than focus on the transmitters, government can regulate the receiving of indecent communication. Some ways of regulating the receiver are tied to the physical world. Potential regulation of this type would include library employees monitoring printers or installing privacy screens on computers used by adults. The greatest potential for regulating receivers, however, is to use computer code to impose conditions on the receipt of information. A blunt way of using code is how many libraries restrict computer terminals to their online catalog.

Internet filters are the most important recipient-based restriction on Internet content. Filters are software programs that selectively block domains based on the incidence of certain characteristics. Companies such as Net Nanny have long offered the service to parents. This private use of filters prompts no legal issues. It is a different story, however, when a governmental entity, such as a public library, imposes filters. The First Amendment applies to government entities. Any content restriction by a government entity raises First Amendment issues. Yet, many libraries want to filter Internet content to avoid having their terminals used to view pornography.

The filtering dilemma for those providing public Internet access was quickly established. Without filters, schools and libraries may face an environment in which computers are being used for noneducational purposes. Patrons consuming pornography might create an uncomfortable environment for others, including one that might rise to the level of sexual harassment or child endangerment. On the other hand, filters impose content-based restrictions that inhibit free expression and may violate the First Amendment. Examining the legal landscape, those responsible for public access terminals would find conflicting messages.

A landmark decision by the Minnesota Equal Employment Opportunity Commission (EEOC) in 2001 showed the dangers of not using filters. The Minneapolis Public Library chose not to impose filters or limit Internet access to educational uses. The end result was that computer terminals frequently were being used by those viewing pornography. A group of twelve employees filed suit against the library on the grounds that the frequent consumption of pornography was creating a hostile work environment based on gender—sexual harassment. One employee framed the issue in terms of expectations: "When I signed up to work at the library, I didn't sign up to work in a porn-shop-type atmosphere."[17] The Minnesota

EEOC investigated the matter and found that a hostile work environment resulted from the Internet access policy of the library. Officially called a "determination," the EEOC decision found enough evidence to suggest that sexual harassment had occurred and the matter should proceed in the legal process.[18]

On the other hand, a landmark ruling by a federal district court in Virginia suggested that filters on library terminals were a violation of the First Amendment. In the case, the court examined the policy of the Loudoun County, Virginia, public library to install filters on all Internet terminals. The library defended the policy as necessary to prevent sexual harassment in the form of an uncomfortable environment for patrons and employees. The court, however, was not persuaded. It found that the library was a public forum and that filters were a content-based restriction on free speech. Under these circumstances, government must prove that the restrictions on content are narrowly tailored as the least restrictive means for achieving a compelling objective. The court ruled that the library policy did not meet this standard. The court suggested that other less restrictive alternatives, such as privacy screens, filtered machines set aside for children, and staff monitoring would accomplish the same purpose. The court concluded its ruling by framing the issue as prior restraint: "Defendant has asserted a broad right to censor the expressive activity of the receipt and communication of information through the Internet. . . . Such a policy offends the guarantee of free speech in the First Amendment and is, therefore, unconstitutional."[19]

In 2000, Congress entered the arena by passing major filtering legislation. The Child Internet Protection Act (CIPA) made eligibility for federal funds under the E-Rate program contingent upon installing filters on Internet access terminals. It did not specify any filter, but requires that libraries and schools use at least some filter. The act was introduced by Senator John McCain (R-AZ). With polls showing 92 percent public support for blocking pornography in schools, supporters pressed forward with the legislation even though a bipartisan congressional commission studying how to protect children online issued a report opposing filtering in October 2000. The proposal became law as part of a year-end omnibus appropriations measure.[20] Proponents hoped that the voluntary nature of receiving federal funds would alleviate any First Amendment concerns. Courts had previously upheld conditions on the receipt of federal funds in a variety of contexts. The most prominent of these is using the threat of withholding federal highway funds to states that do not comply with federal guidelines on the speed limit and drunk driving. Opponents challenged the library portion of the law as a violation of the First Amendment. The legislation was headed for court.

As a buildup to the legal challenge, there was a broader, often quirky, debate over the effectiveness of filtering. Advocates of filtering acknowledged that no software was perfect, but suggested that filters did a good job overall of sorting out noneducational content. Opponents pointed out that filters inevitably stifled protected speech, including political or educational content. Before the court battle began, the Digital Freedom Network held a contest and awarded prizes to those finding the most egregious examples of overenthusiastic filtering. The grand prize winner went to a high school student unable to call up his high school's website from the school library because the word *high* in the title caused the page to be filtered.[21]

The much-anticipated legal challenge began in 2002. The fact-finding stage generated some unusual alliances and salacious details. Both the plaintiffs and defendants objected to a decision by the judges to close to the public the testimony of a filtering company executive.[22] The judges ruled that such action was necessary to protect the trade secrets of filtering programs. The trial included government lawyers showing filter-opposing librarians one sexually explicit image after another and challenging them to defend the right of library patrons to view the image. In May 2002, the district court ruled that CIPA was not narrowly tailored as required by the strict scrutiny standard of content-specific regulation. Ironically, it was a figure given by a witness for the United States—approximately 10 percent of the sites blocked by filters were blocked in error—that was featured most prominently in the opinion. Even if the vast majority of sites were properly blocked, the court said, there was still too much speech that was unnecessarily restricted. Further, this speech was actively excluded, which made the filtering process fundamentally different than the discretion that a library has in choosing what to include in its collection. Finding library filtering to be unconstitutional, the court, then, did not allow the federal government its usual discretion in using financial incentives to encourage state action.[23]

In June 2003, the Supreme Court reversed the district court's ruling that the law was unconstitutional. Finding that filtered access as the default for Internet access terminals in public libraries does not violate the First Amendment, the Supreme Court saw the filtering requirement as an acceptable condition placed on the receipt of federal funds. Writing for a four-person plurality with two concurrences, Chief Justice Rehnquist argued that libraries filtering Internet access on all their terminals—approximately 7 percent when CIPA passed—were fulfilling a classic function: "A library's need to exercise judgment in making collection decisions depends on its traditional role in identifying suitable and worthwhile material; it is no less entitled to play that role when it collects material from the Internet than when it collects material from any other source."[24] Because of the Internet's vast scope, the Court argued, a filtering program that excludes content is a more realistic way of fulfilling this traditional role than affirmatively reviewing all websites. While allowing the law to take effect, the Court's understanding about the "ease with which patrons may have the filtering software disabled"[25] does leave open the possibility of future challenges based on implementation.

Combining the legal status of regulating the transmitters and receivers, it is clear that the legal system has looked skeptically upon measures to regulate indecent content on the Internet. The ruling of the first landmark case in *Reno* v. *ACLU* sets a high bar for regulation. By using analogies such as "pamphleteer" and finding limited bandwidth and the absence of accidental exposure, the Supreme Court has all but ensured that the First Amendment protection of the Internet will be closely aligned to the print model. It is a model that demands narrow tailoring of any regulation. Technological change makes the narrowly tailored regulation somewhat of a moving target. It is a target that has proved difficult for regulators to meet. One reason that regulating the transmitters has posed legal difficulties is that the Internet offers a number of ways in which receivers can be empowered or regulated. The regulation of receivers, in many cases, looks like a less intrusive way of meeting government goals. The comparatively low intrusiveness of receiver-based mechanisms, especially voluntary ones, drew the attention of the court in *Reno* v. *ACLU*. Changing technology has not seemed to alter this calculation. Although age-based verification and filters got off to an inauspicious start, they appear to be more viable as a basis for a longer-term reconciliation of the competing interests involved in regulating indecent communication in cyberspace.

SPAM

While regulating indecency involves questions about the substance of communication, the regulation of spam focuses on the manner in which the communication occurs. *Spam* refers to unsolicited mass mailings on the Internet. A variety of entities ranging from businesses (especially pornographers) to political candidates have been known to spam. The temptation to send mass quantities of e-mail at basically no cost to would-be consumers or would-be voters is great, especially since an equivalent mass mailing through the U.S. Postal Service would be costly. Taken as an individual message, the content of any one spammed e-mail typically would not raise any legal questions. Yet, taken in the context of its quantity and unsolicited nature, spam has become a huge legal issue.

It has become a legal issue largely because spam recipients and Internet service providers (ISPs) want to make it one. Americans have consistently expressed their frustration, if not anger, with spam. Surveys regularly show that people dislike spam. A Gallup poll shows that Americans are evenly divided between those who "hate" spam and those who find it merely "annoying." It's possible that someone is lying, but 0 percent report that they "like" spam.[26] Similarly, ISPs are also displeased with spammers. They are upset when their system is filled with unsolicited mail, especially if spammers target their subscribers.

The dislike of spam has prompted a two-dimensional strategy for curtailing spam. First, ISPs have acted unilaterally to eliminate spam on their system. As part of the basic service contract, ISPs include an agreement not to spam in the basic service contract. Second, legislators have been petitioned successfully for relief. Not waiting for federal action, several states acted quickly to impose penalties on spam. The number of states passing anti-spam laws went from three in early 1999 to thirty-three in 2003.[27] Penalties were significant, such as the possible five-year prison sentence for malicious spam causing over $2,500 in damage under a 1999 Virginia statute.

The judicial system has generally looked favorably on both strategies for reducing spam. In deciding these cases, the courts recognize that First Amendment issues are involved. Spam, after all, is e-mail. Courts, however, have not found the substance of content to be what is being regulated. Rather, courts have focused on the manner in which the content is being delivered. On this ground, courts have found the rights of recipients and ISPs to outweigh the First Amendment rights of spammers.

ISPs have a long history of legal success in trying to stop spam. The earliest cases involved ISPs challenging spam under traditional property rights. In essence, the ISPs argued that spammers were trespassing by using the system in a manner prohibited by the service contract. In general, the courts have accepted this argument. In the first major case, *CompuServe* v. *Cyber Promotions* (1997), the Court made a trespass analogy: "The legal concept . . . that private citizens are entitled to enforce laws of trespass against would-be communicators is applicable to this case."[28] Later cases continued to view spam as trespass. The argument that ISPs are being damaged by the unauthorized use of their property is demonstrated in *AOL* v. *LCGM* (1998). In the case, LCGM admitted to mailing as many as 300,000 unsolicited messages promoting pornographic sites per day, amounting to perhaps 90 million e-mail messages over a six-month period. In making a trespass determination, the court was impressed by the damage caused to AOL in the form of having the network down, needing to replace equipment, and angering its customers.[29]

The case for ISPs is strengthened when the spammer also engages in some form of deception. The incentive for deception is high since most recipients would choose not to read an unsolicited communication if they are aware of the source. Thus, many spammers try to disguise the mail as more attractive than it really is. One possibility is to use the name of the service provider as the apparent source of the message. This technique has been ruled to be a trademark infringement of the service provider and a violation of fraud laws. Another form of deception is to collect the names of ISP subscribers in a manner that violates the service contract. Spam may also be sent from a "post-only" address, to which receivers are unable to reply. Other spammers use deceptive advertising by suggesting that people are eligible for some item of value. Where misleading, spam can be prosecuted as a deceptive business practice.

Courts also have made generally favorable rulings on legislation imposing penalties on spam. The first important case involved Washington's strong anti-spamming law of 1998 that imposed fines of up to $2,000 per violation. In June 2001, the Supreme Court of Washington ruled that Washington's law prohibiting misleading spam was constitutional. The argument of opponents that the law was a restriction on free speech was rejected. The court saw a number of beneficiaries from the law: "The Act protects the interests of three groups—ISPs, actual owners of forged domain names, and e-mail users."[30]

The support for spam laws includes a willingness to impose penalties, albeit usually small ones. In April 2001, the first spam award in a California small-claims court was $50. Where awards are higher, a cottage industry has developed of people seeking compensation for being harmed by spam. Indeed, after the first three years of the Washington law, Martin Palmer's $18,000 collected made him the self-proclaimed leader of an informal competition among spam victims.[31]

FACILITATE CRIME

One type of Internet content that is clearly not protected is communication undertaken to facilitate criminal activity. Using the Internet to commit a crime does not lessen the crime. Crimes are still crimes. Internet communication has been viewed as an element of crimes ranging from drug trafficking to child pornography. Torts are still torts. Compensation for civil offenses such as defamation can still be pursued even if the offense occurred online.[32] Compiling complaints about online activity, the FBI found auction fraud to be the single most common scam reported by Internet users.[33]

The way in which the Internet can offer another vehicle for an existing crime or tort is seen in its use in stalking. Internet communication can be used to threaten or intimidate. The crime is not lessened because the stalking occurred online. This was the clear message of the first prosecution under a cyberstalking law in California. Gary Dellapenta, upset at having his romantic overtures rejected, began using the Internet to stalk a woman. He posted messages online in her name that gave her address with an accompanying security code and invited men to stop by her home to carry out a "rape fantasy." After discovering why men were showing up at her home, she pursued stalking charges. Dellapenta pleaded guilty under the law, which provides up to a six-year prison sentence.[34] Stalking is a real crime even if facilitated in the virtual world.

In fact, use of the Internet can make a crime worse. In 1998, Congress passed a law instructing the Sentencing Commission to raise the penalty in child pornography cases if a computer is used.[35] Considering whether this statute was constitutional, the Tenth Circuit Court of Appeals ruled that Congress could make the use of a computer an aggravating factor in sentencing guidelines. The court noted that Congress had many valid reasons for such action. Congress could legitimately regulate those who might use a child's natural interest in technology to lure a child. A computer also facilitates the copying and distribution of images, thereby increasing the victimization of the child.[36]

While the Internet may provide an extra avenue for criminal activity, there is growing evidence that the Internet has made it easier to identify some types of criminals. This seems particularly true of the prosecution of child pornography. While the Internet has facilitated the distribution of child pornography, it has also led to some investigative efficiencies. Rather than tedious individual identifications, investigators have been able to identify a network of people visiting a particular website or subscribing to a newsgroup. The identification of one person may quickly lead to exposing a network of criminals. In addition, the gravitation of child molesters and pornographers to the Internet has given police a place to concentrate their efforts. The frequent patrols of chat rooms by police trying to identify child molesters have prompted hyperbole from Shari Steele of the Electronic Freedom Foundation: "At least half the 13-year-old girls in chat rooms are probably policemen."[37] When engaging in online stings, police benefit from the fact that perpetrators often have their inhibitions weakened online and may be forthcoming about their illegal activities. The rate for convictions in these cases has been reported to be as high as 99 percent, since the perpetrators typically plead guilty to avoid facing a jury of their peers.[38]

In applying criminal and tort law to Internet activities, an important caveat is that the communication must be directly related to the proscribed acts. Anything short of that is likely to be considered protected speech. Communicators have a broad freedom to transmit a variety of messages, including messages that many will find objectionable. The legal justification for prohibiting hate speech has never strayed far from the standard of Justice Holmes whether the words taken under the particular circumstances "create a clear and present danger."[39] When mediated by the Internet, speech that promotes hatred includes a time-and-place gap that reduces the likelihood of creating a clear and present danger. Thus, people undertaking hate speech on the Internet are generally not going to be held accountable if others are motivated by their message to carry out crimes. There must be an immediate link between the communication and the crime. Those providing information, even inflammatory information, will be protected by the First Amendment unless the communication constitutes a true threat.

Sometimes the line between a true threat and speech is difficult to discern, as shown by the conflicting decisions in *Planned Parenthood* v. *ACLA*. As part of its antiabortion advocacy, American Coalition of Life Activists (ACLA) made traditional fugitive "Wanted" posters for doctors providing abortions. Continuing the "Wanted" motif, the ACLA website listed the names, addresses, and family members of doctors providing abortions and offered a "reward" to those able through "perfectly legal" means to convince doctors to stop performing abortions. The information was promoted as the "Nuremberg Files," accumulating evidence of crimes against humanity to the unborn. Based on the targeting—and in a few cases, murder—of abortion doctors on similar lists, doctors providing abortions were intimidated by the information; some resorted to wearing bulletproof vests. Arguing that this constituted a violation of legislation guaranteeing free access to clinics, Planned Parenthood and other abortion providers sued the ACLA in civil court, saying that the files amounted to "a hit list for terrorists."[40] Deciding the case in favor of Planned Parenthood, a jury in Portland, Oregon, assessed a $107 million penalty against ACLA. On appeal, a three-judge circuit court panel threw out the jury award. They ruled that the speech of the ACLA was protected by the First Amendment since it had not "authorized, ratified, or directly threatened violence."[41] Continuing the case, Planned Parenthood appealed to the full circuit court. In a 6–5 decision, the full circuit court overturned the panel decision and said that the jury could hold ACLA responsible for this "true threat." It ruled, however, that the jury award was too high.[42]

REGULATION OF EMPLOYEES

In documenting the broad freedoms of the First Amendment that protect Internet communication, it is important to emphasize that the freedoms apply only to government regulation of citizens. In fact, the First Amendment originally applied only to the federal government: "Congress shall make no law . . . abridging the freedom of speech." By selective incorporation through the Fourteenth Amendment, the First Amendment now applies to state and local government. The First Amendment, however, does not apply when entities other than government are restricting speech.

Companies, therefore, are legally free to regulate the Internet communication of their employees. They can ban sexually explicit Internet content in the workplace. They can impose sanctions up to and including dismissal for violations of their policy. There are no legal issues associated with filters. Employers can program filters to block any type of content.

Companies do, in fact, routinely regulate employees to minimize communication unrelated to work. The interest of the company in restricting personal use of the Internet at work is obvious. Time spent on personal matters takes away from time spent on work. Companies lose billions of dollars annually from employees using company time and equipment for personal use. If the personal use involves downloading music or video files, a company may lose more than just the time of one employee. The entire computer system of the international software company Net Reality was once frozen by an employee who was illegally downloading a copy of the movie *The Lion King*.[43] Another employer who is unlikely to take the *hakuna matata* ("no worries") perspective to employee use of company equipment for downloading entertainment is the technology consulting firm Integrated Information Systems, Inc. (IIS). In April 2002, IIS announced that it was paying the Recording Industry Association of America $1 million to settle a claim that its employees had infringed copyright by downloading music at work. As part of the agreement, the record companies are allowed to use the settlement as "a means of educating the public about copyright infringement."[44]

Companies are not without recourse against what has come to be called "cyberloafing." Most companies at minimum have a generally understood policy that discourages personal use of the Internet. Many companies have outright prohibitions on personal use. These restrictions on personal use are routinely supported by the use of filters. Surveys show that 40 percent of employers use some kind of filter at work.[45] Companies back up these content restrictions with monitoring and stiff sanctions. Over 20 percent of companies have fired an employee for improper use of the Internet, and over half have undertaken some disciplinary action.[46]

A situation that might complicate the question of whether employers can regulate Internet content is if the employer in question is the government. Government, after all, is the entity prohibited from abridging speech under the First Amendment. Does the First Amendment prevent government from regulating the Internet content of its employees? This is a particularly important question considering that the federal government is the single largest employer—with nearly three million employees. This number is far exceeded by the number of employees of state and local government.

Legally, the issue is resolved by determining that government workers function in two capacities: citizens and employees. Government must adhere to the First Amendment to regulate the content of government workers or any other individual in their capacity as citizens. On the other hand, government does not have to adhere to the First Amendment to regulate the content of government workers in their capacity as employees. Thus, like other employers, government can take steps to ensure that its employees use employer time and equipment to further the completion of work. Government, therefore, can install filters and set policies on the acceptable use of the Internet in the workplace.

Perhaps the most significant ruling on the ability of government to regulate its employees is the Virginia case *Urofsky v. Gilmore*. In 1996, Virginia passed a law that prohibited state employees from accessing "sexually explicit" material on computers owned or leased by the state.[47] The law included an exception if a state employee received authorization from a state agency head who certified that the research was for work-related purposes. The law was challenged by a group of professors who argued that the policy constituted an infringement of the First Amendment and academic freedom. The district court agreed with the professors, noting that the law might preclude research on sexual health and "sexual themes in art, literature, history, and the law."[48] On appeal, the circuit court upheld the law and issued a stinging rebuke to the district court. The court emphasized that the First Amendment did not apply, since the government was acting as an employer: "[T]he challenged aspect of the Act does not regulate the speech of the citizenry in general, but rather the speech of state employees in their capacity as employees."[49] The circuit court was even less kind to the academic freedom argument. The court criticized the "audacity" of the academic freedom argument and rejected the suggestion that a professor should have more First Amendment rights than a state-employed psychoanalyst.

Having a well-established right to regulate content in the workplace, government has followed in the footsteps of private employers in regulating content. These policies are often promulgated as state laws, such as the Virginia law provoking the unsuccessful lawsuit from a group of professors. Government has also established enforcement mechanisms. When government workers speak as citizens, they are fully protected by the First Amendment. Yet, the same communication undertaken in an employee capacity can be seriously punished.

The seriousness of the penalty was apparent in a high-profile case of content regulation at the Central Intelligence Agency (CIA). Demonstrating an ironic lack of confidence in the detection abilities of their employer, a group of employees established an unauthorized chat room on the CIA computer network. During a thirteen-year period, over 150 employees were given the location of the discussion group and participated to some extent. Like many equivalent online discussion groups, the forum included off-color humor and complaints about management. Belatedly learning of the discussion group, the agency launched a seven-month investigation into its activities. At the end of the investigation, the CIA recognized that no classified information had been improperly divulged: "The investigation uncovered no information involving unauthorized disclosure of classified information."[50] Yet, the punishment was severe. Framing the issue as a breach of trust, the CIA announced the broadest disciplinary action in its history. Seventy-nine employees received warnings, and eighteen were formally reprimanded. Nine contractors were prohibited from ever working with the CIA. One married couple and two other women lost their jobs as a result of their role in the discussion group. The four fired employees defended the discussion group as a way of promoting workplace dialogue, arguing that "some of the agency's worst stutterers and most terminally shy people were able to become extraordinarily articulate within its bounds."[51]

CONCLUSION

Internet communication is given broad protection under the First Amendment. Examining existing models, the courts have chosen to apply the print model of the broadest content protection to the Internet. This protection applies to both the transmission and receipt of Internet communication. The First Amendment, however, applies only to government. Internet service providers and employers retain substantial discretion in regulating content.

11

Domain Name Law

Although Madonna, the pope, Julia Roberts, Michael Andretti, and Emeril Lagasse may seem to have little in common, they all have been involved in significant domain name disputes. Their shared experience, however, extends beyond being involved in disputes. They all won. Both the existence and resolution of these disputes provide insight into domain name law.

The existence of disputes is inevitable given the nature of domain names. A domain name is the string of characters that identifies the location of something on the World Wide Web. The inventor of the Web, Tim Berners Lee, identified his critical innovation as creating a "common naming and addressing space" in which each Web item has a "unique" address.[1] His use of the word *unique* captures a fundamental reality of domain name ownership in cyberspace. Only one person or entity can own any one domain name. Of course, many people may want the same address. Any competing claims must be resolved.

The resolution of these disputes involving well-known people shows how the legal system has balanced competing claims for domain names. In each case, the original claim was made on the principle of first-come, first-served. The first person to properly register a domain name with a governing authority secures ownership. Subsequently, a competing claim was made on the basis of traditional property rights. In each case, the legal system found the traditional property rights claim to outweigh the first-come, first-served claim. Despite the high-profile victories by traditional property owners, the first-come, first-served model is still an important part of domain name law. In most cases, it is the determining factor. Yet, where disputes arise, the courts increasingly apply a traditional property rights model. This chapter will highlight the interplay of the two competing models as it outlines the key events in the history of domain name law in both the American and international legal environment.

AMERICAN LAW

The American legal system lays the framework for the distribution of domain names. After all, the Internet was created within the Department of Defense. Later, oversight was transferred to the National Science Foundation. Instrumental in its development, the U.S. government has taken the initiative to keep domain name registration under the rubric of American law.

The first registrar was the U.S. government. Early registration was free and overseen by the Defense Department and the National Science Foundation. The key component of the domain name system was a limited number of top-level domains—.com, .net, .org, .edu, .gov. As the Internet grew, the government contemplated privatizing the process of allocating domain names. In theory, the government could have encouraged distributing domain names based on a first-come, first-served model or by some form of an auction model in which domain names would go to the highest bidder. The government also could have set up a monopoly provider or allowed competition. In 1993 a private firm, Network Solutions Inc. (NSI), was given a monopoly contract to register domain names outside of the government sector. NSI registered domain names for free until 1995, when it sought and received permission to begin charging.

Under NSI, the key principle of registration was first-come, first-served. This principle was the basis of the entire revenue structure of NSI. After 1995, the company registered domain names under a first-come, first-served policy at a rate of $100 for the initial two-year registration period. The flat rate structure built into the contract briefly even included a provision that NSI would pay $30 of the $100 to the government for Internet development. The incentive for NSI, then, was to process registrations, not sort out property rights issues. Although the registration contract made purchasers state that they were not knowingly violating trademark law, the policy was not actively enforced. In its description of the service provided, NSI made it clear that it had no obligation to actively sort out trademarks: "Like a telephone book publisher, NSI presumes that an applicant for a domain name has the legal right to use that name."[2] The race for domain names began. The stakes were high.

The difference in how first sales and second sales were governed created the potential for significant profits by reselling domain names. The first sale of the domain name from NSI was governed by a first-come, first-served flat rate of $100. On the other hand, there were no restrictions placed on the second sale. Having purchased the domain name, an owner was able to sell it to the highest bidder. In fact, at the peak of the domain name rush, business.com was initially sold for $100 and later sold for $7.5 million.[3] This was a nice reward for being the first to claim an address. The common use of the word *business* meant that there was no possibility of a competing legal claim based on trademark or other property rights.

In other cases, people purchased a domain name for which another entity had a valid legal claim. This phenomenon came to be known as cybersquatting. The term is a natural derivative from adding *cyber* to *squatting,* which broadly refers to occupying property for which another has legal claim. As NSI initially began to sell domain names, the potential for cybersquatting was tremendous. The Web had a fairly low profile, and a lot of companies did not notice as their trademark name was being purchased by a cybersquatter. McDonalds, for instance, failed to notice as mcdonalds.com was purchased. Having purchased the names, the owners often hoped to sell the name at a much higher price to the entity with the trademark. Other cybersquatters contented themselves with mischief, trying to trick people into viewing pornography. In time, cybersquatters drew the attention of holders of traditional property rights.

The first approach to asserting traditional property rights to secure domain names was to apply non-Internet-specific trademark law to the Internet. In some form or another, trademark law has been codified in federal law for well over a century. The foundation of modern trademark law is the Lanham Act of 1946. The legislation was designed to protect companies from others using their trademark or a close variation of it. As enacted, the key concept in the Lanham Act was that trademark infringement occurs when an entity uses an identical or similar trademark in a way that leads to a "likelihood of confusion" as to the source of the product. Invoking the Lanham Act, trademark holders argued that the fundamental purpose of cybersquatting was to create confusion. Several courts indicated a willingness to apply classic trademark law to domain names.

An example of an early case that was decided primarily on the basis of the Lanham Act's long-standing framework was *Planned Parenthood* v. *Bucci.* Antiabortion advocate Richard Bucci purchased the domain name www.plannedparenthood.com. Visitors to Bucci's site were greeted with the message "Welcome to the Planned Parenthood Home Page" and presented with generic link names that led to antiabortion materials. After discovering that Bucci was using its trademarked name as a domain name, Planned Parenthood sued on the basis of trademark infringement. Basing her decision primarily on the Lanham Act's long-standing prohibition against using a trademark in a way causing a "likelihood of confusion," Judge Kimba Wood ruled in favor of Planned Parenthood. She saw Bucci's acts as "classically competitive" in that "he has taken plaintiff's mark as his own in order to purvey his Internet services."[4]

The framework of Lanham Act protection was significantly expanded with the passage of the Federal Trademark Dilution Act of 1995. This amendment to the Lanham Act expanded trademark protection to prevent any commercial use resulting in a dilution of the distinct qualities of the trademark. *Dilution* was defined as a "lessening" of the ability to "identify and distinguish a product."[5] This represented a significant increase in protection to the trademark owner. The trademark owner would no longer have to show that a customer was likely to be confused as to the source of the product.

Although the Trademark Dilution Act does not include any Internet-specific language, it is clear that Internet applications were considered at adoption of the act. The legislation had been in the works for some time. Its main purpose was to add greater consistency to trademark law. Over the years, twenty-five states had adopted anti-dilution statutes.[6] Proponents of the legislation said that they wanted to bring these statutes together under a federal law. Thus, most of the discussion was about dilution broadly. There was, however, one mention in the Senate debate about a possible Internet application. Even in the way he brought it up, Patrick Leahy suggested that the Internet was not a huge motivation for the law: "Although no one else has yet considered this application, it is my hope that this antidilution statute can help stem the use of deceptive Internet addresses taken by those who are choosing marks that are associated with the products and reputations of others."[7] It is not surprising that Internet applications were not paramount in the minds of legislators, since NSI had just started selling domain names.

Fulfilling the prediction of Senator Leahy, the Anti-Dilution Act quickly became a way for trademark owners to assert property rights in cyberspace. The law became the major basis for a number of early domain name cases. Trademark holders were able to obtain domain names from cybersquatters whose sites were unlikely to be confused with a product of the trademark holder. In 1998, for instance, panavision.com was awarded to the electronics firm Panasonic after the court found that the cybersquatter had undertaken commercial use by trying to sell the domain name to Panasonic and had diluted the trademark by frustrating Panasonic customers, who would intuitively go to the website.

The strength of the law could be seen in its application in a high-profile case in St. Louis surrounding the visit of the pope. The backdrop for the case was a rare visit of the pope to the United States in 1999. In anticipation, the Archdiocese of St. Louis trademarked the phrase "Papal Visit 1999" in July 1998. As the event approached, Internet Entertainment Group purchased the domain name papalvisit1999.com. The company used the site to market its pornography. Those promoting the papal visit were unhappy to learn that those intuitively visiting papalvisit1999.com were greeted by pornographic images. Clearly, in this case, the traditional arguments of likelihood of confusion would not be helpful to the trademark holder. It was unlikely that anyone would be confused into thinking that the pope was the source of the pornography. The organizers of the papal visit, however, sought damages under the antidilution statute. Finding that the pornographer violated state and federal antidilution statutes, Judge Stephen Limbaugh ordered the site turned over to the organizers of the papal visit.[8] A frustrated pornographer directed blame at the family ties of the judge instead of the new antidilution statute: "This was an absurd ruling that oppresses our freedom of speech . . . and it is not surprising that a ruling from the uncle of Rush Limbaugh came down in this way."[9]

Despite such prominent domain name transfers as papalvisit1999.com, Congress wanted to strengthen trademark protection with Internet-specific legislation. The Anti-Cybersquatting Consumer Protection Act (ACPA) was introduced in 1999. The legislation was Internet-specific, with penalties imposed on cybersquatting. Although there were criminal penalties in the original version, the final form had only civil penalties. Supporters defended the measure as applying existing legal frameworks to cyberspace. House sponsor James Rogan (R-CA) explained that his bill did not represent new regulation: "Essentially, all my bill is doing is taking traditional trademark law—which has been recognized for almost our entire nation's history—and applying it to the Internet."[10] Senate sponsor Spencer Abraham (R-MI) made an analogy of his legislation to broader laws about mislabeling products: "If you order a Compaq or Apple Computer that should mean that you get a computer made by Compaq or Apple, not one built by a fly-by-night company pirating the name [and] the same goes for trademarks on the Internet."[11] Although the amended legislation had substantial support in Congress, it would not become law on its own because the Clinton administration opposed the legislation as undermining international efforts at regulating domain names. The problem was resolved by adding the legislation to a satellite technology bill that the White House supported. The satellite bill was further folded into a massive appropriations bill that President Clinton signed into law on November 29, 1999.[12]

As passed, the ACPA is heavily focused on intent. The definition of cybersquatting is based on a "bad faith intent to profit." The legislation promulgates a list of guidelines as to what the courts should consider in assessing intent. At their core, the guidelines embody two principles. First, the courts are to consider the extent to which the domain name purchaser has some genuine relationship to the name in question. Second, the actions of the purchaser are to be examined to determine if there is a pattern of behavior, such as trying to sell it to the trademark holder, that suggests mischief or extortion was the true goal of the purchase. Those found to be cybersquatting in violation of the law face a penalty of up to $100,000 per domain name. Consistent with antidilution legislation, it is not necessary to show that the intent was to confuse or compete with the trademark holder. The legislation represents a substantial tool for trademark holders to assert their property rights in cyberspace.

The benefits to trademark holders were seen in the first ACPA decision by an appellate court. Oral argument had been heard in *Sporty's Farm* v. *Sportsman's Market* and a decision was pending when Congress passed the ACPA. The new law could be applied to the case because it allowed courts to act on domain names registered before the legislation was passed. Using the case-by-case analysis of bad faith outlined in the law, the court found that the intent to keep a domain name away from a competitor with a trademark interest in the name showed bad faith regardless of whether there was an attempt to sell the domain name. In its decision, the court suggested that the stronger trademark protection in the ACPA may have shifted the outcome: "We think it is clear that the new law was adopted specifically to provide courts with a preferable alternative to stretching federal dilution law when dealing with cybersquatting cases."[13]

Combined, the amended trademark law and the Anti-Cybersquatting Act represent strong protection for trademark holders. In cases that have gone to court, the trademark holder usually wins. Of course, the legal system can be slow. Some companies, to avoid litigation, will just pay for a domain name that has been cybersquatted. Increasingly, however, relief in the courts is available. Prominent domain name victories by trademark holders include Volkswagen vw.net,[14] Ernest & Julio Gallo Winery ernestandjuliogallo.com,[15] and cosmetics company Clarins clarins.com.[16] The victories for trademark holders also have included cases involving misspellings and parodies.

Symbolic of the strong protection of the ACPA even when parody is involved is the case of *PETA* v. *Doughney*. The case arose from a lawsuit initiated by the animal rights organization People for the Ethical Treatment of Animals, commonly referred to as PETA. PETA argued that Michael Doughney had infringed its trademark by purchasing the rights to peta.org. Doughney registered the name peta.org in 1995 and subsequently created a website for an Internet-based organization called "People Eating Tasty Animals." The site compiled links to a variety of meat, fur, hunting, animal research, and other enterprises that PETA finds objectionable. Doughney defended his site as parody and political disagreement. The court, however, rejected his parody argument, suggesting that legally parody must make it apparent that it is referring to the original, yet it is not the original. Looking only at the domain name and not the site's content, the appellate court ruled that peta.org did not reach parody because the domain name conveyed only the message that it was the original. Nothing about the address said that it was not the original. Having rejected the parody defense, the court proceeded to find that Doughney acted in bad faith to weaken the PETA trademark. The court found that Doughney had no genuine interest in peta.org and engaged in a pattern of behavior, including asking PETA to "make him an offer," that suggested the goal was to profit from another's trademark.[17]

For PETA, the case represented a chance to be on a different side of the same legal principle. In 1998, PETA itself was sued as an alleged cybersquatter. It had purchased the domain name ringlingbros.com. PETA used the site to describe incidents in which animals were injured in circuses. When the circus company Ringling Bros. and Barnum & Bailey sued, PETA relinquished the site and agreed not to use the Ringling Bros. trademark in its advocacy.[18]

The strength of the protection to trademark holders is also symbolized by the legal vulnerability of typosquatters. A subset of cybersquatting, typosquatting refers to the act of purchasing domain names that represent misspellings or typographical errors of famous people or companies. A typosquatter, for instance, purchased the domain name hewlittpacker.com,[19] which is close to the name of Hewlett-Packard. Why is typosquatting a significant issue?

A nation of poor typists and poor spellers, Americans are thought to be particularly vulnerable to visiting websites that are close to their intended target. Thus, the struggle over domain names has moved from the literal trademark to myriad permutations of the trademark. Expecting errors in typing, people have bought misspelled versions of trademarked names for the purpose of making mischief, money, or a political statement. Companies have responded by trying to buy the most frequent misspellings of their domain name to ensure that potential customers are not lost just because they type the name incorrectly. The legitimate fear of companies about the damage caused by misspellings is perhaps best seen in a case involving the launch of the Gateway 2000 campaign. Gateway Computers owned the gateway2000.com domain name. Yet, Gateway paid a reported $100,000 to purchase gateway20000.com to avoid the risk of alienating customers who might find objectionable the hard-core pornography at gateway20000.com.[20] In most cases, however, the company is not willing to pay the cybersquatter and looks to the legal system for redress.

In their battle against typosquatters, trademark holders have had significant success. They had mixed early success, based on classic trademark law, in arguing that those unknowingly misspelling a domain name are likely to be confused.[21] The chances for success increased with passage of the ACPA. The legislative history of the ACPA makes it clear that typosquatting is one of its key targets. Indeed, typosquatting was the first example used in one of the few major speeches in Congress on the ACPA. Orrin Hatch highlighted the issue of typosquatting: "I was also surprised to learn that the "dosney.com" domain name was being used for a hard-core pornography website."[22] With the intent of Congress clear, the courts have enforced the ACPA against typosquatters.

The landmark decision on typosquatting is the 2001 decision by the Third Circuit in *Shields* v. *Zuccarini*. In the case, the animator working as "Joe Cartoon" and selling his work at joecartoon.com was able to secure the rights to joecarton.com from a cybersquatter who freely admitted to a practice of registering likely misspellings of famous names and trademarks. The court said that the phrase "confusingly similar" would encompass deliberately "causing an Internet user who makes a slight spelling or typing error to reach an unintended site."[23]

Misspelling was taken to a new level in a case involving the search engine Northern Light. Northern Light Technology had been offering a Web search engine at nothernlight.com since 1997. Among many variations on famous trademarks that he held, Jeff Burgar bought the rights to northernlights.com shortly after northernlight.com was purchased. For a while, it appeared that the Burgar site was causing minimal annoyance to the nothernlight.com search engine. This changed dramatically after the newspaper *USA Today* ran a story on search engines that misspelled the address of northernlight.com as northernlights.com. Not buying Burgar's fan site for the *aurora borealis*, the court awarded the domain name to the search engine on the basis of likely confusion and Burgar's history of registering misspelled names and demonstrating bad faith under the ACPA.

The penalties for typosquatting can be severe. In *Electronic Boutique* v. *Zuccarini,* for example, the court upheld the maximum amount for each violation. The typosquatter who registered five misspelled variations of Electronics Boutique was fined $100,000 per violation for a total of $500,000. In imposing a fine, the court made it clear that it did not regard habitual typosquatting as a minor offense: "Mr. Zuccarini boldly thumbs his nose at the rulings of this court and the laws of our country."[24]

Despite the frequent success of trademark holders in American courts, it is by no means inevitable that a prominent company will win. Perhaps the most effective defense for the original purchaser has been to show a legitimate interest in the name. A court, for instance, was unwilling to take the name clue.com from the firm Clue Computing to award it to the makers of the classic board game "Clue."[25] The Third Circuit refused to take checkpoint.com from Check Point Software to give it to the security company Checkpoint Systems.[26] When the toy company holding a trademark for Gumby's horse Pokey tried to take a website from a 12-year-old who had long been nicknamed Pokey, the only thing the company was successful in obtaining was bad publicity. Inevitably, there will be cases when parties acting in good faith have a bona fide disagreement. In these cases, first-come, first-served will be the determining factor.

INTERNATIONAL LAW

Since 1999, domain name registration has been overseen by an international organization, the Internet Corporation for Assigned Names and Numbers (ICANN). The organization was established to oversee a competitive registration system after the monopoly contract of NSI ended. The organization is headquartered in California and has members from all over the world. ICANN's first major action was to introduce competition into registering the major top-level domain names of .com, .org, and .net. NSI would now be one of a number of organizations authorized to register domain names in a competitive process. The second major action was to approve seven new top-level domain names—.biz, .info, .name, .museum, .pro, .coop, .aero. The process of competitive registration was opened to additional firms. Registrars now typically have a preliminary period during which registration for newly introduced domains is limited to trademark holders.

Consistent with the international paradigm for registration, an increasing number of disputes are being resolved at the international level under ICANN authority. The Uniform Domain Name Dispute Resolution Program (UDRP) was formally launched in 1999. The goal of the program was to resolve disputes quickly and conveniently outside of the regular court system. Resolution in an international forum would help reconcile jurisdiction issues and different applications of trademark throughout the world. The basic framework for decisions was set by ICANN. The criteria for what constitutes cybersquatting are almost identical to those of the American system. In general, a domain name will be transferred if the trademark holder can prove: (1) the domain name is identical or confusingly similar to trademark; (2) the purchaser has no legitimate interest; and (3) it was registered in bad faith. Having established general guidelines, ICANN contracts out to a number of organizations that provide arbitration services consistent with the general charge. Typically, the arbitrators will have Internet expertise that far outweighs the Internet experience of a judge in the regular legal process.

The first prominent organization to provide arbitration services was the World Intellectual Property Organization (WIPO). An international organization promoting intellectual property, WIPO had a strong claim to expertise in trying to apply property rights law to cyberspace. In 1999, WIPO became the first organization approved to hear cases. Consistent with broader guidelines, the goal of WIPO was to resolve disputes in forty-five days. The entire process could be conducted online. Depending on the services provided in the arbitration process, the entity seeking the domain name was charged between $1,500 and $4,000.[27]

The first case before WIPO resulted in the cybersquatter being body-slammed. A day after WIPO was approved to provide arbitration services, a complaint was filed with WIPO. The World Wrestling Federation (WWF) sued for the domain name of worldwrestlingfederation.com. Forgoing the American legal system, the WWF sought to get a quick ruling in the expedited arbitration process. In a straightforward case, the WWF showed that it had a clear trademark in the name World Wrestling Federation. For his part, the original owner could show no genuine interest in the name and was ruled to have purchased the domain name in bad faith. The WWF had its domain name.[28]

The first case began a pattern at WIPO and other ICANN arbitration panels in which trademark owners fare well. In fact, trademark owners prevail in over three-fourths of arbitrator decisions.[29] Over the years, trademark owners have prevailed in a number of high-profile cases. The victories for trademark owners include awarding Botox.net to the manufacturer of Botox[30] and foreveryoung.com to the makers of the "Forever Young" television series.[31] Concern, however, has been expressed that the panels are too deferential to trademark owners. Critics cite an early case involving the clothing manufacturer J. Crew as a prominent example. Despite the fact that *crew* is a generic word meaning "a group of rowers," a WIPO panel awarded the domain name crew.com to the company J. Crew.[32]

One of many companies that have won the rights to a domain name is the owner of C-SPAN. Televising the proceedings of Congress and other public affairs events on its channels, C-SPAN sought to claim cspantv.com from a company that was using the site to display pornographic images and sell sexual services. In ruling for C-SPAN, the arbitrator focused on the lack of interest in the name. The decision dutifully noted that the pornography company has a mirror site at girlhire.com and "has not come forward to establish that it is commonly known by the cspantv.com domain name."[33]

One type of case that has proven relatively simple for companies to win in ICANN arbitration is a domain name representing a spelling or typographical error of a trademarked name. Similar to American courts, ICANN arbitrators have viewed typosquatting as inherently confusing. This has been true even for companies with easily spelled names. Bank of America, for instance, was awarded ankofamerica.com[34] and banofamerica.com.[35] Fending off typosquatters is most important for companies whose names are difficult to spell. The department store Neiman Marcus, for example, has won the rights to niemanmarcus.com,[36] nemenmarcus.com,[37] and neimenmarcus.com.[38] The underlying message of the cases is that a company has a right to all its customers, even those who are keyboard challenged.

WIPO and other arbitration panels also have been more supportive than American courts of trying to convert a personal name into a domain name in cyberspace. Trademark law, central to American property rights claims, has typically not been very helpful for protecting a personal name. On the other hand, arbitration panels often have a broader view of name protection. They are more likely to find common-law property rights where a name is widely identified with a particular individual. Of course, the names widely identified with people are those of celebrities. Thus, celebrities have found it beneficial to take their claims for domain names to ICANN rather than to American courts. The potential number of claims is high. The names of celebrities were quickly gobbled up by an assortment of fans, mischief makers, and profit seekers. In trying to claim a domain name, such as juliaroberts.com, celebrities have been quite successful in front of arbitration panels. The list of celebrities winning domain name cases includes Will Smith,[39] Michael Andretti,[40] Chuck Berry,[41] Garth Brooks,[42] Celine Dion,[43] Mick Jagger,[44] Emeril Lagasse,[45] Dan Marino,[46] Paul McCartney,[47] and Julia Roberts.[48] Kevin Spacey was even able to acquire the misspelled version of his name—Kevinspacy.com.[49] The common-law rights do not even have to be based on an individual's "good" name. As an example, Hollywood madam Heidi Fleiss, who served jail time for prostitution, was able to take heidifleiss.com from a pornographer.[50]

Symbolic of ICANN support for celebrities is the high-profile case involving the singer Madonna. The domain name madonna.com was purchased by habitual cybersquatter Dan Parisi. The singer sued for the rights to the domain name. Of course, the pop singer is not exclusively identified with the name, which is a common term often accompanied in illustrated dictionaries by centuries-old artwork. During the case, there was much speculation about who was more identified with the name. Trademark attorney Neil Smith suggested that Madonna had likely exceeded the fame of the Virgin Mary.[51] Abstract debate aside, the court ruled that the cybersquatter purchased the domain name in bad faith and found that the singer Madonna was identified with the name.[52]

Although trademark owners and celebrities have had much success under ICANN's UDRP, there have been some notable defeats where the requirements have not been met. One type of original purchaser who often is able to retain a domain name on the grounds that it is not identical or confusingly similar is the corporate critic or disgruntled customer who buys a domain name that represents a derogatory term added to the name of a company. Although there are a number of exceptions,[53] the derogatory component makes confusion as to the source unlikely. A good example is the failure of CompUSA to take bancompusa.com from a disgruntled customer.[54] Perhaps the most common type of case in which the trademark owner fails to prove that the original purchaser has no legitimate interest in the disputed domain name is when two companies in different areas have been using the same name. An arbitrator, for instance, refused to take channel-d.com from Channel-D of Australia to give it to Channel D Corporation in New Jersey.[55] Lastly, trademark owners may fail to prove bad faith. A case involving victoriasecretexposed.com, for instance, shows that this can be another defense available to the corporate critic after an arbitrator found that Victoria's Secret had met the first two requirements but failed to show bad faith.[56]

Another ICANN-arbitrated dispute where bad faith was not proved has important implications for political campaigns. An individual who disliked gubernatorial candidate Mark Warner purchased markwarner2001.com and warner2001.com. In challenging ownership, Mark Warner successfully demonstrated that the domain names were confusingly similar to his name and that the purchaser had no legitimate interest in the name Mark Warner. The arbitrator, however, refused to transfer the domain name to Mark Warner because he did not find bad faith. The arbitrator's equation of bad faith with a commercial gain is a bad sign for politicians trying to secure a domain name: "While the use of a candidate's name or campaign as a domain name will attract internet users, the attraction is arguably for *political*, not *commercial* gain."[57]

Making it challenging to prove any of the three elements, the type of case in which the trademark owner or celebrity has the most trouble is when the domain name is a generic word. The fact that the word is used regularly outside the context of the domain name seeker makes confusion less likely and increases the likelihood that the original purchaser has acted in good faith with some legitimate interest in the word. Thus, ICANN arbitrators have often refused to take generic words from their original owner. The musician Sting, for instance, lost an early dispute over sting.com.[58] The rock band Foreigner failed to win foreigner.com from a pornographer.[59] An arbitrator refused to award the domain name dogs.com to the well-known online pet company pets.com.[60] UltraFem, maker of the tampon substitute Instead, was unsuccessful in its attempt to take instead.com from an individual hoping to sell ecological friendly alternatives to other products.[61] An individual paying homage to the bird with a tuxedo-like appearance was able to prevent penguin.com from being taken by the book publisher Penguin.[62] Continuing the tuxedo theme, Prom software was unable to take prom.com from a company that was using the domain for teen-related links.[63] Although it is a huge advantage, purchasing a familiar word is not literally a guarantee of being able to keep it. Indeed, an American company was required to transfer familiar.com to the British computing services firm Familiar Limited.[64]

CONCLUSION

The principles for resolving domain name disputes in the American and international legal systems are consistent. The benefit of the doubt goes to the original purchaser of a domain name. Ownership in the vast majority of domain names is conferred on a first-come, first-served basis. The original allocation system, however, is supplemented with a respect for traditional property rights. In cases where traditional property rights are held in a name, the legal system allows a domain name to be taken from those with no legitimate interest who are acting in bad faith to profit from the name. Long-standing principles of trademark and common-law property rights are an increasingly important part of how domain name ownership is determined.

Surveying the legal landscape, it is clear that the ICANN process is now the preeminent way in which domain name disputes are resolved. The ICANN system is faster and cheaper than the American courts. Disputes are settled inexpensively in a matter of weeks in the ICANN process, compared to often expensive multiyear battles in American courts. Thus, the ICANN process resolves thousands of disputes annually while the American court system might see at most a few dozen cases.

Although the ICANN process has become dominant, the American legal system is likely to have a continuing role. There are two major reasons. First, the American system allows the opportunity for financial damages to be assigned. Action in ICANN procedures is limited to a domain name transfer, while the American system can award damages of up to $100,000 per cybersquatting violation. Second, American courts will get appeals from ICANN. This appeal is built into the structure of both ICANN and American law. Under ICANN, which was created by the U.S. government, it is explicitly stated that its decisions do not supersede the actions of courts having jurisdiction. The Anti-Cybersquatting Consumer Protection Act also explicitly states that losers in ICANN procedures can appeal. American courts have, therefore, been willing to take appeals from the ICANN process.

There is, however, a big difference between being willing to take a case and overturning the ICANN decision. After all, the principles for deciding cases are essentially the same. Traditional property rights are superimposed on an original allocation system. The fundamental definition of cybersquatting—a bad-faith purchase of a domain name in which the purchaser has no legitimate difference—is the same in both systems. Having the same basis for decision, American courts are likely to uphold decisions made by ICANN arbitrators.

12

Piracy and Privacy in Cyberspace

In an early cyberlaw case, Pamela Anderson Lee and Tommy Lee asserted legal rights over their pornographic honeymoon video. The couple had sold some limited Internet rights to their video and asserted that unauthorized uses of the video constitute both piracy and a violation of privacy. Although not often combined as explicitly as in this case, both piracy and privacy are huge legal issues in cyberspace. Litigants in important piracy and privacy cases are household names, like Napster and Timothy McVeigh.

This chapter examines how piracy and privacy are regulated in cyberspace. In both cases, the cyberspace environment poses significant challenges to applying existing law. Lawmakers, however, have generally resisted creating new frameworks to address these challenges. They have applied long-standing legal principles to the Internet. Where new laws have been written, they typically have been framed as attempts to extend current law to the Internet.

PIRACY

The advent of digital technology poses difficult challenges to those seeking to prevent piracy, or theft, of their intellectual property. Works in digital form can be easily copied and distributed. It is quite easy to copy and save the combination of 0s and 1s that make up any digital product. Furthermore, when digital works are copied, they can be copied in identical form with no decrease in quality. Any medium in which digital works can be preserved is, therefore, a possible forum for making copies. As a computer-enabled combination of print, audio, and visual content in digital form, the Internet can potentially be used to copy almost anything. Indeed, one common early metaphor for the Internet was the world's largest copy machine.

Property Rights

In the face of these challenges, policymakers have used the long-standing principle of copyright to protect owners of intellectual property from piracy. Copyright is embedded in Article I, Section 8 of the U.S. Constitution: "The Congress shall have Power . . . To promote the Progress of Sciences and useful Arts, by securing for limited Times to Authors and Inventors the exclusive Right to their respective Writings and Discoveries." Congress exercised this power in 1790 when it passed a copyright law granting creators of maps, charts, and books protection for up to twenty-eight years. A 1909 revision extended the protection period to fifty-six years and expanded the type of work protected to include movies and other visual media. Substantial revision did not occur again until the passage of the Copyright Act of 1976. The law, which expanded protection to the life of the creator plus fifty years, remains the foundation for modern copyright law. Part of the reason that the 1976 legislation has persisted is its flexibility. The law tried to envision future scenarios: "Copyright protection subsists . . . in original works of authorship fixed in any tangible medium of expression, now known or later developed, from which they can be perceived, reproduced, or otherwise communicated, either directly or with the aid of a machine or device."[1] Building on this foundation, Congress extended copyright protection to life of the author plus seventy years in the Digital Millennium Copyright Act of 1998. In January 2003, the Supreme Court ruled that the extended copyright period did not violate the "limited time" copyright standard in the Constitution.[2]

The desire to utilize the flexibility of copyright law to protect intellectual property on the Internet has been apparent since the earliest intellectual property cases in cyberspace. One early case involved the wholesale copying of articles appearing in newspapers. FreeRepublic.com copied articles from the *New York Times* and *Washington Post* to its site and then inserted an area on the article in which people could post comments. Finding in favor of the newspapers, the court ruled that the use of the articles as a backdrop for a discussion forum did not absolve freerepublic.com of its copyright infringement.[3] While the court saw it as a copyright issue, Free Republic saw it as a political issue: "Free Republic is engaged in a life and death struggle with elements of the socialist propaganda machine, namely, the *Los Angeles Times* and the *Washington Post*."[4]

Ironic in light of government efforts to limit sexually explicit content, one type of content that has been granted strong government protection is original sexually explicit work. One of the first copyright law cases involved a person who scanned his copies of *Playboy* magazine and then posted the images on the World Wide Web. *Playboy* preserved its property rights in these photos in a quirky court opinion that considered the age-old question of why people read *Playboy* magazine: "The Court is not implying that people do not read the articles . . . [but] a major factor in PEI's [Playboy Enterprises Inc.] success is the photographs."[5] Demonstrating clearly the adage that the law is slow, Pamela Anderson teamed with her ex-husband Tommy Lee to partly win a federal appellate case asserting property rights in their pornographic honeymoon video.[6] Although this work may stretch their conception of progress in the arts, the Framers of the Constitution laid the basis for its legal protection in 1787. Creators are granted an exclusive right in their work.

There are legal consequences for piracy. For large-scale infractions, the penalties can be severe. As leader of the piracy group DrinkOrDie, John Sankus Jr. supervised university students and others in breaking copyright and then distributing the products over the Internet. After being caught by law enforcement, he pleaded guilty to the felony of conspiring to commit copyright infringement. Although he received the shortest sentence allowed under federal guidelines, Sankus was required to serve forty-six months in prison.[7] For smaller infractions, jail time may not be imposed. The first person convicted for pirating MP3, for instance, was a college student who was arrested after University of Oregon officials notified the FBI about unusual activity on his university account. Facing up to three years in prison for illegally downloading music and movies, Jeffrey Levy pleaded guilty to receive two years probation, limited Internet use, and periodic urinalysis (pretrial tests found marijuana in his system).[8]

The commitment to enforce copyright in cyberspace is seen clearly in *A&M Records* v. *Napster,* which was the first landmark intellectual property cyberlaw case. The case pitted the record companies against an Internet startup that had emerged from the creation of the MP3 digital format for music. MP3 is a format in which the information content of music can be compressed by eliminating sounds that are generally not perceived by the human ear. An MP3 file is typically created by copying a CD on a computer—colloquially known as ripping a CD. Once copied, MP3 files can be easily shared. All that remains is to find people with whom to share files. That is where Napster came in. In May 1999, nineteen-year-old college student Shawn Fanning made public his Napster software facilitating the sharing of music files in MP3 format. Named after a childhood nickname of its founder, Napster soon developed into a company capable of providing full service for transferring MP3 files from one person to another person. Although its server did not store any music, Napster did provide both the software and central server necessary to search and download music files directly from the entire community of Napster users. The appeal of the service was obvious. Napster users could obtain a seemingly infinite variety of music, which in CD format might cost nearly $20, for free on the Internet. The popularity of Napster was staggering. It became a community of 60 million users and peaked at 2.8 billion files traded in the month of February 2001 alone.[9]

Napster quickly drew the attention of record companies, which sought to assert the legal protections of their work. The record companies did not relish the thought of suing 60 million users for copying music files in violation of copyright. It was far more efficient to sue Napster. Suing Napster, however, meant that the record companies were suing a company that provided a means to copyright infringement, but generally did not do the infringing itself. Thus, record companies relied on the doctrine of contributory infringement in that Napster knew infringement was occurring but did not use its power to stop it.

The absence of actual infringement by Napster gave it hope for legal success, especially in light of the legal standing of the videocassette recorder (VCR). The Napster defense team placed much hope in the VCR analogy. In a 1984 case, *Sony v. Universal,* the Supreme Court refused to prohibit manufacture of VCRs even though the vast majority of their use would technically constitute copyright infringement. In a 5 to 4 decision, the Supreme Court ruled that development of the VCR could not be thwarted because it was capable of substantial noninfringing uses.[10] Napster hoped that the Court would apply the VCR analogy to Napster. Although an estimated 87 percent of the activity on the Napster service constituted copyright infringement,[11] a significant amount of material was in the public domain or was made freely available by the creators. So long as Napster was capable of substantial noninfringing uses, the Napster argument went, the technology could not be banned by government consistent with the First Amendment.

In a strong statement promoting legal enforcement of copyright in cyberspace, the Ninth Circuit Court of Appeals ruled in favor of A&M Records in February 2001. The court rejected the major Napster defense. The court refused to adopt the VCR analogy. It argued that Napster users distribute material to the general public, while VCR users generally watch the taped material at home. It drew a further distinction in that Napster has the knowledge of copyright infringement and an ability to do something about it that VCR manufacturers do not. Thus, the court was willing to apply the doctrine of contributory infringement to Napster. It articulated a three-pronged test for assessing contributory infringement in the digital era: (1) made aware of specific copyrighted files; (2) knows or should know that files are available on the system; and (3) fails to act to prevent distribution.[12] With potential liability mounting, Napster closed its file-sharing service in July 2001 and filed for bankruptcy within a year. Although the record companies earned a key legal victory, they continued to have a practical problem of enforcement. In the absence of Napster, other file sharing services emerged. Many of the new services were designed to address the issues that had made Napster vulnerable to legal challenges. Instead of being based on a central server, new services avoided a central server by creating a network of interconnected users serving each other directly. One such file sharing software, Morpheus, had become the most downloaded software on the Internet by August 2001, one month after Napster closed.[13] By 2003, the KaZaA file sharing software created by three Estonian programmers had a global following twice the size that Napster had reached.[14]

Struggling to keep control of their content, the record companies have pursued other avenues to reduce piracy. One alternative that has shown promise for record companies is a provision in the Digital Millennium Copyright Act that makes it easier for copyright holders to force Internet service providers (ISPs) to identify copyright infringers. In the first prominent test of the provision, a federal district judge ordered the disclosure of the name of a customer who regularly used KaZaA to download hundreds of copyrighted songs in *RIAA* v. *Verizon* (2003).[15] Beyond the legal arena, record companies have stepped up efforts to develop a technology that prevents the initial copying.

Anticircumvention

As record companies and other content providers try to make their product copy-proof, they have legal support from the Digital Millennium Copyright Act (DMCA). The law, enacted in 1998, gave additional protections to copyright owners. One important protection is known as the anticircumvention provision. In essence, the law bans the distribution of programs or devices capable of defeating copyright protection measures. Thus, for example, if someone wrote a code that deactivated anti-copying code on a CD, they could face criminal and civil liability. The penalties are severe; a violator can be sentenced to up to twenty-five years in jail.

The passing of the law has set up a huge legal fight. On one hand, the entertainment industry and Congress defend their rights under the Constitution to protect creative works for an exclusive period to promote progress in the arts. The measure is argued to be a necessary and proper measure to carry out this power in the digital age. The challenge that Internet technology is too fast for the law is properly met by writing laws capable of addressing whatever technology emerges. On the other side, critics have argued that the law is an infringement of free speech. It is viewed as a classic case of censorship in which speech is prohibited prior to being uttered. Since no actual infringement is required, the law violates the First Amendment by precluding a number of legal uses in order to stop illegal uses.

The first major legal test of the law involved the circumvention of the copy protection of digital video disks (DVDs). The anticircumvention device at issue in the case is a software program known as DeCSS. It obtains its name from the fact that its purpose is to deactivate the Content Scrambling System (CSS) of DVDs. DeCSS is essentially a computer program—it is a combination of 0s and 1s that can be stated as a series of commands in a variety of computer programming languages. DeCSS was written by a young Norwegian programmer and ultimately posted on the Web. The "forbidden" nature of the distribution of the code only increased its appeal, prompting among other things a thriving business of selling T-shirts with the short DeCSS program printed on the back. One individual who was active in posting the code was Eric Corley, an editor of an online hacker magazine. Mr. Corley freely circulated the software program on his hacker website. His actions drew the attention of the entertainment industry, including Universal Studios, which filed suit against Corley under the DMCA's prohibition on dis-

Chapter 12

tributing anticircumvention technology. Since Corley's defense attacked the constitutionality of the DMCA, the United States was added as a party to the case to defend the law.

Central to the case was the issue of what type of content regulation the law constituted. Was it content neutral or content specific? The difference between the two types of regulation is based on whether government regulation targets a particular viewpoint. A classic example of a content-specific regulation would be limitations on pornographic material; a classic example of a content-neutral regulation would be a ban on using loudspeakers at 2 a.m., whereby government doesn't care what people are expressing but only that the ability of people to sleep is hindered. If the anticircumvention ban were a content-specific regulation, it would be subject to strict scrutiny and would likely fail the requirement that such regulations must be narrowly tailored in the least restrictive way to achieve a compelling public interest. Corley and opponents of the law wanted the law to be considered a content-specific regulation. They argued that a software program is speech and that government is regulating it for the message that it is communicating. On the other hand, the government and defenders hoped to have the law considered under the less demanding test of intermediate scrutiny for content-neutral speech. The government's opening statement in oral argument emphasized that it was the related action, not the substance of the speech, that was being violated: "Your Honor, if we were here today talking about a software program that shut off navigational systems on airplanes or shut down smoke detectors in public buildings, I don't think anyone could reasonably argue that the First Amendment would bar the government from prohibiting the dissemination and distribution of that software."[16]

In a highly anticipated decision, the Second Circuit Court of Appeals upheld the constitutionality of the law and ruled in favor of Universal Studios. The court ruled that the law was a content-neutral regulation. It argued that the overriding purpose of the law was to regulate the functional, not substantive, component of the speech. Government, therefore, was not favoring or disfavoring any specific viewpoint. As a content-neutral regulation, the burden for government was much less. According to the court, the DMCA met that burden.

More controversial than the case involving Corley, who did not write the original program, was the prosecution of the actual author of a software program designed to circumvent a copy protection measure for electronic books. In early 2001, while working for his employer ElcomSoft, Russian Dmitry Sklyarov wrote a program that circumvented Adobe's eBook copyright protection technology. ElcomSoft, a Russian firm, subsequently sold the program online to U.S. customers. Adobe asserted its rights under the DMCA. The government filed charges against Sklyarov and ElcomSoft. Prosecution would be difficult since Sklyarov and ElcomSoft were both Russian. Sklyarov, however, was scheduled to travel to the United States to speak at a programmers' convention. Discovering his travel plans, the government arrested Sklyarov when he arrived in the United States and charged him under the DMCA with a potential penalty of twenty-five years in prison. After being held for a month, Sklyarov was released on bail provided that he stayed in California. In his legal battles, Sklyarov gained strong allies. An editorial by the *Washington Post* on August 21, 2001, characterized the law as "oppressive" and defended Sklyarov: "It seems wrong for Mr. Sklyarov to be subject to criminal penalties for writing a program that has potentially legal uses, without any obligation on the government's part to prove that he intended to aid piracy." In December 2001, with criticism mounting, the government allowed Sklyarov to return to Russia without prosecution on the condition that he provide information about the program.

PRIVACY

Privacy is one area in which the technical challenges of the Internet are formidable. The challenges constitute a paradox. From the perspective of policymakers, the Internet makes it too difficult to find out things about those determined to maintain privacy for unlawful purposes and too easy to find out things about the unsuspecting, law-abiding, average person. The technology provides a substantial amount of anonymity to those who skillfully employ various software packages to disguise their identity and location from law enforcement. While there are bona fide reasons for seeking to remain anonymous from authorities, the desire for anonymity is often a result of trying to avoid criminal prosecution or civil liability. On the other hand, unsuspecting people who leave identifying marks in cyberspace and provide information to various entities may find their personal information being circulated without their knowledge. Confronting this paradox, the primary goal of policymakers has been to apply long-standing legal principles to cyberspace privacy.

Privacy of Personal Information

Individuals have an interest in maintaining privacy of their personal information. In the modern world, records are kept about everything from purchasing habits to medical history. The circulation of personal information is facilitated by the digital nature of the Internet. Blocks of digital information can be aggregated, manipulated, or copied with the click of a mouse.

The collection of personal information can have positive and negative consequences. On the positive side, many people enjoy the customization of service that is possible when records are kept. The most dramatic examples are related to the speed of customized service. The patient brought in for an emergency medical procedure may benefit from readily accessible information about allergies or other special concerns. The consolidation of credit information from various banks and credit cards makes what could be a time-consuming process of assessing credit history into a potentially rapid approval of a loan. Less dramatic, the collection of personal information can lead to targeted marketing that makes it easier for companies to provide products to people likely to want them. As an example, discount sellers of pet medication can use public pet vaccination records to communicate with pet owners. Obviously, the company saves money through more efficient marketing, but consumers may also benefit by becoming aware of a less expensive option for needed products. Indeed, this may explain why veterinarians in Florida, who sell full-price medication to patients, successfully lobbied to remove pet vaccinations from the public record to create what Barbara Peterson of the First Amendment Foundation calls the "stupidest exemption in the history of open government."[17]

On the negative side, there is potential for misuse of personal information. At the least, it can be annoying to receive communication from marketers who have purchased a database of people meeting certain criteria. The disclosure of personal information can be embarrassing. Beyond annoyance or embarrassment, there can be other ramifications of information disclosure. If privacy of medical records is not maintained, people may be discriminated against by entities ranging from potential employers to health insurance companies in a way that can have serious repercussions. Lack of privacy of personal information can also result in crime. Criminals can use personal information to target victims for scams or stalking. If enough information is assembled, identity theft is possible.

An example of the mixed blessings of data collection is the technology of cookies. A *cookie* is an identifying mark left by a computer each time a person visits a website. In essence, it allows the website operator to identify a site visitor as a repeat customer and to track behavior subsequent to a visit. Awareness of cookies increased dramatically when they became part of the Netscape browser in 1994. The feature was promoted as a way for Web users to customize their experience. Cookies have clearly done this. Web users benefit every time they do not have to retype a password or redo work because the Web host can recognize the user by this identifying feature. On the other hand, cookies have received criticism for their privacy implications. Even if not identified by name, the cookie leaves a lot of information about a website visitor.

On balance, the potential of negative consequences seems to be weighed most heavily by the public. Public opinion polls have consistently revealed that a significant percentage of the public is concerned about online privacy. In a 1998 Harris poll, more non–Internet users named improved privacy protection over reduced cost or simpler technology as something that would make it more likely for them to go online. Asking both Internet users and nonusers, Harris found that the public was more concerned about e-mail privacy than the privacy of telephone, U.S. mail, or fax communication.[18] Later polls have confirmed the early results. A Pew Research poll found that the number of people who saw online tracking as harmful was double the number who saw it as helpful. Only 10 percent of Internet users are "very confident" that the things they do online will remain private.[19]

The concern of the public with Internet privacy has been supported by a number of prominent studies pointing to shortcomings in privacy protections of businesses. The first major online privacy study was conducted by the Federal Trade Commission (FTC) on websites directed at children. Released in June 1998, the study found that 89 percent of the sites were collecting personal information from children, but less than 10 percent had a role for parents in the process.[20] In a related study, the FTC found that only 14 percent of all sites disclosed their privacy policy. Although disclosure had increased to 88 percent by 2000, the FTC found that few companies implemented the fair information principles of providing notice, giving choice, allowing access to collected information, and ensuring security of the information.[21]

Shortcomings in privacy protection have been found not only by business, but by government. Government, especially the FTC, was an early critic of business practices. Yet, when others looked into the practices of government, significant shortcomings were identified. In 1997 and 1999, surveys by public interest groups found that only one-third of government sites posted privacy policies.[22] An electronic privacy organization chided the White House in 2000 for collecting information from children. By 2000, a General Accounting Office (GAO) report found that posting privacy policies was nearly universal on federal websites, but found that 34 percent of agencies did not fully comply with federal rules on articulating privacy policies.[23] Lower levels of government also did not fare well under privacy scrutiny. In 1999, only 38 percent of states and 4 percent of the largest cities posted privacy policies on their websites.[24]

Public concern also has been heightened by a number of high-profile incidents related to privacy. One early well-documented incident occurred at a 1998 conference on technology. Scott McNeeley—president of the largest networking company, Sun Microsystems—was asked whether his company's increased integration of digital products raised privacy concerns. Many were shocked by the casual note of his response: "You already have zero privacy—get over it."[25] Privacy concerns were also raised when online marketing firm Double Click announced in 1999 that it would combine its information about Web behavior with non-Internet data to create a large database of information organized by name. A negative media and public reaction prompted an abandoning of the plan and a massive decline in the value of Double Click stock.

Perhaps the most dramatic incident demonstrating the privacy implications of the Internet was the bankruptcy of Toysmart.com in 2000. It wasn't the bankruptcy itself, however, that attracted attention. A number of Internet companies had already gone bankrupt by that time. What was striking was the asset assessment conducted as part of the bankruptcy proceedings. The company was determined to have only one significant asset. The asset was its database of personal information about customers. Under typical bankruptcy proceedings, the asset would be sold to pay off creditors. There was a catch, however. The customers of Toysmart had been told that their information would be kept private by Toysmart. Yet, the Toysmart making the promise ceased to exist. The question arose whether the database should be sold. Reaction to the proposed sale was overwhelmingly negative. Ultimately, the database was destroyed, but the incident left a vivid reminder of the value of personal information.

In addressing concerns about information privacy, policymakers have combined the strategies of self-regulation with the granting of legal rights. The self-regulation strategy emphasizes that business will be able to find a proper balance between the desire to collect personal information and privacy protection. If people do care about privacy, the market will confer advantages on companies that use personal information responsibly and disadvantages on companies that do not. Customers who feel that their privacy has been violated will not return. On the other hand, a legal rights strategy guarantees privacy rights in law and imposes government regulations on the collection of personal information. The assumption is that market forces alone will not provide enough incentives for privacy protection. Throughout the history of the Internet, there is a strong component of each strategy. Over time, there has been an increased focus on a legal rights strategy.

Policymakers have long identified a role for self-regulation in privacy protection. A dramatic early statement of this was a July 1999 FTC report on privacy. Despite its report showing low privacy protection, the FTC formally recommended that Congress take no new action on privacy. The FTC emphasized that privacy provisions outlined on a website are part of an online contract.[26] Violations of the contract can be prosecuted by the FTC as a deceptive business practice.[27]

The self-regulation strategy continues to find many advocates. The technology industry has consistently articulated a vision of how data collection can lead to customized service and efficient marketing of products. Legal scholars have expressed concern that limits on information sharing may violate the First Amendment.[28] Many members of Congress are hesitant to impose new restrictions on business. Even those who typically favor expanded regulation of business are wary of slowing economic commerce. Democrat Richard Gephardt, for instance, has said, "Responsible companies know intuitively that it's in their deep self-interest to protect the privacy of the consumer, so I believe they have all the incentives they need in order to get this done."[29]

Self-regulation is increasingly supported by a legal rights strategy of imposing obligations on the collection of personal information. Still prominent, the first legal rights strategy was to apply privacy law established in a non-Internet context to the Internet. Well-established laws limiting government use of personal information include the Privacy Act of 1974 and, with an eye to the Internet, the Electronic Communications Privacy Act of 1986. On the business side, laws were in place to protect the confidentiality of financial and medical records. These laws have been brought forward to the Internet context.

Building on the application of existing law, Congress passed its first important Internet-specific privacy legislation in late 1998. The Children's Online Privacy Protection Act (COPPA) passed by large majorities in Congress after being folded into a large appropriations bill.[30] The legislation was intended to severely restrict the ability of businesses to collect information from children. Formal responsibility for the policy was delegated to the FTC. As implemented, the major FTC regulations required commercial websites to get the permission of the parent before collecting information about children under age 13.

While there was rapid consensus on legislation to protect the privacy of children, legislation to grant broader privacy protection has been more contentious. The ease of resolving the issue of children's privacy was a product of the long-standing principle that those who are not old enough to understand the implications of their actions are unable to legally consent. On the other hand, adults are legally able to consent and expected to understand the implications of providing personal information. The way in which consent is provided, however, is a hotly contested issue.

In general, consent to use private information can be provided on an opt-in or opt-out basis. Under opt-in, an individual must formally grant permission to allow private information to be collected and used. Under opt-out, it is assumed that private information can be collected and used unless a person takes the initiative to inform the data collector of the desire to be excluded. Since people tend to take the path of least resistance, whether the default is collecting or not collecting becomes a huge issue. Many privacy debates, in fact, are manifested as some variation of opt-in versus opt-out. Business interests are usually aligned in favor of opt-out in order to reduce the burden of obtaining consent and to facilitate data collection. Privacy advocates typically favor some sort of opt-in procedure. The difference between perceived business and consumer interests is seen clearly in survey data that has shown 86 percent of Internet users preferring opt-in procedures, while only 16 percent of the 100 most popular websites offer opt-in.[31] Privacy legislation is a nonstarter without some agreement on the fundamental question of consent.

In the years following the 1998 Children's Online Privacy Protection Act, privacy bills proved difficult to pass. Legislative failure dogged even seemingly popular legislation, such as the legislation banning the sale of social security numbers named in honor of Amy Boyer, a young woman who was brutally murdered by a stalker who obtained information from the Internet. The legislation was abandoned in 2000 after being tied into a broader conflict between privacy advocates and information industry groups.[32]

The slow response of the federal government prompted state action. Many states already had in place privacy laws stronger than federal standards. By 1999 Marc Rotenberg, Executive Director of the Electronic Privacy Information Center, saw a strong move by states to strengthen their privacy protections: "It's not surprising that states are moving when Washington policy legislators are largely sitting on their hands."[33] The subject of addressing shortcomings in online privacy protection was a major theme at the 2000 meeting of the National Association of Attorneys General.[34] In May 2002, Minnesota broke new ground by becoming the first state to pass legislation that gave subscribers the legal right to set limitations on how their ISPs can use personal data.[35]

The inconsistency of state laws has prompted some to call for federal legislation. Business groups began to come out in favor of a federal standard to avoid the complexity of complying with fifty different laws. This call also came from people such as former Speaker of the House Newt Gingrich, often a voice for state autonomy over federal involvement. Newt Gingrich was uncharacteristically critical of state autonomy in advocating for a single national standard of privacy protection:

> In the long run, the very nature of the Internet will lead us to want some kind of federal preemption [on privacy] because in virtually every state legislature you are getting a variety of ideas, many of them from people who do not know what a computer is and aren't sure why it does all those strange things but, by God, doesn't want it doing it to them.[36]

Increasingly, the legal rights strategy for privacy has been pursued as a federal matter. This has come from Congress and the courts. In 1997, for instance, one district court ruled privacy-related state legislation unconstitutional.[37] Numerous privacy bills are introduced in Congress every session. Although support for a federal approach to privacy protection has grown, passing legislation remains a challenge.

Privacy of Personal Communication

Besides information privacy, the law-abiding individual also has a privacy interest in the substance of personal communication. This would include such issues as retaining privacy in the substance of e-mail or websites visited. There are very different legal protections depending on whether the individual wants to keep it private from a private employer or the government.

The workplace online activity of employees has limited privacy protection from monitoring by their employers. In general, the employment contract is heavily weighted in favor of the right of the employer to control company office equipment and secure workplace productivity. The number of companies that believe monitoring is in their interest has increased significantly. In 1997, the American Management Association found that only 15 percent of firms ever stored or reviewed the substance of e-mail messages. By 2003, the number had more than tripled to 52 percent. Most of these companies have taken some disciplinary action based on what they found. About one in five companies has fired someone on the basis of improper e-mail.[38]

On the other hand, the protections from government are more substantial. The Bill of Rights applies to government. Specifically, the Fourth Amendment protects citizens against "unreasonable" searches and seizures. Government intrusions into privacy must follow a formal legal procedure. In most cases, government will need to get a warrant from the courts.

The high-profile case of *McVeigh* v. *Cohen* symbolizes the additional protections that people have from government. The case was initiated by Timothy McVeigh, who is unrelated to the Oklahoma City mass murderer, after being dismissed from the Navy for being a homosexual under the "Don't Ask, Don't Tell" policy. The Navy began to suspect McVeigh's sexual orientation when a civilian Navy volunteer reported that the public America Online directory included an individual named Tim, who said he lived in Hawaii, worked for the military, and identified his marital status as gay. His identity was confirmed when a Navy official identifying himself as a "third party" successfully persuaded America Online to disclose the person's full name and contact information. The government defended its actions by saying that McVeigh's statement on a member profile violated military policy and that a warrant was not required since America Online had voluntarily given up the identity of the subscriber. The court rejected the government's defense. In his opinion, Judge Sporkin described the effort to identify McVeigh as a "search and destroy mission" violating the Don't Ask, Don't Tell policy. He also argued that the failure of the government to obtain a warrant constituted a violation of the Electronic Communications Privacy Act. The judge concluded with a strong statement about bringing forward privacy protection established outside of the Internet context: "In these days of 'big brother,' where through technology and otherwise the privacy interests of individuals from all walks of life are being ignored or marginalized, it is imperative that statutes explicitly protecting these rights be strictly observed."[39]

While the Internet makes it easier to get information about the unsuspecting law-abiding person, it generally makes it more difficult to find out about those determined to use technology to conceal their unlawful activities. In confronting this challenge, policymakers have built on a history of applying the Fourth Amendment requirement for a warrant to new technologies. The advent of the telephone prompted the development of the authorized wiretap. The Internet was formally incorporated into the wiretap legal framework in the 1986 Electronic Communications Privacy Act. The legislation was framed as a way to make the scrutiny of electronic media equivalent to that for other media.

In reality, finding a precise equivalent is not possible. The reason is based on the way in which communication is transmitted on the Internet. One key Internet innovation was the use of packet switching to transmit data, instead of the circuits used for telephone communication. With a circuit reserved, it is far easier to target surveillance on something like a telephone. With packet switching, the path of the communication is unclear. The process of interception, therefore, will likely require taking in more communication than just what is desired. This presents a dilemma. Internet surveillance may "seize"—if only briefly, to filter—more communication than targeted and would thereby invade more privacy. If the search is allowed, the Internet may be seen as having weaker privacy protection than other communication techniques; but if it is not allowed, the Internet would have stronger privacy protections. There may not be an equivalent. Yet policymakers and the public clearly demonstrate a commitment to the idea of treating all media equally. Thus, public debate on privacy invariably becomes a battle between privacy advocates and law enforcement, both staking their claim as the heir of previous law and the fundamental equivalent of other media.

For a while, it appeared that the benefit of the doubt in the Internet environment would go to privacy protection over law enforcement. In 1994, Congress passed the Communications Law Enforcement Act, which expanded federal wiretap laws to allow for cell phone monitoring—largely by placing requirements on cell phone manufacturers. The legislation specifically excluded the Internet. In approving the legislation, the House Committee felt it necessary to explain that classic wiretap law still applied to the Internet, even as the new heightened cell phone requirements did not apply: "This does not mean that communication over the Internet offers a safe haven for illegal activity."[40] Internet users with a cable modem enjoyed even greater protection as a result of the 1984 Cable Act requiring notification and an opportunity to challenge before cable monitoring can occur.

Privacy advocates also had the upper hand in the early debate over Carnivore. Introduced in 1999 by the FBI, Carnivore is a software program that is physically attached to the network of an ISP. Unlike a telephone wiretap, which is targeted to a particular line, the Carnivore program necessarily momentarily scrutinizes all communication on a segment of the network as it runs search terms approved in a court order. In defending the program before Congress in September 2000, the FBI used terrorism as the first example of how Carnivore could prevent crime: "Convicted terrorist Ramzi Yousef, the mastermind of the World Trade Center bombing, stored detailed plans to destroy United States airliners on encrypted files on his laptop computer."[41] On the other hand, privacy advocates told Congress that authorities had not found an online equivalent to existing privacy protections: "The demand that every current offline capability be directly implemented online should not become an excuse for creating a massive technical architecture for surveillance that, given the nature of the Internet, could be far more invasive than anything we have seen to date."[42] With criticism mounting, the FBI announced in February 2001 that it was changing the name of the software from Carnivore to DCS1000. In announcing the name change, the FBI said that the new name "doesn't stand for anything" but avoids the "unfavorable" connotations of the old name.[43] In its first two years of existence, Carnivore had been implemented by the FBI about twenty-five times pursuant to court orders.[44]

The nature of the privacy debate changed dramatically after the September 11, 2001, attacks on America. Authorities quickly discovered that the Internet had been used by the hijackers. Although there is little evidence to suggest that the Internet was essential to the attacks, it has been attributed some guilt by association. There is evidence that the perpetrators used the Internet in public libraries in the days preceding the attacks. Numerous e-mails were exchanged. Some of the hijackers used the Internet to purchase airline tickets using their own name, and in some cases, their own frequent flier numbers.[45] Information about potential targets may have been gleaned from government websites.[46]

The intent of policymakers to elevate government scrutiny of the Internet is apparent from the very top. President Bush signed the U.S.A. Patriot Act (PL 107–56) on October 26, 2001. The act included several hundred pages of measures with the express purpose of assisting in the fight against terrorism. Considering the scope of the law, President Bush could have focused on any number of measures in the signing ceremony. His choice to discuss the Internet provisions indicates that they were considered an important part of the legislation. President Bush made it clear that the legislation would increase government oversight of electronic communication:

> Surveillance of communications is another essential tool to pursue and stop terrorists. The existing law was written in the era of rotary telephones. This new law that I sign today will allow surveillance of all communications used by terrorists, including emails, the Internet, and cell phones. As of today, we'll be able to better meet the technological challenges posed by this proliferation of communications technology.[47]

The goal of treating the Internet in the same manner as other media is clear from measures adopted in response to September 11, 2001. The key Internet-related component of the U.S.A. Patriot Act is to facilitate law enforcement in ascertaining identity. Under the legislation, the Cable Privacy Act was amended to legally make it as easy for investigators to get information about a cable Internet subscriber as it is to obtain a phone number.[48] The necessity of court approval for Carnivore or other surveillance of Internet communication is lessened.[49] That said, the extent to which the Internet can be treated the same as other media will depend on the logistics of implementation over a period of years. The identification of an equivalent itself will be a continuing process. Fundamental differences between digital and circuit communication mean that Internet scrutiny can be more invasive in some respects and less invasive in other respects.

CONCLUSION

In addressing questions of both piracy and privacy, policymakers have emphasized long-standing principles. This reliance on long-standing principles has persisted despite the challenges posed by the Internet. Even where Internet-era legislation has been adopted, it is invariably framed as simply updating earlier legislation for the new environment. This approach seems to resonate with the public, which tends to view the Internet as one of a series of available communication options, not a reason to fashion a new cyberworld.

This is apparent from how the post–September 11, 2001, goal of treating the Internet like other media is consistent with public opinion before September 11,

2001. In February 2001, Pew Research asked Americans whether they support the surveillance of various media by "law enforcement agencies." There was essentially no difference between media; the surveillance of mail, e-mail, and telephone calls each received support from 51 to 54 percent of the population. There was little difference by demographic or political characteristics; the percentage of those disapproving ranged from 29 to 38 percent for each category of gender, race, and political party.[50] This configuration of public opinion provided little obstacle to measures framed as raising e-mail scrutiny to that of other media.

PART FIVE

GLOBAL LANDSCAPE OF INTERNET POLITICS

13

The Internet in Global Democracies

Since the Internet is a global communications infrastructure, no work on the Internet would be complete without a consideration of the situation outside the United States. Thus, the following two chapters will examine the relationship between the Internet and politics in nations around the world. This chapter will consider the Internet in the context of democracies in which citizens enjoy significant political freedoms. The next chapter will look at the Internet and politics in nations with governments that place significant limitations on political freedom.

This chapter uses the experience of the United States as a reference point to understand the influence of the Internet in democracies throughout the world. It first challenges the tendency to view other democracies as simply a lag of the United States—being where the United States was at an earlier point in time. Next, it finds a similarity between the United States and other democracies in the existence of a digital divide. An additional similarity emerges from the exploration of global Internet content, including the extent to which it is influenced by government regulation. Lastly, the special concerns of lesser developed democracies are addressed.

COUNTERING THE LAG PERSPECTIVE

In the current stage of Internet development, it is simply not accurate to view other democracies as uniformly behind the United States. As shown in table 13.1, several other nations equal or surpass the United States in relation to Internet prevalence. The impressive growth rates in the United States often have been matched or exceeded elsewhere. The growth rate of South Korea has been particularly impressive.

Table 13.1   Top 10 Nations in Per Capita Internet Use

Rank	Country	Percent Online 2002	1997
1	Iceland	61	27
2	Sweden	57	23
3	South Korea	55	4
4	Singapore	54	16
5	United States	54	15
6	Netherlands	53	6
7	Finland	51	19
8	Norway	50	14
9	New Zealand	48	15
10	Canada	48	15

Source: ITU, "Information Technology," April 2003, at int.org.

Not even in the Top 25 in 1997, South Korea is now third. On the other side of the coin, a slower growth rate has been present in Bermuda, which led the world at 24 percent in 1997 but has since dropped out of the Top 10.

The United States trails even more nations in the use of wireless technology, which is increasingly applied to the Internet. A study by the International Telecommunications Union found the United States to rank thirty-eighth in the world, with only 44 cell phone subscribers per 100 inhabitants. The list of highest users was dominated by European nations, including Luxembourg (97 cellular subscribers per capita), Italy (84), Norway (83), Iceland (82), Austria (81), Finland (78), and the United Kingdom (78).[1] Americans and Europeans also use cell phones in substantively different ways. For Americans, the cell phone is typically a supplement to a fixed telephone line. On the other hand, Europeans quickly adopted mobile phones as their primary or only telephone.

In particular, the nation of Finland emerged quickly as a leader in its incorporation of high technology into daily life. Propelled by being home to the world's largest cell phone manufacturer, Nokia, Finland has long been a leader in cell phone usage. It was the first nation to have over half of its citizens be mobile phone users.[2] Finland also got off to a fast start on the Internet and by 1999 had an Internet access rate four times greater than the European Union average.[3] Finland continues to maintain a strong leadership position. Its visionary approach can be seen in the Helsinki Virtual Village Project. By 2010, a recently barren area on the Gulf of Finland is scheduled to become the world's first wireless community. The Helsinki Virtual Village is to include universities, homes, and seven hundred companies that are all networked through the most advanced wireless technology to provide integrated and personalized service. Construction on the initial group of buildings was completed in 2001.[4]

DIGITAL DIVIDE IN ADVANCED INDUSTRIAL DEMOCRACIES

The digital divide represents the uneven diffusion of the Internet. It is typically expressed in relation to socioeconomic and cultural characteristics that make Internet use more or less likely. The digital divide exists both within and between countries. It is an issue that is discussed throughout the world.

The key factor in explaining differences between countries in Internet use is economic development. The major gap in Internet use is between lesser developed nations and advanced industrial nations.[5] While Internet use exceeds 50 percent in a number of advanced democracies, the average for Africa is about 1 percent. Even between advanced industrial democracies, there are important differences in Internet use. As shown in table 13.2, citizens in poorer European nations such as Spain and Portugal are less likely to use the Internet than those in wealthier nations such as Sweden.

In addition to the overwhelming significance of economic development, a cultural variable affects the digital divide between countries. This is the language spoken in a country. Specifically, the greater the prevalence of the English language in a nation, the more likely its citizens are to use the Internet. English has largely become the language of the Internet, accounting for about 85 percent of Internet content.[6] An English speaker, therefore, has more incentive to use the Internet. Some of the highest Internet users are the Nordic nations, in which English is a widely used second language.

Table 13.2   Trends in Internet Use by European Union Nations

	Percent Online	
Nation	2002	1997
Austria	41	8
Belgium	33	5
Denmark	47	11
Finland	51	19
France	31	2
Germany	42	6
Greece	18	2
Ireland	27	4
Italy	30	2
Luxembourg	37	7
Netherlands	53	6
Portugal	36	5
Spain	19	3
Sweden	57	23
United Kingdom	41	7

Source: ITU, "Information Technology," April 2003, at int.org.

In addition to population characteristics, government policy can affect the degree of Internet use. Government can play an important role in promoting the development of a telecommunications infrastructure. Regulation also affects the likelihood for Internet service to be provided. The pricing structure of telephone service adopted by either a government or private provider (especially metered or flat rate) can alter incentives for telephone service. Increasing competition in telephone service has generally resulted in lower telephone prices, which make Internet use cheaper.

One reason, for example, that many European nations outside Scandinavia got off to a slow start on the Internet was the relatively high cost of telephone service. The high prices partly resulted from the existence or legacy of government-endorsed monopoly providers. Over time, European Union regulations have encouraged nations to allow more competition. Legally, the process culminated in December 2000 when the European Union passed a rule opening up the local loop, thereby introducing competition into all aspects of telephone service. Although implementation was sometimes slow, competition did increase, resulting in price reductions and the introduction of more flat-rate access fees that encourage Internet use.

Within other advanced democracies, the nature of the digital divide parallels the American experience. The strongest support for this comes from comparing Europe to the United States at a similar diffusion point. Both the European Union and United States had large, government-sponsored studies of Internet use that coincidentally were taken when about 18.5 percent of the overall population had online access from home. The digital divide in Internet home access within the United States and within the European Union was strikingly similar at this identical stage of diffusion. In the European Union, 24 percent of households headed by a 25- to 54-year-old had home access compared to 8 percent of those headed by a person over 55; the corresponding figures in the United States were 24 and 9 percent. Looking at the age at which formal education stopped for Europeans, 6 percent of those stopping by age fifteen, 17 percent of those stopping at ages 16–19, and 33 percent of those continuing beyond age 20 had home Internet access; in the United States, 10 percent of those with only a high school diploma, 22 percent of those with some college, and 38 percent of those with a college degree had home Internet access. In the European Union, 8 percent of the lowest income quartile, 11 percent of the second quartile, 20 percent of the third quartile, and 37 percent of the highest income quartile had home Internet access; in the United States, the corresponding figures were approximately 5, 13, 26, and 45 percent. Thus, for each of the three primary components of the digital divide, Europe and the United States were having a similar experience at a similar level of diffusion.[7]

As in the United States, the key policy to address the digital divide in democracies has been to wire public facilities, especially schools. In the European Union, government has played the largest role in purchasing computers for schools, although approximately 15 percent of all computers are donated by private entities. By 2001, wiring schools had become virtually universal in the European Union, with over 95 percent of secondary schools connected to the Internet and over 90 percent of schools allowing students access. In fact, the only nation with fewer than 90 percent of its secondary schools connected to the Internet in 2001 was Greece, at 58 percent. Internet use in European Union schools is further enhanced because over 50 percent of school computers are less than three years old.[8]

One policy of promoting Internet use that has not been as popular in Europe as in the United States is tax exemption. Unlike the United States, which allows state and local governments to impose a sales tax on final purchases, European nations tax goods and services at each stage of commerce through a value-added tax (VAT). The European Union quickly applied the VAT to online purchases within the European Union. The European Union, however, did not decide until May 2002 to apply the VAT to Internet sales to European customers from companies outside Europe. Before then, European customers paid the VAT on purchases from European firms, but not from non-European firms. Non-European countries now pay the VAT rate for the country in which the European customer resides. As shown by the statement from a Treasury Department spokesperson, strong objections to the policy change were voiced by the United States: "We continue to be concerned about the potential for discrimination inherent in the new EU VAT regime that applies to downloaded products."[9]

INTERNET CONTENT IN ADVANCED INDUSTRIAL DEMOCRACIES

Similarities in the prevalence of the Internet are reflected in similar content for Internet communication in the United States and other advanced democracies. In fact, political content on the Internet among advanced democracies varies far less than political content in other media. It is not an overstatement to say that political communicators on the Internet are using a comparable template for communication. In other media, the template for communication varies substantially between advanced industrial democracies. An important reason for variation in other media is the pervasive impact of regulation of the media and political process.

The way in which countries regulate television generates huge differences in campaigning around the world. In a few cases, such as France, television ads are subject to restrictions on content and production technique.[10] More typically, broadcasting regulation has implications for the existence and duration of ads. The British, for instance, allow each party a number of five- or ten-minute blocks of free air time to get out its message. This regulation ensures that parties will have a longer span of time than the American thirty-second television spot.

Divergence from country to country in the content of traditional media is also ensured by the intersection of campaign finance regulation and political content. Spending limits have important consequences for political content. Some nations, such as Canada, place similar limits on spending by both parties and candidates in a constituency.[11] On the other hand, limits can be more restrictive on either the party or the individual candidate. In Britain, for example, local candidates have been subject to a strict limitation on constituency spending as far back as 1883. At the same time, the political parties have had an unlimited ability to raise and spend money. This regulation has the predictable consequence of a party-centered campaign in which individual candidates are unable to afford access to significant media advertising.

The impact of regulatory differences is far less pronounced on the Internet. Campaign finance regulation is almost taken out of play on the World Wide Web. It does not matter whether the website is publicly financed, privately financed, or subject to spending limitations. Candidates do not need to purchase their own, or have the government provide, expensive blocks of space on the Web. There aren't any. The operation of at least a primitive website can be done so inexpensively as to elude any but the most restrictive limits on campaign spending. Avoiding important regulation-derived differences in political content, Internet political content has strong similarities in advanced democracies around the world.

Taking a broad look at campaigning style on the Web, differences in the technological capabilities of Web design often seem more pronounced than differences between countries. The British campaign sites of early 1997, for example, in many ways look more like the Canadian campaign sites of 1997 than the British campaign sites of 2001. What can be done with the template has more to do with the state of technology than government regulation. The case, however, should not be overstated; the substance of issue discussion is country dependent. Yet, it does appear that many of the themes present in the discussion of American content are present in other advanced democracies. In looking at these themes, attention will be focused on party campaign websites in Great Britain in 1997 and 2001.[12] This is consistent with the longitudinal design of this book in recognizing the importance of change over time—in this case, change from an early Internet stage in 1997 to a more mature medium in 2001. The consideration of Britain will be supplemented with other noteworthy examples.

The overriding feature of campaign content on the Internet throughout advanced democracies is the preeminence of issues. The Internet is a medium that favors issues over personality. This focus on issues is more important than it might first appear. While issues are a significant part of other dimensions of the campaign, seldom are they as dominant. Unlike the consistent emphasis on issues of Web communication across countries, the emphasis on issues in TV ads has been found to vary substantially from country to country. One study, for instance, found that issues were emphasized in 100 percent of French TV ads, 61 percent of American ads, and only 26 percent of German ads.[13] Media coverage of campaigns also downplays issues. Ascribed most often to the American media, the propensity for so-called horse race coverage about who is ahead and what campaign tactics are being used is prevalent elsewhere. In one study of the 1997 British election, the conduct of the election and sleaze occupied 42 percent of media stories, while issue coverage was characterized as having "disappeared."[14] Television news sound bytes, which are becoming shorter worldwide, are down to 18 seconds in Britain[15] and under 10 seconds in the United States. The sound bytes of party leaders in Canada declined from about 10 seconds in 1993 to about 3 seconds in 1997.[16] Even if issues arise in media coverage, the discussion is often too short to do more than scratch the surface. In contrast, the Web allows a candidate to develop issue positions in far greater detail.

Another common feature of Web campaigning is raising money and recruiting volunteers. A non-accidental audience with an above-average education already has shown enough interest to prompt an advocate to use this interactive medium for some form of solicitation. The ability to use the Internet to solicit funds has increased significantly in recent years with advances in secure credit card technology. Over time, political communicators have become more subtle and effective in making requests for contributions. The most important development is clearly the ability to receive a donation online.

Symbolic of the crucial leap in raising money online is the difference in approach used by the Conservative Party in Britain from 1997 to 2001. The approach in 1997 was clumsy and ineffective. On the main home page, the typeface for the phrase "Credit Card Hotline" was larger than the typeface for the word "Conservative." Even the basic presentation of the request revealed an underutilization of Web technology. When the "Donate" icon was activated, an entire screen was called up with no other material other than a telephone number for credit card contributions. By 2001, the approach was far more subtle and effective. Instead of being the largest text on the home page, the icon for solicitation was one of many icons, and it was smaller than issue-centered material. Further, the icon in 2001 led to a secure form to donate online. For those not wanting to donate online, traditional telephone and mail options were described at the bottom of the donation page.

A third similarity is that the Internet provides a forum for the discussion of issues downplayed in the broader political system. The low cost of disseminating large amounts of information gives advocates the opportunity to expand the scope of issues that are discussed in campaigns and in broader political discourse. Discussion of minority issues, for instance, can receive a broader hearing. During the same 1997 campaign in Canada in which some groups belittled the amount of coverage devoted to aboriginal issues, a large amount of information from parties was available on the Web.[17] In 2001, the major British parties added a section devoted to special issues of concern to university students. It does appear that space capacity is motivating this discussion, since issues with a relatively small constituency still occupy a small percentage of overall content. It is simply a lot easier to find 5 percent of campaign material in a well-ordered menu than in a campaign speech or advertisement. Beyond campaigns, advocates for minority issues are using the Internet to communicate with a potentially large audience at minimal cost in a way impossible in traditional media. Sometimes issues downplayed by the broader political system can be very important. It may take a third party or interest group to raise the issues during a campaign.

A landmark example of an interest group using the Internet to raise the profile of a downplayed issue during a campaign occurred in South Korea in the 2000 parliamentary elections. In this case, the downplayed issue was the low integrity of politicians of both parties. Six hundred interest groups cooperated to form an umbrella citizens' group that disseminated information and mobilized outside of the established political institutions. The most important information disseminated was a list of eighty-six "unfit" candidates that was included on the website. The citizens' group pressured the elections commission for records that revealed that 15 percent of candidates had criminal records. The popularity of the site, which received 1.1 million visits on Election Day, was a significant factor in the defeat of 58 of the 86 unfit candidates. In addition to disseminating information, the site served as a forum for discussion and mobilized the member groups behind a unified purpose.[18]

A fourth characteristic of political content in advanced democracies is a gradual adoption of original uses of the Internet. Similar to the pattern of U.S. politicians, politicians in other democracies seemed content early on to simply have a website to show that they were up-to-date technologically. The website was used almost exclusively to reproduce items already existing in other forms, such as the party campaign manifesto. The language of the Canadian Reform Party's introduction to the Web version of its manifesto in 1997 clearly shows that the Web was perceived as another delivery system for the same material: "This [website] is just one of the ways we're sharing our Fresh Start platform with Canadians from coast to coast."[19] Thus, as in the United States, early sites in other democracies were criticized for a lack of creativity. Recently, more original uses of the Internet have been developed.

One early focus of original content has been to add some fun to politics through interactive games, contests, and computer applications. The Liberal Democrats in the 1997 British campaign, for example, offered a fantasy election game that allowed visitors to pick a constituency and see a simulation of what would happen under various vote swings. In 2001, the use of serious games was continued in Britain with a Labour Party "cut 'n' run" game, in which players took the role of competing prime ministerial candidate William Hague making his way through a maze of angry voters upset at proposed budget cuts. Contests included the 1997 Conservative Party website contest, challenging visitors to guess where the ball should be in a photo of incumbent prime ministerial candidate John Major batting in the game of cricket. A contest on the 1997 campaign site of the Irish party Fine Gael offered participants the chance to win a trip or a *Michael Collins* movie video for answering questions based on information provided on the site. Political advocates also provided visitors with their fill of screen savers, background images, wallpaper, and icons. An odd example of this is the 2001 Conservative site in Britain which, for those who might find it comforting, provides a way to set as perpetual desktop wallpaper the words, "Violent Crime is Rising."

One widespread original Internet function is the site search engine. As sites expand, the ability to conduct a keyword search of a particular site becomes more valuable. It allows site visitors to quickly identify anything a party is saying about an issue of particular concern to them. It can be especially effective for identifying discussion of minority issues that is not prominently featured on the site but is more accessible online than through other media. In 1997, neither the Conservative nor Labour Party sites in Britain offered a site-specific search engine. By 2001, both sites had site-specific search engines allowing a visitor to pinpoint items of interest.

Another development in original content is the use of targeting on websites. As an example, the 1997 Labour and Conservative sites employed little targeting. By 2001, targeting was fundamental to the sites. On the Labour site, visitors could pick their constituency from a map and call up two sets of documents: "What Labour's done for you" and "Tories in your area." Within a basic template of information about what "good" Labour has done and what "bad" the Tories have done were data fields that varied by constituency. There were still some rough edges in the software, as the field for unemployment by constituency defaulted to a number of decimal points seldom seen outside the number pi. The same decimal format for Bethnal Green & Bow was replicated in all constituencies: "The Tories would axe the New Deal and all Labour's measures to help people off benefit and into work that has seen unemployment fall by 1780 (or 27.2488001238582%) in Bethnal Green & Bow since May 1997."

The Conservative effort at targeting in 2001 was highlighted by the opportunity to "shape the conservative manifesto." Visitors were asked for information about their age, marital status, children, health status, employment, and region. The information was then used to generate a "personal manifesto." For instance, if a person inputted "single with no children," the "raising a family" part of the manifesto was candidly downplayed: "We realize that our policies in this area are not of primary concern to you at this stage in your life." Those living in the city found a manifesto speaking about urban renewal and the tube (subway); country dwellers received conservative positions on greenfields and agriculture. The personal manifesto was sympathetic to the visitor's individual situation. As an example, the elderly were told that "older people are among our most responsible citizens and give a great deal to their communities, but they have been demeaned and patronized by this government."

One group that has been targeted by Internet communication is young people. As a percentage of Internet users, young people are invariably overrepresented. The Internet offers a unique opportunity to communicate with young people about politics and counteract the low youth participation that characterizes many democracies. Far more attention is devoted to the issues of young people on the Internet than in other media. Often, this material is clearly distinguished. In 2001, the Conservatives set up a "Conservative Future" section that focused on the issue of university student loans and listed university-based

opportunities to participate in politics. In some cases, the party has set up a separate site for young voters. These sites usually go out of their way to mix fun
with a discussion of issues. It also helps to have a domain name that looks more
like a personalized license plate than a political website. The 2001 Labour Party
website for young people, located at www.ruup4it.org.uk, had separate sections
for celebrity interviews and descriptions of how to vote. The questions section
starts with pub closing time and is followed by discussion of the Internet, university fees, genetically modified food, and an account of Tony Blair's university days playing in a rock band. Although the issue discussion may take stereo-
types too far, it is undoubtedly true that young people are more interested in
university fees than in the Widowed Parent's Allowance. Overall, the discussion
of youth issues on the Internet can help young voters see the intersection of politics with their daily lives.

One milestone, albeit an awkward one, in directly addressing young people
occurred in the 1999 New Zealand elections. During the campaign, nocrap.org.nz
became well known for its irreverent treatment of politics. Its discussion of policy was sprinkled with humor and profanity. The site attacked youth apathy:
"But despite the fact politics can be boring it is in fact quite important—especially, to those of us under 30—as we have to live longer with the consequences of what Government does."[20] After some investigation, it was discovered that the site was not independent, but was established by the National
Party. The opposition Labour and Alliance parties criticized the anonymity of
the site and described it as "filthy" and perhaps illegal.[21] Building on a tradition
of mobilizing youth online, New Zealand became the first nation to allow
young people to sign up for the military through an online application in September 2001.[22]

Outside the context of campaigns, Internet communicators in advanced democracies are pressing ahead with efforts to improve the content of e-government. As
in the United States, the history of e-government in advanced democracies is one
that begins with information dissemination and is increasingly supplemented by
interactive services. In November 2001, the European Commission issued its first
report on e-government. The report found that e-government services to business
were 33 percent more interactive than e-government services directed at citizens.
An important exception, however, was the citizen tax service, which was the most
interactive of all services.[23]

One type of e-government function that has had difficulty gaining popularity is
online voting. Overall, little effort has been made to implement online voting.
There are, however, a number of limited implementations of electronic voting.
One of the most notable is the Australian Capital Territory, which became the first
Australian territory to allow online voting for Parliament in October 2001. Although only 9 percent of votes were cast online, the effort was praised as the first
time that blind Australians (using headphones and keying in choices online) could
vote without a sighted person being present.[24]

INTERNET REGULATION IN ADVANCED DEMOCRACIES

In advanced industrial democracies, regulation of Internet communication has been low. Use of the Internet has been integrated into the basic freedoms held by citizens in democracies. There has been no systematic effort to control the amount and nature of communication. Democratic governments have not required government approval of websites. People are free to obtain accounts for Internet access. Political content, including criticism of the government, has been allowed to flourish on the Internet.

One rare exception is the parliamentary elections in Japan in June 2000. Campaigns in Japan are highly regulated events. Historically, the most visible mode of campaigning is for the candidate to drive through the streets with a megaphone. This is because the public airwaves for television and radio have not been made available to candidates. Japan defends the ban as a way to prevent the public airwaves from being used for political advocacy that is not necessarily in the public interest. The emergence of the Internet posed an interesting dilemma for the Japanese. Should the ban on broadcasting of political messages apply to the Internet? Ultimately, Japan decided that it should. In 1996, Internet communication joined neon signs and billboards as violators of the restrictions on image-based campaigning. After efforts to permit Internet campaigning failed, candidates in the 2000 election were not allowed to actively campaign on the Web during the twelve-day campaign period. Instead, they followed tradition and used an automobile and a megaphone to get their message out to passersby.[25]

Other notable efforts to regulate online content include the enforcement of language restrictions. In 1997, a branch campus of Georgia Tech in France was sued by an interest group under a French law requiring all goods and services to be in French. A French court made it clear that the university could face a fine of up to 25,000 francs per site visit.[26] Another example occurred in Quebec. Enforcing a province law requiring that printed material be in French, the Office de la Langue gave a computer store operator a brief grace period to set up a bilingual page.[27] The computer store's ultimate conversion to a bilingual site revealed that for website operators in a jurisdiction where the French language regulations apply, the best approach is a simple acknowledgment: I made a mistake (*Je me suis trompé*).

Within the context of low regulation, democracies still try to apply existing criminal law to the Internet. Of course, the fact that democratic governments have not established central control of providers and end users makes it difficult to restrain criminal communication on the Internet. Yet, communication that is illegal elsewhere is not made legal simply because it is communicated in a medium that governments have been reluctant to censor. Thus, those using the Internet to facilitate criminal activity have been vigorously prosecuted in democracies. The first major international treaty coordinating laws about using the Internet to commit a crime, the Council of Europe's Convention on Cybercrime, was signed in November 2001 by the United States and twenty-nine other nations.

Democracies also have instituted regulations to protect privacy on the Internet. The major substantive issue related to privacy in democracies is the role of the Internet in facilitating the collection of personal information. Records of all types (including sensitive financial and health information) are now in digital form, which can quickly and easily change hands. Throughout advanced democracies, policymakers have tried to reduce the privacy costs of new technologies.

In general, government regulation of privacy on the Internet has been stricter in Europe than in the United States. The differences in privacy regulation emerged early in the diffusion of the Internet. As the European Union Data Privacy Directive was introduced in 1995, a clear difference in approach had emerged. In the United States, privacy regulation was targeted to particularly sensitive industries and to protecting children. The European Union, on the other hand, took a more comprehensive approach encompassing all industries and individuals. Indeed, the European Union Data Privacy Directive, which took effect in 1998, was landmark legislation giving consumers control over how personal information can be collected. The directive made the difference in privacy protection between the United States and the European Union a substantial political issue. Under the directive, non–European Union entities must provide "adequate" privacy protection before doing business in the European Union. With the United States law failing to meet required privacy levels, American firms worried that they would be excluded from the European market. After an extended period of negotiation, an agreement took effect in November 2000 that allowed individual companies to meet the privacy guidelines even though American law generally did not. American companies agree to follow European Union–based privacy protections overseen by the Federal Trade Commission in order to be given the status formerly known as "safe harbor" to transfer data from Europeans. As companies throughout the world try to meet European privacy standards, data privacy protection is increasingly seen as an example of a process known as "trading up," in which the global economy can result in a race to the top to meet high regulatory standards.[28]

INTERNET IN LESSER DEVELOPED DEMOCRACIES

In lesser developed democracies, the overriding issue related to the Internet is expanding access. These nations typically have low use of the Internet. Where the large masses of people are relatively poor and uneducated, it has been difficult to broaden access. As shown in table 13.3, the Internet is rare in the heavily populated African nations. There is a weak social and economic infrastructure for widespread Internet use. Aside from the wealthy and inroads among the young, the Internet does not affect the daily lives of people.

Governments of lesser developed democracies have tried to directly address the digital divide. As in advanced industrial democracies, the emphasis is on wiring

Table 13.3   Internet Use Trends in the Most Populous African Nations

Nation	Population (Millions)	Percent Online 2002	1997
Nigeria	120	0	0
Egypt	70	1	0
Ethiopia	66	0	0
Congo	54	0	0
South Africa	44	7	2
Tanzania	37	0	0
Sudan	33	0	0
Kenya	32	2	0
Algeria	31	2	0
Morocco	31	2	0

Sources: United Nations Population Fund, *State of World Population* 2002; ITU, "Information Technology," April 2003, at int.org.

public facilities. One common technique is to wire schools. By including some Internet skills in primary education, governments will ensure that a generation of young people can be exposed to the Internet, even if it is unlikely that there is a computer in the home. Beyond schools, a variety of other public facilities can be established as public Internet locations. In Brazil, for example, a $400 million project in 2001 emphasized putting Internet terminals in post offices.[29] Closing the digital divide will be tough work, but strides have been made. Although the future is impossible to predict, there are some reasons for optimism about the narrowing of the gap between advanced nations and lesser developed nations.

The growth of the open-source movement is one reason for optimism about the ability of lesser developed nations to become more technologically advanced. Open-source technology, which entails computer code being visible and freely reproduced, dramatically reduces the cost of computer technology. In operating systems, the most prominent open-source vehicle is Linux. Officially released in 1994, Linux has been committed to open source since its creation. In part because of its complexity, Linux has had little success against the proprietary Microsoft Windows in the PC market in advanced democracies, although it has done well for local networks. On the other hand, Linux has made significant inroads in lesser developed nations. The UN Development Program regularly provides forty-five lesser developed nations with Linux-powered machines.[30]

Another reason for optimism about closing the digital divide in lesser developed nations is the move to wireless technology. Wireless offers the potential for nations to skip a prohibitively expensive stage of infrastructure development. With fewer vested interests in an established infrastructure, governments may be free to innovate. A United Nations report finds a silver lining for poor nations: "Often those with the least have the least to fear from the future, and certainly their governments are less encumbered by special interests committed to yesterday's technology."[31]

Although Internet use is not widespread in lesser developed nations, it has been adopted by some governments and political actors. Their use of the Internet echoes the themes of use in advanced democracies. One striking example of similar content is the use of the Internet for issue discussion, especially issues important to young people.

Symbolic of the emphasis of the Internet on issue discussion is the Peruvian 2001 presidential election. On the whole, the 2001 campaign between Alejandro Toledo and Alan Garcia was dominated by personal innuendo, including allegations of corruption, prostitution, illegitimate children, cocaine use, and general low integrity. Where issues were discussed in the traditional campaign, the state of the economy dominated. On the other hand, looking at cyberspace, one might be tempted to think that the campaign was highly focused on a variety of issues. Issue discussion was often detailed and constituted the primary focus of the presidential and party websites. Further, issues of particular importance to young people were disproportionately represented on Peruvian sites. Symbolically, this can be seen in the largest typeface used on candidate Alan Garcia's main page. The words *La Generación Internet* jumped out at site visitors. As part of a seven-page statement on youth issues, Garcia outlined his position on universities, including the funding of sports teams at universities. He tied the issue of promoting technology in universities to the broader campaign issue of the economy: "Information technology . . . is the key to employment" [author translation]. The sites of both Garcia and his opponent also included an express commitment to Internet expansion in schools below the university level.[32]

CONCLUSION

As described throughout this book, the American experience broadly reflects the politics of Internet communication in other advanced democratic nations. The United States is joined by a number of other nations in an era of the Internet as a majority medium. Yet, in lesser developed nations the Internet is still rare. Regardless of their development stage, governments have promoted the Internet by providing access in public facilities, especially schools. With widespread diffusion, the Internet has come to play a role in politics. This role represents a net gain for democracy by enhancing information dissemination and mobilization.

14

Walls and Ladders in Nations Limiting Political Freedom

The potential impact of the Internet is greatest in nations limiting political freedom. In free democratic nations, the Internet enhances democracy by providing an efficient additional outlet for mobilization and information dissemination. Yet with other communication outlets available, it is unrealistic to expect one additional outlet—indeed, one that represents a computer-enabled combination of earlier outlets—to facilitate a revolutionary transformation of politics in democracies. On the other hand, in nations limiting political freedom, the Internet is more than an additional outlet building on an infrastructure of many outlets for mobilization and information dissemination. It may be the only outlet. Where other outlets of communication are shut off, the effectiveness and resilience of the Internet as a tool of mobilization and information may facilitate a revolutionary transformation of politics. By no means does the Internet guarantee this transformation, but in several prominent cases it has played a prominent role in enhancing the voice of ordinary citizens against a repressive government.

INTERNET TECHNOLOGY

It does not take much imagination to identify how Internet technology poses a threat to repressive governments. As identified throughout this book, the fundamental political characteristic of the Internet is as an outlet for mobilization and the dissemination of information. A repressive government is going to be threatened by both the capacity for mobilization and the spreading of information. This is particularly true insofar as the Internet functions as a decentralized, anonymous, and resilient outlet.

The Internet does not exist in any central location. A repressive government has no identifiable headquarters to target. From the perspective of the repressive government, Internet communication represents a confounding paradox of being everywhere but nowhere. Although there is no central location, Internet communication can occur in many locations simultaneously as ordinary citizens become content providers and mobilizers.

The Internet allows communicators to remain anonymous through a variety of techniques. Accounts can be established under fictitious names. The use of the Internet in public facilities can minimize the risk of tracing use to a particular individual. Anonymous remailers can disguise the source of communication. Through encryption, the actual message of the communication can be hidden. On the international scene, software is readily available for hiding messages. While software to enhance privacy has often struggled to find a market in democratic nations, it is in great demand from dissidents in nations limiting political freedom. Indeed, human rights organizations quickly identified the Internet as crucial to their efforts to disseminate information about repression. Originally released in 1991, the seminal encryption software Pretty Good Privacy was created by Phil Zimmerman with the explicit goal of assisting human rights organizations.[1]

Lastly, the Internet is a resilient technology. Redundant channels are available for communication. A variety of methods of transmission are available. Even in the unlikely case that a repressive government was willing to shut down all telephone lines, those seeking to mobilize or disseminate information could still use wireless modes of Internet communication.

DOUBLE-EDGED SWORD

For a repressive government, the most pressing concern about the Internet must surely be its capacity to mobilize and disseminate information in opposition to the government. The Internet constitutes an ever-present threat to the government monopoly on information and its ability to prevent the opposition from mobilizing. Further complicating the situation for repressive governments is the speed of the Internet. These technological features make it clear that the Internet can become a sword capable of seriously wounding the ability of the government to repress opposition.

Once hidden, the other edge of the sword is becoming easy to identify. With the rapid expansion of e-commerce, Internet technology is becoming increasingly important to economic growth. An Organisation for Economic Co-operation and Development (OECD) report estimates that electronic commerce could lend itself to approximately 30 percent of a nation's gross domestic product (GDP).[2] The price for failing to keep up with Internet technology will continue to rise.

This dilemma has been most widely documented in Asian nations, such as Singapore, which have become accustomed to substantial economic freedom but limited political freedom. These nations constitute some of the most technologically advanced nations on Earth. Moves to restrain Internet development might threaten their prominent place in the global economy. Falling behind in communications technology can undermine economic success. Yet, there may be a temptation to prevent the unfettered growth of the Internet in order to prevent criticism of the government. Although these nations do not reach the level of complete repression, there is a tradition of the government placing limitations on political freedom in the name of the broader good. Governments will have to weigh the balance between the political risks and economic benefits of unfettered use of the Internet.

This dilemma applies not only to these economically advanced nations but also to any nation that seeks economic progress in the context of limited political freedom. Restrictions placed on the Internet for political purposes will undoubtedly have economic consequences. Nations will vary in their willingness to sacrifice economic growth for perceived political benefits. Strategies for restricting political freedom on the Internet must be made in light of the economic costs.

WALLS

Some nations have sought to build a metaphorical wall preventing undesirable Internet content from entering. The walling out of politically undesirable content is usually accompanied by the walling out of "morally" undesirable content, especially pornography and gratuitous violence. Of course, many open democratic nations have made efforts at limiting pornography and violence. What distinguishes the nations in this chapter is the substantial limitation of the most fundamental political freedoms.

Indeed, the restriction of political content on the Internet is consistent with a broader climate of repression. Efforts to restrict the Internet typically fall under the broader legal authority to prohibit acts that undermine the government or foster civil unrest. This broad grant has been used to regulate the use of previous technologies, from the telegraph to television, that have been seen as a threat to the government. Repressive governments have also justified Internet regulation based on its capacity to upset tranquility. In many cases, repressive governments acted quickly to apply the broad grant of authority. China, for instance, formally announced in 1996 that the Internet would fall under broader laws prohibiting social disturbances. With the Internet formally under broad laws of repression, governments can take their time in crafting Internet-specific measures.

A classic example of using broader authority to build a wall for the Internet occurred in Malaysia. In 1999 Malaysia passed the Communications and Multimedia Act, which regulated every "screen" in Malaysia. Passed under government authority to preserve Malaysia's multiracial society, the law regulated all broadcasting and telecommunications services. The government argued that regulation was necessary because the Internet might be used to foster dissent between ethnic groups. The chair of the enforcement agency provided assurances that the new law would not be abused: "Nobody should be overtly concerned except perhaps those who have immoral and illegal things in mind."[3]

In regulating the Internet, repressive governments can use a comprehensive or selective strategy to minimize the likelihood that the Internet will be used as a vehicle for political opposition. The comprehensive strategy involves placing significant restrictions on both the transmission and receipt of Internet communication. In contrast, a selective strategy employs targeted ad hoc denials of service. The distinction between a comprehensive and selective strategy closely mirrors an early distinction made by Reporters Without Borders in an early report on the Internet. The organization identified twenty countries that were true "Enemies of the Internet" and an additional twenty-five countries that had significant, but less severe, restrictions.[4] Almost exclusively composed of Asian, African, and Mideastern dictatorships, the list is made up of countries for which Internet restrictions are only a part of an overall strategy of limiting freedom.[5]

The defining characteristic of a comprehensive approach to Internet control is formal governmental approval of access and content. Under a comprehensive approach, all Internet content must be approved by the government. Further, access to the Internet must be granted by the government. Of course, the most restrictive version of a comprehensive approach would be if the government refused to approve any access or content—an outright ban. With only the rare exception, outright bans on the use of the Internet have been abandoned. In some cases, these bans have been lifted for a significant period of time. The Internet ban, for example, was lifted in China in 1995.

Symbolic of the move away from an absolute ban on Internet content is Iran lifting its ban on the Internet in 1997. Prior to this move, all use of the Internet in Iran was criminalized. Although the ban was lifted, customary restrictions remained on Internet use. The first Internet café opened in 1998 with veils required on women and the genders segregated on different floors. There was substantial filtering of political and pornographic content.[6] Although the ban was lifted, the cost of Internet use remained a significant barrier for many Iranians.

Although typically stopping short of a ban, comprehensive strategies impose significant restrictions on Internet communication. Regulation is imposed on both transmitters and receivers. On the transmitter side, repressive governments often require anyone wishing to establish an Internet server to obtain permission from the government. Essentially, government is the sole registrar of domain names and can place various restrictions on registration. Another option is to systematically deny content. A comprehensive strategy typically entails extensive blocking and editing of content.

On the recipient side, there are a variety of options. Many repressive governments require that all Internet access be provided through government or government-approved Internet service providers (ISPs). In some countries, computers themselves must be formally registered. The high price of Internet service also substantially limits use in countries with repressive governments. As a result of the expense and limited accounts, much Internet use in repressive regimes occurs in public cafés. With Internet use in public, monitoring is easier for the government. China, for instance, has a long history of regulating cybercafés. Under legislation passed in 2000, cybercafés must block access to pornographic or subversive websites. Within the first year of implementation, approximately 20 percent of the 94,000 cybercafés were closed for inadequate blocking of prohibited content.[7]

A tragic reminder of the heavy reliance on Internet cafés was the extent of casualties from a Chinese fire on June 16, 2002. At 2:30 a.m., the Lanjisu Cyber Café was suddenly engulfed in flames. Despite the time of day, the café had a number of customers, mostly university students. The windows of the unlicensed café were barred to avoid detection, and customers struggled to escape; twenty-four lost their lives. The next day, Beijing temporarily closed all Internet cafés in the city. Officials said that only 200 of the 2,400 cafés would be allowed to re-open. Framed as a safety measure, the action also reveals an eagerness to maintain control of Internet recipients.[8]

A landmark event in the implementation of a comprehensive strategy is the 1999 declaration of Saudi Arabia that it had effectively controlled the Internet. Although total control is impossible, Saudi Arabia proclaimed victory on the basis of a comprehensive strategy implemented by the bureaucracy King Abdulaziz City for Science & Technology (KACST).[9] On the transmitter side, all Internet connections are channeled through a server in the capital of Riyadh. Approved Web pages are saved on the Riyadh server. Other sites are subject to ongoing filtering. The Saudi Arabian government has justified its regulations as necessary to ensure that people do not have their values offended online: "[We] focus on pornographic material and will block any site that contains such material as it becomes aware of it."[10] Filtering is supported by public input, which is facilitated by convenient forms to suggest additional sites that should be blocked. The approximately five hundred daily suggestions for blocking are analyzed by the government, which on average blocks about half of the suggested sites.[11] The combination of methods prevents a vast amount of content from being transmitted. Significantly, sites opposed to the government are not allowed. On the recipient side, Internet service is provided only through licensed ISPs. As early as 2001, the government said that there was "no plan to have new ISPs" beyond the thirty in existence.[12] In effect, the government authorizes all Internet accounts.

To obtain the best technology, repressive governments have been willing to seek out blocking services from companies in democratic nations. Saudi Arabia, for instance, took at least ten bids in 2001 from American, British, German, and Dutch companies for the contract to update its blocking services. The original Saudi filtering contract had been awarded to Secure Computing, a California-based firm, in 1999. In offering their services, international filtering companies add customized features to methodologies already identifying content such as pornography for their democratic customers.[13]

The defining characteristic of a selective strategy of Internet control is targeted ad hoc denials of service. In a selective strategy, formal approval of transmission and receipt is not necessary. Government, however, does selectively deny service. Typically, some modest filtering is implemented. Overall, this strategy values economic growth over political restrictions, but at least symbolically wishes to restrain political freedom on the Internet in the name of the broader social "good."

An important example of how selective strategies are used is the late 1990s response of Singapore to the Internet. Singapore is a country of significant economic freedom and growth in the context of a tradition of limited political freedom. The development of the Internet posed a dilemma for Singapore. After wrestling with the issue, Singapore opted for a selective strategy. At first, selective measures were aggressively imposed. In 1994, for instance, there was a wide sweep of all university-based accounts looking for pornography. Under the guise of seeking a virus, 80,000 accounts were searched. Over time, the attempts were less rigorous. Later Singapore decided on a less aggressive strategy that included blocking sites on an ad hoc basis. As implemented, the government blocks over one hundred sites. Although some significant sites are blocked, it is recognized that access is available to many sites with "undesirable" content. The economic potential of the Internet won out over political claims for restrictions. As described by Singapore's trade and industry minister, the selective site blocking for political purposes is largely symbolic: "The Internet will reduce government's ability to restrain you to a set of behavior; we just symbolically block off a few sites to make a point."[14]

Although Internet bans are now rare and some countries have substantially reduced regulation, there is certainly no widespread movement toward easing restrictions. In fact, the track record of some Internet strategies associated with repressive governments has prompted adoption elsewhere as a way to minimize the perceived harms of the Internet. In June 2002, for example, the South African parliament gave preliminary approval to a plan to give the government a monopoly on domain name registration. Frustrated with the move, the bureaucrat in charge of domain names took the unusual step of hiding the computer file that generates the nation's Web addresses.[15] Earlier in 2002, the Turkish Parliament by a 202–87 majority passed a restrictive Internet law requiring government approval of new websites and imposing fines for vague offenses such as "airing pessimism" online.[16]

With either the selective or comprehensive strategy, the government may choose to buttress the strategy with criminal prosecution of violators. The legal justification for prosecution can be a broad grant of power or an Internet-specific statute. The broad grant of authority to secure tranquility that is used to nominally justify measures of Internet control is usually accompanied by criminal penalties. These penalties can be imposed on those using the Internet in a manner that is determined to violate the broader statute. On the other hand, Internet-specific violations relate only to the Internet context. An example of an Internet-specific statute is the 1996 Communications Computer Law in Myanmar, imposing a lengthy prison sentence on accessing the Internet without permission, and its January 2000 follow-up law banning all political speech on the Internet. In many nations, violators of either the broad or Internet-specific statute will not have the benefit of a fair trial.

The landmark criminal prosecution for using the Internet to communicate undesirable political content is the case of Lin Hai in China in 1999. The backdrop for the prosecution is the publication of a newsletter *VIP Reference* in the United States by Chinese dissidents advocating for political freedom. Unwilling subscribers themselves, government officials considered the newsletter to be subversive spam. At the time of the prosecution, the newsletter was estimated to go to over 250,000 accounts in China. To increase the influence of the newsletter, the publishers of *VIP Reference* were always trying to obtain databases of e-mail addresses. Working at a software company, Lin Hai had access to a list of approximately 30,000 e-mail accounts. In early 1998, Lin allegedly gave the list of e-mail addresses to the publishers of *VIP Reference*.

The 1999 prosecution of Lin Hai by the Chinese government drew international attention. He was prosecuted under a Chinese statute that prohibited political subversion. Unfortunately, Lin Hai could not find refuge in a fair trial. Human rights groups throughout the world responded with outrage as Lin Hai was sentenced to two years in prison. He was quietly released six months before his term expired. The leniency was short-lived as the Chinese crackdown on *VIP Reference* continued in September 2001 with a three-year sentence to Zhu Ruixiang for forwarding some *VIP Reference* articles to twelve of his friends.[17]

International outrage with the Lin Hai prosecution did little to prevent future prosecutions by China and other repressive nations. China has continued to build a reputation as the most active prosecutor of Internet offenses. Some of the strongest penalties, including death to detention, have been handed out as part of a Chinese crackdown on using the Internet to distribute information on the outlawed spiritual movement Falun Gong.[18] China, however, is not alone in imposing harsh sentences for online political dissent. In possibly the first murder of an online journalist, Ukranian Georgiy Gongadze was found beheaded after his Internet reports on corruption prompted death threats from the president.[19] In June 2002, a thirty-month prison sentence imposed on the editor of a freedom-advocating Tunisian news site was widely condemned by international human rights organizations.[20] Unfortunately, these notable cases represent only a small portion of the known and unknown prosecutions by repressive governments.

LADDERS

In nations limiting political freedom, the Internet can be an effective tool to circumvent government monopolies of information and restrictions on political assembly. The effectiveness of the Internet in mobilization and information dissemination makes it an important tool for those opposing the government. The Internet can function metaphorically as a ladder to scale the walls imposed by a repressive government. It can help scale broader and Internet-specific walls. Where broader restrictions are imposed, the Internet may stand out as the only medium in which the government is unable to maintain a monopoly. Where Internet-specific walls are imposed by government, the decentralization of Internet technology makes it likely that private efforts can successfully surmount them. The Internet, therefore, may serve as the most powerful technology yet in the struggle against repressive governments.

The capacity of the Internet for mobilization can help the cause of freedom in countries where the right to political assembly is limited. Through the Internet, large numbers of people can be contacted and mobilized in a manner that can avoid detection by the government. The government opposition can use the anonymity of the Internet for protection. Face-to-face meetings that pose great risk of government discovery can be minimized. The early stages of protest that can be so dangerous to participants can be held quietly. The extent of the mobilization may quickly surpass a level that the government can reasonably contain.

A landmark example of the use of the Internet to mobilize against a government occurred in Indonesia in 1998. At the time, Indonesia was ruled by a military government led by General Suharto. Under its control, political freedoms had been significantly restricted. The government was engaged in extensive corruption. The military government made it difficult for citizens to use traditional means to organize a protest against the government. Demonstrators needed to operate under the radar screen of the government, but on a scale significant enough to make a strong case for change. The Internet proved to be an ideal tool for this challenge. It could be used to quietly mobilize significant numbers of people. Further, the Internet was a technology most often utilized by young, often college-age Indonesians. Thus, a large movement of young people was able to use the Internet to arrange meetings and protests. With an important role for this Internet-based mobilization, wide-scale protests of the government in Indonesia occurred throughout 1998.[21] The strong demonstration against the government emboldened opposition forces within the government. In May 1998, General Suharto succumbed to pressure and resigned. A new government promising more political freedom took power.

The capacity of the Internet for disseminating information can help the cause of freedom in countries where the government seeks to maintain a monopoly on information. Repressive governments have been fairly successful in shutting down opposition newspapers, radio, and television stations. The existence of these media outlets in a specific geographic location has made them targets for government crackdown. In contrast, the Internet offers the benefit of decentralization and makes suppression less likely. Information on the Internet arrives from a multitude of sources in a multitude of locations. Repressive governments have found it far more difficult to shut down the decentralized voices on the Internet than to shut down a television station. Official government sources of information may find themselves competing with Internet sources in opposition to the government. Information, in turn, can empower people.

A dramatic example of the significance of the Internet in disseminating information occurred in the Serbian elections on September 24, 2000. The incumbent leader, Slobodan Milosevic, encountered strong opposition. Historically, Milosevic had used the government monopoly on information to perpetrate electoral fraud. Without alternative sources of information, the public found it difficult to challenge the election results presented by the government. In 2000, however, the Internet had changed the electoral landscape. As election returns were counted, opposition parties posted the results immediately on the Internet. People saw online the votes being tabulated, with a majority going to the opposition party. Thus, the Serbian population was very surprised to "discover" that Milosevic had won when the official government results were released later in the week. Empowered by Internet-based information about the results of the election, the public was unwilling to accept clear election fraud.[22] Opposition parties with international support demanded that the results of the election be observed. Under extreme pressure, Milosevic relented and allowed the results of the election to be observed. Milosevic stepped down and would soon face prosecution for war crimes perpetrated against ethnic Albanians.

While the Serbian example emphasizes getting information out within a country, the dissemination of information on the Internet can extend far beyond the borders. Information disseminated on the Internet may suddenly find itself with a global audience. Those fighting against government repression might find allies far from the original location of conflict. Spreading information may expand the sphere of conflict and fundamentally change the balance of power. Expanding the parties involved in the conflict may be the best strategy for a small opposition facing a powerful government. Spreading information over the Internet may be the best way to bring new parties into the conflict.

The watershed example of a dissident group using Internet-disseminated information to find a broader audience is the Zapatistas. Their early use of the Internet became a model for political minorities throughout the world and a catalyst for creating online networks of protest organizations. Interestingly, the dissidents were not in a totalitarian nation but in a democracy that was limiting freedom. The Zapatista National Liberation Army is a guerilla force of indigenous groups in southern Mexico. Upset with a recent law against community property and general conditions for indigenous peoples, the Zapatistas rebelled against the Mexican government in 1994. Subsequently, the Mexican army took control of the indigenous villages—including a blackout of all traditional outlets of information. Although the villagers themselves did not use the Internet, they gave information to reporters and others to tell a global audience about what was going on in Chiapas.[23] Under political pressure, the Mexican government was forced to scale back a search for guerillas that Amnesty International called a "general brutalization" of civilians.[24] More than a one-time phenomenon, Internet mobilization is fundamental to the Zapatista strategy in their ongoing conflict with the Mexican government. A global infrastructure of websites and Internet-based communities joins journalists, academics, and advocates in support of indigenous peoples in Mexico. In essence, their use of the Internet has enabled the Zapatistas to convert a struggle of force that they were unlikely to win into a struggle of words that they are far more likely to win.

There are many other ways in which the Internet is enhancing the expression of dissent by the repressed. The editors of independent news sites in nondemocratic nations are true heroes fighting for freedom at great risk to themselves. Cuba, for example, has an estimated one hundred independent reporters regularly posting local news on foreign websites at risk of receiving a twenty-year sentence for associating with foreign media.[25] Even for organizations without an explicit political agenda, the Internet may be their sole hope for survival in a repressive regime. Indeed, after being repressed since 1999 for violating tenets of atheism, the Chinese spiritual movement Falun Gong relies almost exclusively on Internet interaction.[26] Focused on breathing exercises and made more political by repression, Falun Gong has transformed itself from a top-down organization to a decentralized organization that is well suited to the Internet architecture.

INTERNET IN WAR

In wartime, the Internet may be the last channel of communication remaining after others have been destroyed. It is relatively easy to attack a television or radio station. These traditional outlets may be co-opted by the government for its own purposes. In contrast, the decentralization of the Internet makes it a difficult target for the military to destroy. The Internet can stand as an outlet available to ordinary citizens during wartime. They can share information that can counterbalance the official government line. Ordinary Iraqis, for instance, would have been better able to assess the claims of Saddam Hussein that Iraq was winning the 1991 Gulf War conflict if the Internet had been available. Reports from the countryside about the process of bombings could counter official government information. Not surprisingly, getting news about the location of bombings was to become the main use of the Internet in the first war in which a significant population had access to the Internet.

This first significant use of the Internet in wartime occurred in 1999 in Kosovo. Attempting to stop the genocide of ethnic Albanians by Bosnian Serbs, international forces bombed Serbia for months. The Serbians at the time were fairly advanced technologically and had a strong Internet infrastructure. Thus, as bombings continued, the Serbian people used the Internet to disseminate information about the progress of the war. In addition to the inevitable rumors, reports about the bombings had accurate and detailed information from ordinary citizens. The accuracy was possible in part because the citizens were in the best position to chronicle the bombings. The decentralized nature of Internet communication meant that many were describing a bombing that occurred nearby. This information would often stand in contrast to what the Serbian government was reporting. Unlike the Iraqis in the Gulf War, the Serbs were under no illusion about who was winning the war. Symbolic of the resilience of the Internet compared to traditional media is that when the major independent radio station was shut down, it was able to continue broadcasting over the Internet.

The information had an enthusiastic audience among Serbians. The reporting of bombings was the main reason that participation in chat rooms during the war was six times greater than before the war.[27] The Serbian audience for this information included those remaining in Serbia plus Serbians who had fled the country. The latter were able to use the Internet to reunite with family and friends outside of Serbia. The posting of names and locations on the Internet was an effective way to determine who had survived or escaped.

The audience outside Serbia, however, was largely disinterested. This is definitely not a parallel to the ability of the indigenous peoples in the Chiapas to inspire a global audience to take action. A large international force was attacking Serbia in an effort to put an end to a Serbian-perpetrated genocide. Information disseminated about bombing damage, therefore, was unlikely to generate sympathy from an international audience. Deana Srajber captured the futility felt by those in Serbia: "With the Internet we have the means of telling the world about how we feel . . . [but] the frustrating part is that the world seems not to care how we feel."[28]

GOVERNMENT PROPAGANDA OVER THE INTERNET

Whether in wartime or not, governments may try to use the Internet as a tool for political propaganda. For a government limiting political freedom, a government website is not a particularly useful addition to other state-run media. A state-run website must inevitably compete with other opportunities for information over the Internet. In contrast, state-run monopolies in television, radio, or newspaper seldom encounter the vigorous competition present on the Internet. Traditional media, therefore, are a far more effective means of propaganda than a website.

Although less effective than state-run monopolies in the traditional media, government websites will be used by repressive governments to dispense propaganda. Little of this propaganda is probably consumed domestically, because there is little incentive for citizens to pay the high price of Internet access to find another manifestation of the state-run news source. Thus, the propaganda on government websites is presented mostly for the benefit of an international audience. This is a highly skeptical international audience, of course. There is, however, little downside to a promotional government website, and these sites are regularly maintained by repressive governments.

As part of the Internet propaganda effort, a repressive government may wish to create the impression that it listens to ordinary citizens. In 1998, for instance, China set up an Internet forum to solicit public opinion on an upcoming five-year plan. Government officials were pleased to receive over a thousand comments in the first week. The vast majority of these comments were positive statements about government performance. A forum rule prohibited comments in opposition to the government.[29]

The propaganda ideal for a repressive government would be to have ordinary citizens voluntarily use the Internet to express opinions consistent with the official government position. It's not easy to do, but it can be very effective. Information gained from traditional state-run media might be retransmitted by ordinary citizens over the Internet in a way that looks more spontaneous than if it were government led. An example of this is the outpouring of emotion on the Internet in China following the death of pilot Wang Wei. Using information from state-run media, ordinary citizens took to the Internet to express their grief and respect for the pilot who "collided" with an American spy plane in April 2001. For ordinary Chinese, the pilot became a martyr in cyberspace. The genuine emotion transmitted online was far more effective than what the Chinese government could have produced on its own.[30]

The propaganda effort is typically complemented by a broader government reliance on the Internet. Often, Internet restrictions have been targeted at the private sector, while government entities are encouraged to use the Internet. Repressive governments are very likely to be wired and transmit government business over the Internet. These governments will want to take advantage of the increase in efficiency provided by the Internet. Symbolic of this is the disparity between government and private use of the Internet in nations limiting political freedom. In Saudi Arabia, for instance, the expansive period of the late 1990s resulted in government entities having a 75 percent likelihood of being on the Internet compared to the 30 percent likelihood of private sector businesses being online.[31] Allowing the Internet to be used by the government sector, including state-run businesses, is a fairly easy way to pursue economic growth without altering broader political and social realities.

CONCLUSION

The Internet poses a strong threat to governments limiting political freedom. It jeopardizes the government monopoly on information and provides a means for opponents to mobilize. Thus, repressive governments have tried to build walls to limit competing influences. A need to use the Internet in commerce and the nature of technology mean that the walls will not be perfect. The Internet will remain a potential tool for the opposition. In most cases, the Internet has not led to dramatic change. There are, however, important ways in which the Internet is changing politics. The Internet is often quietly improving information dissemination. It also can facilitate mobilization. Overall, these changes are more dramatic in repressive governments than in democracies. While democracies have a variety of available means of information dissemination and mobilization, the Internet may be the only option in nations limiting political freedom. Guo Long, researcher at the Chinese Academy of Social Sciences, captures well the reason for greater change in nondemocracies: "The Internet will affect China more deeply than other societies because China is a closed society and the Internet is an open technology."[32]

Conclusion

Net Gain for Democracy

In a crucial early moment of Internet politics, the U.S. government acted as if the Internet were literally alien to politics. In 1992, a measure to lift the prohibition on commercial traffic on the Internet was added to legislation on NASA funding. The Internet-related measure received little attention compared to other aspects of the bill. Floor debate in the Senate centered on whether the United States should continue funding a project that regularly monitored the skies for aliens. Internet politics and aliens will forever share some history. Politics, however, has never been alien to the Internet.

INALIENABLE POLITICAL ESSENCE

Politics is inseparable from Internet communication. The Internet began within the Department of Defense. Many early developments from e-mail to the expansion of the network were done by or at the behest of the U.S. government. As government gave up actual oversight of the network, it shifted into a more familiar role of regulator. In that capacity, government has continued to affect how people communicate on the Internet. This role persists despite a long-standing ethos that government should leave the Internet alone. While some advocate for government non-intervention, there are more who ask the government to do something about the Internet. Government continues to be involved with the Internet because people ask it to get involved.

With the significant exception of tax measures, Congress has frequently acted to regulate the Internet. Congress has passed laws regulating matters from pornography to privacy. Congress has passed sweeping legislation on several occasions to regulate content on the Internet. In 1996, the Communications Decency Act prohibited the transmission of any "indecent" communication to minors on the Internet. In 1998, the Child Online Protection Act prohibited using the World Wide Web to transmit communication that was "harmful to minors." Both measures had substantial criminal penalties, including jail time. The ultimate impact of content legislation, however, has been muted by the intervention of the courts, which have applied traditional First Amendment protection to the Internet.

Despite the willingness of Congress to act, the alien legacy can be seen in a lack of serious debate on Internet issues. Most early Internet legislation was enacted without serious debate. The allowing of commercial traffic was part of a NASA bill. The Communications Decency Act was a late addition to the Telecommunications Act of 1996, a monumental piece of legislation in development for years. The Child Online Protection Act, thought dead, found new life when attached to a $0.5 trillion must-pass appropriations bill. The Anti-Cybersquatting Act of 1999 was added to a satellite technology bill that was folded into a massive appropriations bill. Much of this legislation was passed without any significant hearings or fact finding. Although government has never been alien to the Internet, policy-makers have been reluctant to recognize the role of government or at least talk about it. Whether it wants to talk about it or not, government plays an important role in shaping the environment of Internet communication.

The politics of Internet communication, however, entails more than government setting rules for communication. Crucial to the health of a democracy, mobilization and information dissemination are facilitated by the Internet. Political parties and interest groups of all viewpoints and resource levels are using the Internet. The website is now a fundamental part of campaigns for public office. Government has benefited from gains in efficiency and openness. The amount of information available from journalists has increased. Citizens are empowered. The Internet represents a net gain for democracy.

Despite the gains for democracy, Internet politics is still awkward. There is no reason to believe that political leaders will be the first or best at using a new technology. Politicians can be slow to learn. Legally, the Internet poses challenges. The allocation of domain names in a global spectrum leads to competing claims from multiple jurisdictions. The legal system faces the constant challenge of ascertaining location and identity. The end result is that we get a quirky Internet politics. That is part of what makes Internet politics so fascinating. The existence of vote trading, spam victim contests, friendly Web page users, cybersquatting, and flash campaigns gives vitality to Internet politics.

ICANN

Symbolic of the uneven nature of the Internet's promotion of democracy is the experience of the Internet Corporation for Assigned Names and Numbers

(ICANN). As described in chapter 11, ICANN is the international body established to oversee administration of domain names. It formally replaced the government-conferred monopoly Network Solutions, Inc., in 1999. Much of what ICANN does is technical work distributing registration responsibility so as to ensure growth and avoid duplicate registrations.

Consistent with its technical nature, ICANN governance started as a closed group of experts. The board met in closed meetings to discuss issues. Members were chosen by the Department of Commerce based on the recommendation of major figures in the development of the Internet. When the board decided to expand, the first expansion was scheduled to be representatives from various sectors of Internet technology, such as browsers, semiconductors, and servers. The board came under criticism for its closed decision-making process.

As 2000 progressed, the pressure to change the method of voting grew. The appointment of the industry representatives was canceled. In its place, the board agreed to have the broader public assume a role in membership selection. Ultimately, the plan announced would have all members chosen by the public. This would be phased in gradually. At the outset, the nine existing members would remain in power. They would be joined by nine members selected by the people. The first five would be selected in elections held in October 2000. To avoid a North American bias, the board would have equal representation by continent.

The 2000 ICANN board elections constitute a landmark event in the history of the Internet if not politics more broadly. Elections were held in which every person in the world was theoretically eligible to vote directly for representatives to a worldwide governance authority. Typically, representatives to worldwide governance authorities are appointed. Americans, for instance, have never seen their UN representative on the ballot. The UN representative was appointed by the president. Nor has anyone in the world seen the name of the Secretary-General of the UN on the ballot. The Secretary-General is an appointee of one country's government and is later elected by the appointed UN representatives. For ICANN elections, however, a worldwide electorate saw names of candidates on the ballot and directly voted for representatives.

Within a decade of its existence, the Web had prompted the creation of a true worldwide electorate. Anyone in the world was eligible to vote as long as they met the requirements for voter registration. First, the person had to be at least 16 years of age. Second, the person had to have an e-mail account. Third, to reduce duplication and provide a link to the "real" world, the person had to have a postal address to which the access code for voting would be mailed. Even with the socioeconomic bias of the e-mail address requirement, the potential electorate was enormous and diverse. When the registration period concluded, however, only 76,500 people had registered. Voter apathy is not new to democracy.

The landmark election had its share of technical glitches, but did conclude as scheduled. The campaign for ICANN membership, not surprisingly, was contested online through debates and chat sessions. The main issue in the election was

ICANN itself, especially the extent to which its membership was dominated by commercial interests. Candidates varied from people who were harshly critical of ICANN to those who were generally supportive. Registered voters could vote anytime from October 1 to 10 using a code received by mail. The first few days of the election exposed problems with online voting. The system had significant glitches, and there were difficulties accessing the site. The problems diminished over the election period, and ultimately 34,000 of 76,500 registered voters cast a ballot.[1] In the hotly contested North American contest, an ICANN critic wanting to fire the ICANN president handily defeated those more supportive of ICANN.

Although these elections constituted a landmark for global democracy, they did not parallel exactly the democratic principle of one person, one vote. First, the principle of equal weighting of votes is violated by any electoral system in which representation is based on geographic areas not adjusted for population. Less-populated continents received the same representation as more heavily populated continents. Second, there were qualifications for voting in addition to age. Voters were required to have an e-mail account, which skewed the worldwide electorate in favor of the socioeconomically advanced. Third, the members elected by the global electorate were added to a board that had some members elected by other means. Those divergences from textbook models of modern democracy, however, do not diminish the importance of the global election. Time would tell whether ICANN would build on this democratic milestone.

A preliminary answer came quickly. Frustrated by the election of critics and on-line voting glitches, the ICANN board suspended the next round of public elections. In March 2002, ICANN formally ended direct elections and replaced them with appointments from public and private institutions. Membership would return to the experts. The act spurred protests. The board reiterated its commitment to ending popular elections. Democracy can be uncomfortable.

The experience of ICANN symbolizes the implications of the Internet for democracy. It shows the flashes of amazing potential. In a few short years, the Web had prompted the creation of a true worldwide electorate. Yet, the ICANN experience shows the difficulty of sustaining the flashes of heightened democratic activity. Sustaining this activity is especially difficult when people are used to doing things in another way. Instilling new Internet habits will take time. Internet time occurs in the context of ordinary time. As with the building of ICANN, a lot of democratic politics is the slow building of institutions. The Internet's ability to facilitate information dissemination and mobilization will assist in this process.

FUTURE VIEWS

Although it will be awkward, the Internet will ultimately strengthen democracy. Whether this will constitute a "revolutionary" change depends on semantics and a lot more time. At this stage, however, it is clear that the evidence of substantial information dissemination and mobilization is strong. Over time, technology may change our interface with the Internet, but the globally networked nature of the Internet guarantees its use for information dissemination and mobilization.

As the Internet increasingly becomes part of life, the Internet is destined to grow as a political issue. The importance of its use in politics is growing. It is more integrated into the lives of people. The number of cyberlaw cases continues to grow. These issues will be debated in domestic and international environments. The conception of the Internet as alien to politics surely will fade. It will become more difficult to ignore the politics of Internet communication.

Notes

INTRODUCTION

1. C-SPAN, Speech at American University, 10 January 2002.
2. M. H. Aylesworth, "Radio's Accomplishment: The Part It May Play in National and International Affairs," *The Century Magazine,* June 1929, 214–21.
3. Paul F. Lazarsfeld, *Radio and the Printed Page: An Introduction to the Study of Radio and Its Role in the Communication of Ideas* (New York: Duell, Sloan, and Pearce, 1940), 172.
4. Christopher Harper, *And That's the Way It Will Be: News and Information in a Digital World* (New York: New York University Press, 1998), 3.
5. NBC, "The Tonight Show with Jay Leno," 17 June 2003.

CHAPTER 1

1. Federal Networking Council, "FNC Resolution: Definition of 'Internet,'" 24 October 1995, at www.itrd.gov/fnc/Internet_res.html.
2. *Reno* v. *ACLU,* 521 US 844, 849 (1997).
3. Robert H. Reid, *Architects of the Web: 1,000 Days That Built the Future of Business* (New York: Wiley, 1997), 16, 38.
4. Thomas A. Watson, *Exploring Life: The Autobiography of Thomas A. Watson* (New York: Appleton, 1926), 79.
5. "The Story of the First News Message Ever Sent by Telegraph," *The Century Magazine,* July 1888, 475; Tom Standage, *The Victorian Internet: The Remarkable Story of the Telegraph and the Nineteenth Century's On-line Pioneers* (New York: Walker, 1998), 46–53.
6. Watson, *Exploring Life,* 111.
7. PBS, "Nerds 2.01: A Brief History of the Internet [Documentary by Robert Cringely]," 25 November 1998.

8. Barry M. Leiner et al., "A Brief History of the Internet," at isoc.org/internet/history/brief.shtml (accessed February 2003).

9. PBS, "Nerds 2.01."

10. R. T. Griffiths, "Internet for Historians, History of the Internet, E-mail, Newsgroups, and Lists," at let.leidenuniv.nl/history/ivh/chap3.htm (accessed February 2003).

11. Leiner et al., "A Brief History."

12. Robert E. Kahn and Vinton G. Cerf, "What is the Internet (and What Makes it Work)?" at internetpolicy.org/briefing/12_99_story.html (accessed February 2002).

13. Bill Stewart, "NSFNet," livinginternet.com/i/ii_nsfnet.htm (accessed January 2002).

14. Richard Bryan, *Congressional Record,* 7 October 1992, S17395.

15. Tim Berners-Lee, *Weaving the Web: The Original Design and Ultimate Destiny of the World Wide Web by Its Inventor* (New York: HarperCollins, 1999), 50.

16. Herb Brody, "The Web Maestro: An Interview with Tim Berners-Lee," *Technology Review,* July 1996, 33–42.

17. Reid, *Architects,* 7.

18. Reuters, "Web's First Image Gets Retired," *MSNBC News,* 12 March 2001, at msnbc.com/news/540664.asp.

CHAPTER 2

1. Pew Research Center for the People and the Press, "The Internet News Audience Goes Ordinary," 14 January 2000, at people-press.org/techn98sum.htm.

2. Pew Internet & American Life Project, *Who's Not Online: 57% of Those without Internet Access Say They Do Not Plan to Log On* (Washington, D.C.: Pew Internet & American Life Project, 2000), 16.

3. Department of Commerce, *A Nation Online: How Americans Are Expanding Their Use of the Internet* (Washington, D.C.: Department of Commerce, 2002), 44.

4. Department of Commerce, *Nation Online,* 43.

5. Department of Commerce, *Falling Through the Net: Toward Digital Inclusion* (Washington, D.C.: Department of Commerce, 2000), 47.

6. National Center for Education Statistics (NCES), *Internet Access in U.S. Public Schools and Classrooms: 1994–2000* (Washington, D.C.: Department of Education, 2001), 2.

7. John Carlo Bertot and Charles R. McClure, *The 1998 National Survey of U.S. Public Library Outlet Internet Connectivity: Final Report* (Washington, D.C.: U.S. National Commission on Libraries and Information Science, 1999), 1; NCES, *Internet Access,* 2.

8. Bertot and McClure, *1998 National Survey,* 2.

9. David Birdsell, Douglas Muzzio, David Krane, and Amy Cottreau, "Web Users Are Looking More Like America," *The Public Perspective,* April–May 1998, 33–35.

10. Norman T. Mineta, preface to *Falling Through the Net: Toward Digital Inclusion* by Department of Commerce (Washington, D.C.: Department of Commerce, 2000).

11. Donald L. Evans, introduction to *A Nation Online: How Americans Are Expanding Their Use of the Internet* by Department of Commerce (Washington, D.C.: Department of Commerce, 2002).

12. Pew Research Center for the People and the Press, "Public's News Habits Little Changed by September 11," 9 June 2002, at people-press.org/reports/print.php3?ReportID=156.

13. The parsimonious logit model of age, education, and income correctly predicts whether a person uses the Internet 77 percent of the time. Controlling for age and income, those whose last year of education completed is less than a high school degree, a high school degree, and some college are 6 percent, 16 percent, and 38 percent, respectively, less likely to be Internet users than college graduates. Controlling for age and education, those making under $10,000, $10,000–$30,000, and $30,000–$50,000 are 19 percent, 23 percent, and 55 percent, respectively, less likely to be Internet users than those making above $50,000. The β for age is −.045, and all variables are significant at the .001 level (income disclosure refusal category not reported). Results are based on author analysis of the Pew Research Center for the People and the Press, "Biennial Media Consumption, 2002," Data Set.

14. Department of Commerce, *Toward Digital Inclusion*, 8, 51.

15. Department of Commerce, *Falling through the Net: Defining the Digital Divide* (Washington, D.C.: Department of Commerce, 1999), 50.

16. Department of Commerce, *Nation Online*, 46.

17. Department of Commerce, *Nation Online*, 28.

18. Pew Internet & American Life Project, *Retired Seniors: A Fervent Few, Inspired by Family Ties* (Washington, D.C.: Pew Internet & American Life Project, 2001), 1.

19. Pew Internet, *Retired Seniors*, 12.

20. Times Mirror Center for the People and the Press, "Technology in the American Household," at democracyplace.org/~democracy/polls2.html (accessed June 1996).

21. Pew Internet, *Who's Not Online*, 2.

22. Department of Commerce, *Toward Digital Inclusion*, 65.

23. Birdsell et al., "Web Users," 33.

24. Times Mirror, "Technology," at democracyplace.org.

25. Pew Research Center for the People and the Press, "News Attracts Most Internet Users: One-in-Ten Voters Online for Campaign '96," 16 December 1996, at people-press.org/tec96–1.htm.

26. Bruce Bimber, "Toward an Empirical Map of Political Participation on the Internet" (paper presented at the annual meeting of the American Political Science Association, Boston, Mass., September 1998), 16.

27. Department of Commerce, *Defining the Digital Divide*, 49.

28. Department of Commerce, *Nation Online*, 28.

29. The number of women grew at 9 percent while the number of men grew at 3 percent. Dick Kelsey, "US Women's Net Use Grows at Triple the Rate of Men's," *Washington Post* [*Newsbytes*], 18 January 2002, at newsbytes.com/news/02/17378.html.

30. Birdsell et al., "Web Users," 33.

31. Bimber, "Empirical Map," 17.

32. Department of Commerce, *Toward Digital Inclusion*, 15.

33. Bimber, "Empirical Map," 21.

34. Politics USA, "Technology in the American Household," at PoliticsUSA.com/PoliticsUSA/news/1106ip08.html.cgi (accessed June 1996).

35. PBS, "The News Hour," 22 October 1996.

36. Ann Reilly Dowd, "The Net's Surprising Swing to the Right," *Fortune*, 10 July 1995, 113–15.

37. Department of Commerce, *Nation Online*, 28.

38. Department of Commerce, *Defining the Digital Divide*, 30.

39. Department of Commerce, *Nation Online*, 10.

40. Everett M. Rogers, *Diffusion of Innovations* (New York: Free Press, 1995), 42–43.

41. Department of Commerce, *Toward Digital Inclusion,* 3.

42. Adapted from aggregate data on households and household presence. Department of Commerce, *Historical Statistics of the United States: Colonial Times to 1970* (Washington D.C.: GPO, 1975), 43, 796.

43. Estimates for 1902 are based on projected ratios of number of telephones per 1,000 persons to households controlling for average household size. The year 1902 showed a 30 percent gain from 1901 as the number of telephones went from 23 per 1,000 people to 30 per 1,000 people. The average household was about 4.7 members in 1902, but some had multiple telephones. Telephone growth slowed in the period surrounding the world wars. In 1920, telephones were in 35 percent of households. In 1940, they were in only 37 percent of households. Telephones also had a long exclusive period, going from one telephone per 1,000 persons in 1880 to five telephones per 1,000 persons in 1895.

44. U.S. Census Bureau, *Statistical Abstract of the United States,* 96th ed. (Washington, D.C.: U.S. Census Bureau, 1975), 518.

45. U.S. Census Bureau, *Statistical Abstract of the United States,* 110th ed. (Washington, D.C.: U.S. Census Bureau, 1990), 550.

46. *The World Almanac and Book of Facts* (New York: World Almanac Books, 2002), 280.

47. Pew Internet, *Who's Not Online,* 11.

48. Department of Commerce, *Defining the Digital Divide,* 38.

49. National Cable & Telecommunications Association, "Industry Statistics," at ncta.com/industry_overview/indStats.cfm?statID=14 (accessed February 2002).

50. Pew Research Center for the People and the Press, "Technology in the American Household: Survey Methodology," at people-press.org/tectop.htm (accessed January 2002).

51. Department of Commerce, *Toward Digital Inclusion,* 24.

52. Department of Commerce, *Nation Online,* 39.

CHAPTER 3

1. NBC, "The Tonight Show with Jay Leno," 7 February 2002.

2. Katie Hafner, "Billions Served Daily, and Counting," *New York Times,* 6 December 2001, p. G1.

3. Pew Internet & American Life Project, "Daily Internet Activities," at pewinternet.org/reports (accessed May 2001).

4. Pew Research Center for the People and the Press, "News Attracts Most Internet Users: One-in-Ten Voters Online for Campaign '96," 16 December 1996, at people-press.org/tec96-1.htm.

5. Department of Commerce, *A Nation Online: How Americans Are Expanding Their Use of the Internet* (Washington, D.C.: Department of Commerce, 2002), 65.

6. Andy Wang, "Giving Up the Day Job to Trade Online," *MSNBC News,* at msnbc.com/news/181975.asp (accessed December 1998).

7. Pew Internet & American Life Project, *Women Surpass Men as E-Shoppers during the Holidays: 2001 Sees More E-Commerce, and More Online Socializing* (Washington, D.C.: Pew Internet & American Life Project, 2002), 3–4.

8. Pew Internet & American Life Project, *Getting Serious Online* (Washington, D.C.: Pew Internet & American Life Project, 2002), 21.

9. Pew Internet & American Life Project, *The Online Health Care Revolution: How the Web Helps Americans Take Better Care of Themselves* (Washington, D.C.: Pew Internet & American Life Project, 2000), 13.

10. Council for Excellence in Government, "E-Government: The Next American Revolution," at excelgov.org/egovppoll/datasets/final1.htm (accessed October 2000).

11. Department of Commerce, *Nation Online,* 58.

12. P. J. Huffstutter and Robin Fields, "A Virtual Revolution in Teaching," *Los Angeles Times,* 3 March 2000, p. A1.

13. Pew Internet & American Life Project, *Cyberfaith: How Americans Pursue Religion Online* (Washington, D.C.: Pew Internet & American Life Project, 2001), 2.

14. Aaron Schatz, "Britney Spears: The Web's Most Wanted 2000," 26 December 2000, at lycos.com.

15. Cheryl W. Thompson, "FBI Cracks Child Porn Ring Based on Internet," *Washington Post,* 19 March 2002, p. A2.

16. Philip Elmer-Dewitt, "Cyberporn: On a Screen Near You," *Time,* 3 July 1995, 38–42.

17. Charles Grassley, *Congressional Record,* 26 June 1995, S9017.

18. Donna L. Hoffman and Thomas P. Novak, "A Detailed Critique of the *Time* Article," at hotwired.lycos.com/special/pornscare/hoffman.html (accessed March 2002).

19. Philip Elmer-Dewitt, "Fire Storm on the Computer Nets: A New Study of Cyberporn, Reported in a *Time* Cover Story, Sparks Controversy," *Time,* 24 July 1995, 57.

20. NUA.com, "Alexa Research: Most Popular Search Terms Revealed," at nua.ie/surveys (accessed March 2002).

21. National School Boards Association, "Study Inflates On-line Porn Numbers," *Electronic School,* September 1995, at electronic-school.com/0995ew2.html.

22. Alan Boyle, "Web Growth Outpaces Search Engines," *MSNBC News,* at msnbc.com/news/287392.asp (accessed July 1999).

23. Pew Internet, *Getting Serious,* 20.

24. Stanford Institute for the Quantitative Study of Society (SIQSS), "Internet and Society: A Preliminary Report," 17 February 2000, at www.stanford.edu/group/siqss/Press_Release/Preliminary_Report.pdf.

25. Robert Kraut, Sara Kiesler, Bonka Boneva, Jonathon Cummings, Vicki Helgeson, and Anne Crawford, "Internet Paradox Revisited," *Journal of Social Issues* 58, no. 1 (January 2002): 49–74.

26. Associated Press, "Nearly 6 Percent of Internet Users Are Addicted to It, Study Finds," *St. Louis-Post Dispatch* [online], 23 August 1999, at stlnet.com/postnet.

27. Amy Harmon, "Researchers Find Sad, Lonely World in Cyberspace," *New York Times* [online], 28 August 1998, at nytimes.com/library/tech/98/08/biztech/articles/30depression.html.

28. Robert Kraut, Michael Patterson, Vicki Lundmark, Sara Kiesler, Tridas Mukopadhyay, and William Scherlis, "Internet Paradox: A Social Technology That Reduces Social Involvement and Psychological Well-Being?" *American Psychologist* 53, no. 9 (September 1998): 1017–31.

29. Kraut et al., "Internet Paradox," 1029.

30. SIQSS, "Internet and Society," stanford.edu.

31. SIQSS, "Internet and Society," stanford.edu.

32. Rebecca Fairley Raney, "Study Finds Internet of Social Benefit to Users," *New York Times,* 11 May 2000, p. G7.

33. SIQSS, "Internet and Society," stanford.edu.

34. SIQSS, "Internet and Society," stanford.edu.

35. Raney, "Study Finds Internet," G7.

36. Raney, "Study Finds Internet," G7.

37. Kraut et al., "Revisited," 62.

38. Kraut et al., "Revisited," 68.

39. David W. Moore, "Americans Say Internet Makes Their Lives Better," *The Gallup Poll Monthly,* February 2000, 45.

40. SIQSS, "Internet and Society," stanford.edu.

41. UCLA Center for Communication Policy, *Surveying the Digital Future* (Los Angeles: UCLA, 2003), 33.

42. Robert Putnam, *Bowling Alone* (New York: Simon & Schuster, 2000), 216–46.

43. Kristi Essick, "Web Surfers versus TV Watchers: Who's Lazier?" *CNN Interactive,* 14 August 1998, at cnn.com/tech/computing/9808/14/potatonet.idg.

44. Douglas A. Ferguson and Elizabeth M. Perse, "The World Wide Web as a Functional Alternative to Television," *Journal of Broadcasting & Electronic Media* 44, no. 2 (Spring 2000): 155–74.

45. Pew Research Center for the People and the Press, "Internet Sapping Broadcast News Audience," 11 June 2000, at people-press.org/media00rpt.htm.

46. Democracy Online Project, "Post-Election 2000 Survey on Internet Use for Civics and Politics," at democracyonline.org/databank/dec2000survey.shtml (accessed December 2000).

47. Richard Davis, *The Web of Politics: The Internet's Impact on the American Political System* (New York: Oxford University Press, 1999), 183.

48. Pew Research Center for the People & the Press, "Public's News Habits Little Changed by September 11," 9 June 2002, at people-press.org/reports/print.php3?Report ID=156.

49. Putnam, *Bowling Alone,* 18–24.

50. David M. Anderson, "Cautious Optimism about Online Politics and Citizenship," in *The Civic Web: Online Politics and Democratic Values,* ed. David M. Anderson and Michael Cornfield (Lanham, Md.: Rowman & Littlefield, 2003), 30.

51. No variable reaches the .05 level of significance on chi-square tests for all three activities or in logistic regression for all three activities where independent variables in the logistic regression are limited to the categories specified in table 3.2.

CHAPTER 4

1. Bill Clinton, "Remarks at MIT 1998 Commencement," 5 June 1998, at www.pub.whitehouse.gov.

2. Associated Press, "Clinton Aims to Alleviate Digital Divide," *New York Times* [online], 4 April 2000, at nytimes.com/tech/articles/05clinton-divide.html.

3. James Berstenzang and Matea Gold, "Gore Sets as Goal High-Speed Internet Access for All Homes," *Los Angeles Times,* 16 February 2000, p. A16.

4. Maria Cantwell, "Cantwell 2000," at cantwell2000.com (accessed October 2000).

5. "Debate Over 'Gore Tax' Heats Up," *Tech Law Journal,* 4 June 1998, at techlaw journal.com/telecom/80604.htm.

6. "Debate Heats Up," techlawjournal.com.

7. Dick Armey, "Armey Sharply Criticizes FCC for Increasing Gore Tax on Telephone Users," 27 May 1999, at freedom.house.gov/library/technology/pr9902527.

8. Clinton, "Remarks," whitehouse.gov.

9. David Kennard, "Remarks at the EdLiNC Press Conference," 5 May 1999, at www.fcc.gov/Speeches/Kennard/spwek917.html.

10. Joe Lieberman, "$650,000 to Provide Internet Access in Connecticut Schools, Libraries, and Districts," at lieberman2000.com/erate.htm (accessed September 2000).

11. Charles Robb, "Improving Our Schools," at robb2000.org/record/rec-edu.html (accessed October 2000).

12. *Texas Office of Public Utility Counsel* v. *FCC,* 183 F 3d 393, 440 (5th Cir 1999).

13. Adam Thierer, "GWB's 'Gore Tax,'" 4 April 2001, at nationalreview.com/comment/comment-thierer040401.shtml.

14. National Center for Education Statistics (NCES), *Internet Access in U.S. Public Schools and Classrooms: 1994–2000* (Washington, D.C.: Department of Education, 2001), 4.

15. NCES, "How Much Progress Have Public Schools Made in Connecting to the Internet?" at www.nces.ed.gov/pubs2001/InternetAccess/2.asp (accessed December 2001).

16. Benton Foundation, "Study Finds E-Rate Is Achieving Its Goal of Building Internet Framework for 21st-Century Schools," 2 March 2000, at benton.org/e-rate/pressrelease.html.

17. Robin Clewley, "California Schools Get Hooked," *Wired News,* 10 September 2001, at wired.com/news/print/0,1294,45882,00.html.

18. Gary Chapman, "Political Agendas Have a High-Tech Ring," *Los Angeles Times,* 8 November 1999, p. C1.

19. Clewly, "California Schools," wired.com.

20. David C. Powell, "Taxing the Web: The Potential Impacts on States of the Internet Tax Freedom Act" (paper presented at the annual meeting of the American Political Science Association, Atlanta, Ga., September 1999), 7, 14.

21. Associated Press, "House Extends Net Ban," *Wired News,* 16 October 2001, at wired.com/news/politics/0,1283,47630,00.html.

22. Associated Press, "Congress Will Allow Ban on Internet Taxes to Expire," *New York Times,* 19 October 2001, p. A16.

23. *Quill Corporation* v. *North Dakota,* 504 US 298 (1992).

24. Jeri Clausing, "Foes of Internet Tax Ban Vow to Fight On," *New York Times* [online], 4 April 2000, at nytimes.com/library/tech/00/04/cyber/capital/04capital.html.

25. Associated Press, "Congress," A16.

26. Associated Press, "House Extends Net Tax Ban," *Wired News,* 16 October 2001, at wired.com/news/politics/0,1283,47630,00.html.

27. Markle Foundation, "MRKL-00.Q1: Frequency Questionnaire," at markle.org/news/_news_pressreport_index.stm (accessed January 2002).

28. Brian Krebs, "Senate Passes Two-Year Internet Tax Ban—Update," *Washington Post* [Newsbytes], 15 November 2001, at newsbytes.com/cgi-bin/ . . . story.id=172220.

29. Declan McCullagh, "UN Retreats from Email Tax," *Wired News,* 16 July 2001, at wired.com/news/politics/story/20784.html.

30. C-SPAN, "New York Senate Debate," 8 October 2000.

CHAPTER 5

1. Campaign Solutions, "Campaign 98 Internet Study," campaignstudy.org (accessed December 1998).

2. C-SPAN, "Alaska Senate Debate," 29 October 1998.

3. Pew Research Center for the People and the Press, "Internet Election News Audience Seeks Convenience, Familiar Names," 3 December 2000, at people-press.org/online00rpt.htm.

4. Jennifer Stromer-Galley, "On-Line Interaction and Why Candidates Avoid It," *Journal of Communication* 50, no. 4 (Fall 2000): 111–32.

5. Lawrence T. McGill, Andras Szanto, and Marianne Johnston, "The Voters Speak," at fac.org/publicat/campaign/lth96votespk.htm (accessed May 1997).

6. Wayne Rash Jr., *Politics on the Nets: Wiring the Political Process* (New York: Freeman, 1997), 68.

7. Thomas W. Benson, "The First E-Mail Election: Electronic Networking and the Clinton Campaign," in *Bill Clinton on Stump, State, and Stage,* ed. Stephen A. Smith (Fayetteville: University of Arkansas Press, 1994), 315–40.

8. Steve Piacente, "Politicians Riding Info Superhighway," *Post and Courier,* 27 November 1995, p. A1.

9. Mark Neumann, "Mark Neumann for Senate," at neumannforsenate.com (accessed October 1998).

10. C-SPAN, "First Presidential Debate," 6 October 1992.

11. Bradley Peniston, "Politicians Caught in a Web: Going Online Could Bring New Life to the Local Democratic Process," *The Capital,* 14 January 1996, p. A1.

12. Candidate sites were identified by a thorough search for the candidate's name in the three most popular search engines at the time. This method invariably added names to the sites provided on the national party pages and the election sites of washingtonpost.com and cnn.com. Operationalized as any mention of the opponent with the intent of placing that person in an unfavorable light, negative campaigning is identified by examining the content within the main page, issues section, biography pages, and pages accessible from opponent-alluding links on these pages.

13. The relative measure of financial disadvantage was chosen over an absolute measure to compensate for population size, although in practice the two definitions tend to identify the same candidates. In 2002, for instance, the relative definition identified fifteen financially disadvantaged candidates while an absolute definition of $3 million would have identified the same fifteen plus four candidates from small states. Figures are based on FEC-reported campaign receipts.

14. Dave D'Alessio, "Adoption of the World Wide Web by American Political Candidates, 1996–1998," *Journal of Broadcasting & Electronic Media* 44, no. 4 (Fall 2000): 556–68.

15. Rash, *Politics,* 52.

16. Stephen Ansolabehere and Shanto Iyengar, *Going Negative: How Attack Ads Shrink and Polarize the Electorate* (New York: Free Press, 1995), 9.

17. Michael Young, *American Dictionary of Campaigns and Elections* (Lanham, Md.: Hamilton Press, 1987), 60.

18. Edward Harpham, "Going On-Line: The 1998 Congressional Campaign" (paper presented at the annual meeting of the American Political Science Association, Atlanta, Ga., September 1999), 9, 13.

19. William L. Benoit, "A Functional Analysis of Political Advertising across Media," *Communication Studies* 51, no. 3 (Fall 2000): 274–95.

20. Jennifer Greer and Mark LaPointe, "Meaningful Discourse or Cyber-Fluff? An Analysis of Gubernatorial Campaign Web Sites throughout the 1998 Election Cycle" (paper presented at the annual meeting of the International Communication Association, San Francisco, Calif., May 1999), 13.

21. Jakob J. Nielsen, "A Web Site Design Expert Reviews Candidates' Sites," *New York Times* [online], 20 September 1996, at nytimes.com/search/ . . . %29.

22. Greer and LaPointe, "Meaningful Discourse," 14.

23. David A. Dulio, Donald L. Goff, and James A. Thurber, "Untangled Web: Internet Use during the 1998 Election," *PS: Political Science & Politics* 32, no. 1 (March 1999): 53–59.

24. John Kerry, "John Kerry for U.S. Senate," at kerry96.org (accessed October 1996).

25. Campaign Solutions, "Campaign," campaignstudy.org.

26. Rebecca Fairley Raney, "Former Wrestler's Campaign Got a Boost from the Internet," *New York Times* [online], 6 November 1998, at nytimes.com/library/tech/98/11/cyber/articles/06campaign.html.

27. Deborah Scoblionkov, "Georgia Spampaign Backfires," *Wired News,* 17 July 1998, at wired.com/news/print/0,1294,13815,00.html.

28. Patricia Jacobus, "Candidates Not Tapping the Net for Advertising," *CNET News.com,* 12 October 2000, at news.cnet.com/news . . . 5–200-3174543.html.

29. "Nader Win, Gore Win," at winwincampaign.org/privacy.html (accessed November 2000).

30. "Exchange and Swing a State," at voteexchange.com (accessed November 2000).

31. "Voteswap 2000," at voteswap2000.com (accessed November 2000).

32. CNN, "Exit Polls," at cnn.com/ELECTION/2000/epolls/US/P000.html (accessed January 2001).

33. Aaron Pressman, "Analysis: Internet Lessons for Campaign 2002," *CNN News,* 15 November 2002, at cnn.com/ . . . 11/15/campaign.2004.idg/index.html.

34. Pew Research, "Internet Election News," people-press.org.

35. Rebecca Fairley Raney, "Online Campaign Contributions Still a Promising Experiment," *New York Times* [online], 22 November 1998, at nytimes.com/library/tech/98/11/cyber/articles/22campaign.html.

36. Pressman, "Analysis," cnn.com.

37. Raney, "Former Wrestler's Campaign," nytimes.com.

38. Tina Kelley, "Internet Campaigns Supercharge U.S. Presidential Race," *Globe and Mail* (Toronto), 20 October 1999, p. A11.

39. Jim Drinkard, "McCain Closing in on Bush on the Balance Sheet," *USA Today,* 17 February 2000, p. A8.

40. Michael Janofsky, "Internet Helps Make Dean a Contender, *New York Times,* 5 July 2003, p. A8.

41. FEC, Advisory Opinion 1998–22.

42. FEC, Advisory Opinion 1996–2.

43. FEC, Advisory Opinion 1999–9.

44. Rebecca Fairley Raney, "Letters Ask Election Commission to Leave the Internet Alone," *New York Times* [online], 13 January 2000, at nytimes.com/library/tech/00/01/cyber/articles/13campaign.html.

45. Raney, "Letters Ask," nytimes.com.
46. FEC, Advisory Opinion 1999–17.
47. FEC, Advisory Opinion 1999–25.
48. FEC, Advisory Opinion 2000–13.
49. FEC, Advisory Opinion 2000–16.
50. Ben White, "Group Tests Impact of Online Advertising on 'Unlikely Voters,'" *Washington Post,* 21 January 2001, p. A8.
51. Rebecca Fairley Raney, "Internet Speculators Target Politicians," *New York Times* [online], 2 January 1999, at nytimes.com/library/ . . . presidents.html.
52. Melinda Wittstock, "Everyone has a Megaphone," *The Guardian* (Manchester, U.K.), 5 June 2000, p. 71.
53. Wittstock, "Megaphone," 71.
54. FEC, "Zack Exley," *Tech Law Journal,* at techlawjournal.com/agencies/fec/bush/narrative.htm (accessed August 2001).

CHAPTER 6

1. David Truman, *The Governmental Process: Political Interests and Public Opinion* (New York: Knopf, 1951), 244.
2. NBC, "The West Wing," 2 October 2002.
3. Jennifer Oldham, "Wiesenthal Center Compiles List of Hate-Based Web Sites," *Los Angeles Times,* 18 December 1997, p. A1.
4. Simon Wiesenthal Center, "Wiesenthal Center to Release 'Digital Hate 2002,'" 20 May 2002, at wiesenthal.com/social/press/pr_item.cfm?ItemID=5723.
5. Kevin Hill and John Hughes, *Cyberpolitics: Citizen Activism in the Age of the Internet* (Lanham, Md.: Rowman & Littlefield, 1998), 58, 114, 125.
6. Chris Carr, "Internet Anti-Impeachment Drive Yields Big Pledges of Money, Time," *Washington Post,* 7 February 1999, p. A9.
7. Edie Goldenberg, *Making the Papers: The Access of Resource-Poor Groups to the Metropolitan Press* (Lexington, Mass.: Lexington Books, 1975), 145.
8. Modeled after the movie Oscars with shorter acceptance remarks, the Webby Awards (webbyawards.com) are chosen by an academy of over 350 practitioners.
9. Heritage Foundation, "Dr. Edwin J. Feulner's Remarks for Town Hall Launch," 29 June 1995, at heritage.org/features/5years/kickoff.html.
10. Neil Munro, "The Electronic Lobbyist," *National Journal,* 22 April 2000, 1264–65.
11. Robert Cwiklik, "MoveOn Targets Campaign 2000 Voters: Web Fund-Raiser Tries to Revive Impeachment Angst," *Wall Street Journal,* 2 February 2000, p. A13.
12. Jeffrey M. Ayres, "Transnational Activism in the Americas: The Internet and Mobilizing Against the FTAA" (paper presented at the annual meeting of the American Political Science Association, San Francisco, Calif., August 2001), 9.
13. Sam Howe Verhovek, "Seattle Police Admit Failure in '99 Protests," *New York Times,* 5 April 2000, p. A16.
14. Ayres, "Transnational Activism," 29.
15. Patricia D. Siplon, "Acting up Globally: The Internet, AIDS, and Activism" (paper presented at the annual meeting of the American Political Science Association, San Francisco, Calif., August 2001), 27.

16. Scott Baldauf, "Nobel Laureate's Long Trip from Vermont Farm to Fame," *Christian Science Monitor,* 14 October 1997, 1.

17. Graeme Browning, "Electronic Democracy," February 1997, at onlineinc.com.

18. Michael Margolis, David Resnick, and Joel D. Wolfe, "Party Competition on the Internet in the United States and Britain," *Harvard International Journal of Press Politics* 4, no. 4 (Fall 1999): 24–47.

19. Clerk of the House of Representatives, *Statistics of the Presidential and Congressional Election of November 7, 2000* (Washington, D.C.: GPO, 2001), 74.

20. Margolis, Resnick, and Wolfe, "Party Competition," 32.

21. Leslie Wayne, "On Web, Voters Reinvent Grass-Roots Activism," *New York Times,* 21 May 2000, p. A1.

22. Mark S. Bonchek, "From Broadcast to Netcast: The Internet and the Flow of Political Information" (Ph.D. diss., Harvard University, 1997), 137–39.

23. Patricia Jacobus, "Candidates Not Tapping the Net for Advertising," *CNET,* 12 October 2000, at news.cnet.com/news . . . 5–200-317543.html.

24. Geralyn M. Miller, "Political Participation Channels on the Internet: An Empirical Analysis of American Political Party Web Sites in the States" (paper presented at the annual meeting of the Midwest Political Science Association, Chicago, Ill., April 2001), 13.

25. Rebecca F. Raney, "Flood of E-Mail Credited with Halting U.S. Bank Plan," *New York Times* [online], 24 March 1999, at nytimes.com/library/tech/99/03/cyber/articles/24email.html.

26. Parliamentary Office of Science and Technology, "Online Voting," *Postnet,* May 2001, 1.

27. Daniel Keegan, "Reform Party Online Balloting Thwarts Hackers," *CNN News,* 17 August 2000, at cnn.com/2000/tech/computing/08/17/evote.v.hackers.idg.

28. Janet Wilson, "GOP Hopes to Cast Wide Net with E-Politicking Drive," *Los Angeles Times,* 9 November 1999, p. A1.

29. Patrick McMahon, "Tolerance Ads to Infiltrate Web Sites of Hate Groups," *USA Today,* 2 April 2001, p. D9.

CHAPTER 7

1. Todd Spangler, "Mars Attacks the Web," *Internet.com,* 18 August 1997, at mars.jpl.nasa.gov/MPF/press/webweek/19970818-mars.html.

2. Council for Excellence in Government, "E-Government: The Next American Revolution [Data]," September 2000, at excelgov.org/egovppoll/datasets/final1.htm.

3. John Lancaster, "Farm Subsidy Web Site Sows Discord," *Washington Post,* 19 December 2001, p. A37.

4. Paula Shaki Trimble, "Mission to Mars Reveals Need for More Bandwidth," *Network World Fusion News,* 9 December 1999, at nwfusion.com/news/1999/1209mars.html.

5. Council for Excellence in Government, *E-Government: The Next American Revolution* (Washington, D.C.: Council for Excellence in Government, 2000), 9.

6. Media Matrix, "Top Rankings," at mediametrix.com/TopRankings (accessed June 1999).

7. Richard Davis, *The Web of Politics: The Internet's Impact on the American Political System* (New York: Oxford University Press, 1999), 136.

8. Bill Clinton, "Frequently Asked Questions," at www.whitehouse.gov/WH/html/faq.html (accessed July 1999).

9. Declan McCullagh, "Woe unto White House Site," *Wired News,* 22 May 2001, at wired.com/news/print/0,1294,43993,00.html.

10. David Friend, "Nobody Loved It Better," *Vanity Fair,* December 2000, 33.

11. Richard L. Berke, "The Last (E-Mail) Goodbye, from (gwb) to His 42 Buddies," *New York Times,* 17 March 2001, p. A1.

12. See, for example, Shawn P. McCarthy, "Fifty Government Sites Make List of Most-Visited 600," *Government Computing News,* 6 March 2000, at gcn.com/ . . . story.id=1466.

13. Darrell M. West, "State and Federal E-Government in the United States," September 2002, at insidepolitics.org.

14. "Put Washington Online," *Los Angeles Times,* 4 August 1999, p. B6.

15. William E. Moen and Charles R. McClure, "Final Report: An Evaluation of U.S. GILS Implementation," 30 June 1997, at www.access.gpo.gov/su_docs/gils/gils-eval.

16. Jeri Clausing, "U.S. to Offer Search Service that Links Its Online Sites," *New York Times* [online], 17 May 1999, at nytimes.com/library/tech/99/05/biztech/articles/17gov.html.

17. Greg R. Notess, "The Federal Web, NTIS Database, and More," *Online,* January-February 2000, 57–61.

18. Bob Woods, "Government Search Loses Uncle Sam's Clout," *Washington Post* [Newsbytes], 15 June 1999, at newsbytes.com.

19. William Matthews, "GSA Moving to Open WebGov Portal," *Federal Computer Week,* 23 June 2000, at fcn.com/fcw.

20. Christopher J. Dorobek, "Feds Plan Web Welcome Mat," *Government Computer News,* 24 August 1998, 1.

21. Frank A. Micciche, "FirstGov Web Portal to Launch by October," *GovExec.com,* 30 June 2000, at govexec.com/dailyfed/0600/063000fl.htm.

22. Dipka Bhambani, "Who's Owner of FirstGov Database? Not Uncle Sam," *Government Computer News,* 20 August 2001, at gcn.com/cgi-bin/ . . . story.id=16885.

23. Shawn P. McCarthy, "Heavy Traffic Travels to Federal Web Sites," *Government Computer News,* 30 April 2001, at gcn.com/vol20_no9/tech-report/4050–1.html.

24. Bhambani, "Who's Owner," gcn.com.

25. Jason Miller, "ISO: Search Engine for FirstGov," *Government Computer News,* 21 January 2002, at gcn.com/cgi-bin/ . . . story.id=17808.

26. West, "State and Federal," insidepolitics.org.

27. See, for example, McCarthy, "Heavy Traffic," gcn.com

28. Cheryl Lu-Lien Tan, "Government Gets Wired for Residents," *Baltimore Sun,* 1 March 1999, p. C1.

29. Tan, "Government Wired," C1.

30. Michelle Mariani, "E-Permitting 101," *Governing,* April 2001, 86.

31. Department of Information Services, "DIS Offers Citizens Greater Access in Their Government," 29 December 1997, at www.wa.gov/dis/role/news/stories/301997.htm.

32. Department of Information Services, "Governor Unveils Another First for Washington," 15 December 1997, at www.wa.gov/dis/role/news/stories/281997.htm.

33. Department of Information Services, "Governor Commemorates a National First for the State of Washington," 7 September 1998, at www.wa.gov/dis/role/news/stories/361998.htm.

34. Anne Jordan, "The World Wide Workhorse," *Governing,* April 1999, 52.

35. Dibya Sarkar, "Site Eases Adoption Process," *Federal Computer Week,* 15 February 2002, at fcw.com/geb/articles/2002/0211/web-adopt-02-15-02.asp.

36. George Pataki, "New York Introduces Physician Profile Web Site," *Government Technology,* 15 February 2002, at www.govtech.net/news.

37. *Connecticut Department of Safety* v. *Doe,* 123 S.Ct. 1160 (2003).

38. E. Scott Adler, Chariti E. Gent, and Cary B. Overmeyer, "The Home Style Homepage: Legislator Use of the World Wide Web for Constituency Contact" (paper presented at the annual meeting of the American Political Science Association, Washington, D.C., August 1997), 12; Patrick Barkham, "Parliament Online," *The Guardian* (Manchester, U.K.), 13 May 1999, p. O2.

39. Ralph Nader and Gary Rushkin, "Congress Pulls the Shades on Net: If Members are so Proud of What They Do, They Ought to Post Their Voting Records Clearly on the Net," *Los Angeles Times,* 30 November 1999, p. A9.

40. Richard Davis, *Web of Politics,* 131.

41. John P. Messmer, "Early Politics on the World Wide Web: Congressional Communication on the Internet" (paper presented at the annual meeting of the American Political Science Association, Washington, D.C., August 1997), 10.

42. Adler, Gent, and Overmeyer, "Home Style Homepage," 13, 19.

43. Preeti Vasishtha, "House Sees E-mail Spike," *Government Computing News,* 5 November 2001, at gcn.com/cgi-bin/ . . . story.id=17449.

44. Thomas Edsall, "In Congress, They've Got Mail—Far Too Much of It," *Washington Post,* 19 March 2001, p. A5.

45. Jason Miller, "With Mail Safety Still Iffy, Hill Upgrades E-mail," *Government Computing News,* 7 January 2002, at gcn.com/cgi-bin/ . . . story.id=17720.

46. Jonathan Krim, "House Makes a Plea to Keep BlackBerrys," *Washington Post,* 17 January 2003, p. E1.

47. Timothy C. Barmann, "Weaving Political Webs: Does Promotional Material Belong on State Sites?" *Providence Journal-Bulletin,* 25 October 1998, p. J1.

48. Progress & Freedom Foundation, "Digital State 1998: How State Governments are Using Digital Technology," September 1998, at pff.org/digital98.html.

49. Darby Patterson, "State of the Digital State: Part II," *Government Technology,* August 2001, at govtech.net/magazine/story.phtml?id=5621&issue=08:2001.

50. Darrell M. West, "E-Government and the Transformation of Public Sector Service Delivery" (paper presented at the annual meeting of the American Political Science Association, San Francisco, Calif., August 2001), 5.

51. West, "State and Federal," insidepolitics.org.

52. Council for Excellence in Government, *E-Government,* 9.

53. Council for Excellence in Government, *E-Government,* 16–17.

54. Bill Gates, "Statement before the Joint Economic Committee," 15 June 1999, at microsoft.com/billgates/speeches/06–15jointecon.asp.

55. Rachel Gibson, 2001, "Elections Online: Assessing Internet Voting in Light of the Arizona Democratic Primary," *Political Science Quarterly* 116, no. 4 (Winter 2001–2002): 561–83.

56. Associated Press, "Internet Balloting Called Success," *Washington Post,* 12 August 2001, p. A6.

57. Ben White, "Internet Voting: A Web of Intrigue," *Washington Post,* 7 March 2001, p. A21.

58. Walter R. Houser, "Government Webmasters Need Lots of Wiggle Room," *Government Computer News,* 3 August 1998, 32.

59. *Armstrong* v. *Executive Office of the President,* 1 F 3d 1274, 1283 (DC Cir 1993).

60. J. Robert Oppenheimer, *Science and the Common Understanding: Reith Lectures BBC* (New York: Simon and Schuster, 1954), 94–95.

61. Katie Dean, "Let the Documents Go Free," *Wired News,* 28 June 1999, at wired.com/news/news/politics/story/20461.html.

62. West, "State and Federal," insidepolitics.org.

63. Department of Justice, *Freedom of Information Act Guide* (Washington, D.C.: Department of Justice, 1998), 3.

64. Department of Justice, *Freedom,* 3.

65. J. Timothy Sprehe, "EFOIA: Mixed Bag of Access Benefits and Legal Loopholes," *Federal Computer Week,* 6 January 1997, at fcw.com/fcw/articles/1997/FCW_010697_10.asp.

66. Jennifer Lafleur, "EFOIA Pluses: Getting Electronic Data Still Tough, But Some Internet Sites Are Good Resources," *The Quill,* September 1998, 28–29.

67. *Tozzi* v. *Environmental Protection Agency,* 1998 US Dist Lexis 6234 (DDC 1998).

68. Gregory Slabodkin, "Defense Wipes Sensitive Data from Its Web Sites," *Government Computer News,* 12 October 1998, 6.

69. Bob Brewin and Daniel Verton, "DoD Leaders Mull Internet Disconnect," *Federal Computer Week,* 19 April 1999, at fcw.com/fcw/articles/1999/FCW_041999_337.asp.

70. Patricia Daukantas and Preeti Vasishtha, "New World Order Pits Security against Web," *Government Computing News,* 4 February 2002, at gcn.com/cgi-bin/ . . . story.id=17913.

71. David Colker, "The Web Never Forgets," *Los Angeles Times,* 27 November 2001, p. A1.

72. Daukantas and Vasishtha, "New World Order," gcn.com.

73. Bill Clinton, Executive Order 13011, 17 July 1996.

CHAPTER 8

1. The largest paper in each state is based on daily subscription, as reported in the *Working Press of the Nation* (New York: Farrell, 2002). Ties in circulation are broken in favor of the newspaper covering the highest-population metropolitan area.

2. Don Middleberg and Steven S. Ross, *The Media in Cyberspace Study: 1998 Fifth Annual National Survey* (New York: Euro RSCG Middleberg, 1998), 3.

3. Don Middleberg and Steven S. Ross, *The Media in Cyberspace III: A National Survey* (New York: Euro RSCG Middleberg, 1996), 3.

4. Chip Brown, "Fear.com," *American Journalism Review,* June 1999, 50–71.

5. Pew Research Center for the People and the Press, "One-in-Ten Voters Online for Campaign '96," 16 December 1996, at people-press.org/tec96sum.htm.

6. Alan Boyle, "PoliticsNow Vanishes from the Web," *MSNBC News,* 7 March 1997, at msnbc.com/news/60131.asp.

7. Rusty Coats, "Reflections from the Subscription-Site Pioneers," *The Digital Edge,* October 2001, at naa.org/TheDigitalEdge/DigArtPage.cfm?AID=3201.

8. Borrell & Associates, "Newspapers Report Paid Online Subscribers," *The Digital Edge,* October 2001, at naa.org/TheDigitalEdge/DigArtPage.cfm?AID=3225.

9. Coats, "Reflections," naa.org.

10. Brown, "Fear.com," 50–71.

11. Borrell & Associates, "Newspapers," naa.org.

12. Christopher Harper, *And That's the Way It Will Be: News and Information in a Digital World* (New York: New York University Press, 1998), 20.

13. Don Middleberg and Steven S. Ross, "The Seventh Annual Middleberg/Ross Survey of Media in the Wired World: Executive Summary," at middleberg.com/toolsforsuccess/fulloverview.cfm (accessed March 2002).

14. Middleberg and Ross, *Media Fifth,* 14.

15. Don Middleberg and Steven S. Ross, "The Eighth Annual Middleberg/Ross Media Survey: Executive Summary," at middleberg.com/toolsforsuccess/fulloverview_2002.cfm (accessed May 2002).

16. Matt Drudge, "Address before the National Press Club," 2 June 1998, at frontpagemag.com/archives/drudge/drudge.htm.

17. PR Newswire, "Large Majorities Believe Big Companies, PACs, Media and Lobbyists Have Too Much Power and Influence in Washington," 10 April 2002, 1.

18. Fox News/Opinion Dynamics, "Major Institutions," at pollingreport.com/institut.htm (accessed May 2002).

19. James Fallows, "Why Americans Hate the Media," *Atlantic Monthly,* February 1996, 45–64.

20. Christopher J. Feola, "Net Comes of Age," *The Quill,* December 1998, 16–19.

21. Howard Kurtz, "The Dirt on Matt Drudge," *Washington Post,* 19 May 1997, p. C1.

22. Associated Press, "Salon.com to Charge for Once-Free Content," *CNN News,* 2 October 2001, at cnn.com/2001/showbiz/news/10/02/salon1.subscriptions.ap/index.html.

23. Art Kramer, "Netwatch," *Atlanta Journal and Constitution,* 14 January 1997, p. B5.

24. Mark Tran, "Slate Expectations," *The Guardian* (Manchester, U.K.), 5 March 1998, 4.

25. "Microsoft's Slate Makes Its Web Site Free, *New York Times* [online], 12 February 1999, at nytimes.com/library/tech/99/02/cyber/articles/12state.html.

26. Joan Connell, "Weblog Central Explained," *MSNBC News,* at msnbc.com/news/817121.asp (accessed January 2003).

27. Paul Krugman, "The Other Face," *New York Times,* 13 December 2002, p. A39.

28. Howard Kurtz, "'Webloggers,' Signing on As War Correspondents," *Washington Post,* 23 March 2003, p. F4.

29. Middleberg and Ross, "Seventh Annual," middleberg.com.

30. John V. Pavlik, "The Future of Online Journalism," *Columbia Journalism Review,* July-August 1997, 30–34.

31. Philip Seib, *Going Live: Getting the News Right in a Real-Time, Online World* (Lanham, Md.: Rowman & Littlefield, 2002), 141.

32. Middleberg and Ross, *Media Fifth,* 7.

33. Middleberg and Ross, "Seventh Annual," middleberg.com.

34. These are the most recent findings from a longitudinal study of the content of the freely available leading newspaper sites. Each year, the top stories from the leading state newspaper sites are examined on two days, which together average to be the 183rd day of the year (first day randomly selected). This average is designed to represent the status in the middle of the given year. To ensure that the findings are not biased by the substance of one big story, results of a given day are discarded and the next day chosen if more than 10 percent of the stories are the same story. The top two stories of the day are chosen such that

a minimum of one in-state story is selected. Selection of the top stories is based on distance from the top, with ties being broken by headline size followed by positioning furthest to the left. This process produces an annual sample of 200 stories and a minimum of 100 in-state stories.

35. Donica Mensing and Jennifer Greer, "Above the Fold: A Comparison of the Lead Stories in Print and Online Newspapers" (paper presented at the annual meeting of the American Political Science Association, San Francisco, Calif., August 2001), 14, 19.

36. Doris A. Graber, *Mass Media & American Politics* (Washington, D.C.: CQ Press, 2002), 356.

37. William Powers, "Hello, World," *National Journal,* 30 June 2002, 2082–85.

38. Middleberg and Ross, *Media Fifth,* 2.

39. Carl Lindemann, "No Payoff Yet," *Broadcasting & Cable,* 19 March 2001, 44–52.

40. Lindemann, "No Payoff," 46.

41. Pew Research Center for the People and the Press, "Internet Election News Audience Seeks Convenience, Familiar Names," 3 December 2000, at people-press.org/online00rpt.htm.

42. Pew Research Center for the People and the Press, "Internet Sapping Broadcast Audience," 11 June 2000, at people-press.org/reports/print.php3?PageID=210.

43. Pew Research Center, "Internet Sapping," people-press.org. Percentages are derived from Question 39 asking "how frequently do you go online to get news?" Percentages for online population are multiplied by percentage online to get results for the general public.

44. Pew Research, "Internet Election News Audience," people-press.org.

45. Pew Research Center for the People and the Press and Pew Internet & American Life Project, *Political Sites Gain, But Major News Sites Still Dominant* (Washington, D.C.: Pew Charitable Trusts, 2003), 11.

46. Pew Research, "Internet Election News Audience," people-press.org.

47. Dick Kelsey, "Online Newspapers Top Local News Source on Web," *Washington Post* [Newsbytes], 29 April 2002, at newsbytes.com/cgi-bin/ . . . story.id=176208.

48. Pew Research, "Internet Election News Audience," people-press.org.

49. Pew Research Center for the People and the Press, "Public's News Habits Little Changed by September 11," 9 June 2002, at people-press.org/reports/print.php3?ReportID=156.

50. Pew Research Center for the People and the Press, "Internet News Takes Off," 8 June 1998, at people-press.org/med98rpt.htm.

51. Pew Research, "Little Changed," people-press.org.

52. Pew Research Center for the People and the Press, "Unusually High Interest in Bush's State of the Union," 17 January 2002, at people-press.org/reports/print.php3?PageID=92.

53. Pew Research Center for the People and the Press, "Terror Coverage Boost News Media's Image but Military Censorship Backed," 28 November 2001, at people-press.org/reports/print.php3?PageID=9.

54. Pew Research, "Internet Sapping," people-press.org.

55. Drudge, "National Press Club," frontpagemag.com.

56. Harper, *Will Be,* 26.

57. Drudge, "National Press Club," frontpagemag.com.

58. Harper, *Will Be,* 3.

59. Dirk Smillie, "News Breaks on the Web, But Can You Believe It," *Christian Science Monitor,* 1 October 1997, 1.

60. Larry J. Sabato, Mark Stencel, and S. Robert Lichter, *Peepshow: Media and Politics in an Age of Scandal* (Lanham, Md.: Rowman & Littlefield, 2000), 77.

61. Dave Becker, "News Coverage of Clinton: Has Web Led to Reckless Media Behavior?" *Wisconsin State Journal,* 31 January 1998, p. A1.

62. Pierre Salinger, *P.S.: A Memoir* (New York: St. Martin's Press, 1995), 273.

63. Smillie, "News Breaks," 1.

64. Brian McWilliams, "Pop Singer's Death Hoax a Top Story at Cnn.com," *Washington Post* [Newsbytes], 9 October 2001, at newsbytes.com/cgi-bin/ . . . story.id=170973.

65. Online News Association, "Digital Journalism Credibility Study," at journalists.org/Programs/ona_credibilitystudy2001report.pdf (accessed March 2002).

66. Pew Research, "Internet Sapping," people-press.org.

67. Elizabeth A. Rathburn, "Sly Fox Buys Big, Gets Back on Top," *Broadcasting & Cable,* 23 April 2001, 59–66.

68. Ben H. Bagdikian, preface to *The Media Monopoly,* 6th ed. (Boston: Beacon Press, 2000).

69. Daniel Schorr, *Staying Tuned: A Life in Journalism* (New York: Pocket Books, 2001), 344.

70. Fox News, "The O'Reilly Factor," 17 September 2002.

71. Online News Association, "Digital Journalism," journalists.org.

72. Online News Association, "Digital Journalism," journalists.org.

73. Thomas Jefferson, "Letter to Archibald Stuart," in *The Great Quotations,* ed. George Seldes (Secaucus, N.J.: Citadel Press, 1983 [1789]), 366.

CHAPTER 9

1. Transcribed by author from "Oral Argument [*Reno* v. *ACLU*]," 19 March 1997, *The Oyez Project,* at oyez.org/dynaram.cgi?case_id=842&resource=argument.ra.

2. Alexander Hamilton, "Federalist 73," in *The Federalist,* ed. Henry Cabot Lodge (New York: Putnam, 1888 [1788]), 459.

3. Wayne Rash Jr., *Politics on the Net: Wiring the Political* Process (New York: Freeman, 1997), 138.

4. Mark Grossman, "Cyberlaw: There's No Dumpster Diving in Cyberspace," *Texas Lawyer,* 7 June 1999, 44.

5. *Unauthorized Practice of Law Committee* v. *Parsons Technology,* No 3:97-CV-2859-H, slip op at 9, 19 (ND Tex, Jan. 22, 1999).

6. *Worldwide Volkswagen* v. *Woodson,* 444 US 286, 297 (1980).

7. Shamoil Shipchandler, "The Wild Web: Non-Regulation as the Answer to the Regulatory Question," *Cornell International Law Journal* 33, no. 2 (2000): 435–63.

8. David Johnson and David Post, "Law and Borders—The Rise of Law in Cyberspace," *Stanford Law Review* 48, no. 5 (May 1996): 1367–1402.

9. Lawrence Lessig, "Reading the Constitution in Cyberspace," *Emory Law Journal* 45, no. 3 (Summer 1996): 869–910.

10. Christopher J. Dorobek, "OMB Shelves New Web Policy," *Government Computer News,* 12 October 1998, 56.

11. Associated Press, "Plan B for Cyberspace," *Wired News*, 9 August 1999, at wired.com/news/news/politics/story/21191.html.

12. Transcribed by author from "Oral Argument," *Oyez Project*, oyez.org.

13. *Religious Technology Center* v. *Netcom On-Line Communication Services*, 907 F Supp 1361, 1370 (ND Cal 1995).

14. *Blumenthal* v. *Drudge*, 992 F Supp 44, 49 (DDC 1998).

15. *Bensusan* v. *King*, 126 F 3d 25, 27 (2d Cir 1997).

16. Jonathan Zittrain, "Testimony before the Subcommittee on Courts and Intellectual Property of the Judiciary Committee," at commdocs.house.gov/committees/judiciary/hju66042.000/ hju66042_0.htm (accessed April 2002).

17. Johnson and Post, "Law and Borders," 1381.

18. *Cybersell* v. *Cybersell*, 130 F 3d 414, 419 (9th Cir 1997).

19. *Blumenthal* v. *Drudge*, 992 F Supp 44, 56 (DDC 1998).

20. *Voyeur Dorm* v. *City of Tampa*, 265 F 3d 1232, 1237 (11th Cir 2001).

21. *Yahoo!* v. *LICRA*, 169 F Supp 2d 1181 (ND Cal 2001).

22. *ALA* v. *Pataki*, 969 F Supp 160 (SD NY 1997).

23. *Cyberspace Communications* v. *Engler*, 55 F Supp 2d 737 (ED Mich 1999); *ACLU* v. *Johnson*, 194 F 3d 1149 (10th Cir 1999).

24. Chris Oakes, "Cluing Congress into Net ABCs," *Wired News*, 1999 August 24, at wired.com/news/news/politics/story/21411.html.

CHAPTER 10

1. *Red Lion Broadcasting* v. *FCC*, 395 US 367, 386 (1969).

2. Telecommunications Act of 1996, P.L. 104–104.

3. Pew Research Center for People and the Press, "Technology in the American Household," at people-press.org/tectop.htm (accessed January 2002).

4. PL 104–104.

5. *ACLU* v. *Reno*, 929 F Supp 824 (ED Pa 1996).

6. *Reno* v. *ACLU*, 521 US 844, 879 (1997).

7. *Reno*, 521 US at 879.

8. *Reno*, 521 US at 854.

9. Omnibus Appropriations Bill FY99, PL 105–277.

10. *Congressional Quarterly Almanac 1998* (Washington, D.C.: CQ Press, 1999), 11–22.

11. *ACLU* v. *Reno*, 31 F Supp 2d 473 (ED Pa 1999).

12. *ACLU* v. *Reno*, 217 F 3d 162 (3d Cir 2000).

13. *Ashcroft* v. *ACLU*, No. 99–1324, oral argument at 47, 48 (28 Nov. 2001).

14. *Ashcroft* v. *ACLU*, 535 US 564 (2002).

15. *ACLU* v. *Ashcroft*, No 99–1324, slip op (3d Cir, 6 Mar. 2003).

16. An Act to Prevent Child Abduction and the Sexual Exploitation of Children, and for Other Purposes, 2003, PL 108–21.

17. Leyla Kokmen, "Smut Check," *City Beat*, 20 June 2001, at citypages.com/databank/printing.asp?ArticleID=9637.

18. *Cynthia Smith* v. *Minneapolis Public Library*, EEOC No 265A00651, at techlawjournal.com/internet/20010523eeocdet.asp (accessed May 2002).

19. *Mainstream Loudoun* v. *Board of Trustees of the Loudoun County Library,* 24 F Supp 2d 552, 570 (ED Va 1998).

20. FY2001 Labor, Health and Human Services, and Education Appropriations Bill, PL 106–554.

21. Joyce Slaton, "Hey Armey, You've Been Filtered," *Wired News,* 28 September 2000, at wired.com/news/print/0,1294,39038,00.html.

22. Declan McCullagh, "Porn-Filter Judge Boots Public," *Wired News,* 25 March 2002, at wired.com/news/print/0,1294,51309,00.html.

23. *American Library Association* v. *United States,* 201 F Supp 2d 401 (ED Pa 2002).

24. *United States* v. *American Library Association,* No 02–361, slip op at 11 (U.S., 23 June 2003).

25. *American Library,* slip op at 12.

26. Jeffrey M. Jones, "Almost All E-Mail Users Say Internet, E-Mail Have Made Lives Better," *Gallup Poll Analyses,* 23 July 2001, at gallup.com/poll/releases/pr010723.asp.

27. Mylene Mangalindan, "For Bulk E-Mailer, Pestering Millions Offers Path to Profit," *Wall Street Journal,* 13 November 2002, p. A1; National Conference of State Legislatures, "Unsolicited Commercial E-Mail Advertisements," at ncsl.org/programs/lis/legislation/spam03.htm (accessed July 2003).

28. *CompuServe* v. *Cyber Promotions,* 962 F Supp 1015 (SD Ohio 1997).

29. *America Online* v. *LCGM,* 46 F Supp 2d 444 (ED Va 1998).

30. *Washington* v. *Heckel,* 143 Wn 2d 824, 833 (2001).

31. Jeffrey Benner, "Wham, Bam, Thank You Spam," *Wired News,* 12 December 2001, at wired.com/news/print/0,1294,49089,00.html.

32. *Blumenthal* v. *Drudge,* 992 F Supp 44 (DDC 1998).

33. Margaret Kane, "FBI: Auction Fraud Tops Net Scam List," *MSNBC News,* 10 April 2002, at msnbc.com/news/736783.asp.

34. Greg Miller, "Man Pleads Guilty to Using Net to Solicit Rape," *Los Angeles Times,* 29 April 1999, p. C1.

35. Sexual Crimes Against Children Prevention Act of 1995, PL 104–71.

36. *United States* v. *Reaves,* 253 F 3d 1201 (10th Cir 2001).

37. Greg Miller, "Online Chat the Sting of Choice in Illicit-Sex Cases," *Los Angeles Times,* 25 September 1999, p. A1.

38. Miller, "Online Chat," A1.

39. *Schenk* v. *United States,* 249 US 47 (1919).

40. Sam H. Verhovek, "Creators of Anti-Abortion Web Site Told to Pay Millions," *New York Times,* 3 February 1999, p. A9.

41. *Planned Parenthood* v. *American Coalition of Life Activists,* 244 F 3d 1007, 1015 (9th Cir 2001).

42. *Planned Parenthood* v. *American Coalition of Life Activists,* 290 F 3d 1058, 1063 (9th Cir 2002).

43. Linda Bowman, "Kiss Your MP3s at Work Goodbye," *MSNBC News,* 27 June 2002, at msnbc.com/news/773100.asp.

44. Integrated Information Systems, "Integrated Information Systems Responds to 2001 Settlement with RIAA," 12 April 2002, 1.

45. American Management Association (AMA), "2001 AMA Survey: Workplace Monitoring & Surveillance," at amanet.org/research/pdfs/ems_short2001.pdf (accessed July 2002).

46. AMA, "2003 E-Mail Rules, Policies and Practices Survey," at amanet.org/research/pdfs/Email_Policies_Practices.pdf (accessed July 2003).

47. Va. Code Ann Section 2.1–804-806, Michie Supp 1999.

48. *Urofsky* v. *Allen,* 995 F Supp 634, 636 (ED Va 1998).

49. *Urofsky* v. *Gilmore,* 216 F 3d 401, 409 (4th Cir 2000).

50. CIA, "Central Intelligence Agency Concludes Investigation of Inappropriate Use of Computer Systems," 30 November 2000, 1.

51. James Risen, "Dismissed for Chat Room, CIA Workers Speak Out," *New York Times,* 18 May 2001, p. A13.

CHAPTER 11

1. Herb Brody, "The Web Maestro: An Interview with Tim Berners-Lee," *Technology Review,* July 1996, 33–41.

2. Network Solutions, "Domain Name Policy," 28 July 1995, at lectlaw.com/files/inp07.htm.

3. Andrew Pollack, "What's in a Cybername? $7.5 Million for the Right Address," *New York Times,* 30 November 1999, p. C8.

4. *Planned Parenthood* v. *Bucci,* No 97 Civ 0629 (KMW), slip op at 21 (SD NY, Mar. 24, 1997).

5. Federal Trademark Dilution Act of 1995, PL 104–98.

6. Orrin Hatch, *Congressional Record,* 29 December 1995, S19310.

7. Patrick Leahy, *Congressional Record,* 29 December 1995, S19312.

8. *Archdiocese of St. Louis* v. *Internet Entertainment Group,* 34 F Supp 2d 1145 (ED Mo 1999).

9. Mike Brunker, "Pope and Adult Web Sites Don't Mix," *MSNBC News,* 20 January 1999, at msnbc.com/news/233791.asp.

10. Carolyn Lochhead, "Web-Address Legislation Called Flawed," *San Francisco Chronicle,* 18 November 1999, p. A1.

11. Spencer Abraham, *Congressional Record,* 5 August 1999, S10519.

12. FY2000 Consolidated Appropriations Bill, PL 106-113.

13. *Sporty's Farm* v. *Sportsman's Market,* 202 F 3d 489, 497 (2d Cir 2000).

14. *Virtual Works* v. *Volkswagen,* 238 F 3d 264 (4th Cir 2000).

15. *E&J Gallo Winery* v. *Spider Webs,* 286 F 3d 270 (5th Cir 2002).

16. *Domain Name Clearing Company* v. *FCF,* 16 Fed Appx 108 (4th Cir 2001).

17. *PETA* v. *Doughney,* 263 F 3d 359, 368 (4th Cir 2001).

18. "Ringling Bros. Wins Domain Skirmish," *Wired News,* 14 May 1998, at wired.com/news/print/0,1294,12325,00.html.

19. *Hewlett-Packard* v. *Cupcake Patrol,* National Arbitration Forum, No 95822 (2000).

20. Abraham, *Congressional Record,* S10519.

21. For failed action, see *Lockheed Martin* v. *Network Solutions,* 985 F Supp 949 (CD Cal 1997).

22. Hatch, *Congressional Record,* S10515.

23. *Shields* v. *Zuccarini,* 254 F 3d 476, 484 (3d Cir 2001).

24. *Electronics Boutique Holdings* v. *Zuccarini,* No 00–4055, slip op at 27 (ED Pa, 30 Oct. 2000).

25. *Hasbro* v. *Clue Computing*, 232 F 3d 1 (1st Cir 2000).

26. *Checkpoint Systems* v. *Check Point Software*, 269 F 3d 270 (3d Cir 2001).

27. World Intellectual Property Organization (WIPO), "Schedule of Fees Under the ICANN Policy," at arbiter.wipo.int/domains/fees/index.html (accessed May 2002).

28. *World Wrestling Federation* v. *Bosman*, WIPO, No D1999–0001 (1999).

29. WIPO, "Case Filings and Decisions," at arbiter.wipo.int/domains/statistics/cumulative/results.html (accessed July 2003).

30. *Allergen* v. *Ostad*, National Arbitration Forum, No 92974 (2000).

31. *I.H.N. Awareness* v. *The Web People*, National Arbitration Forum, No 95117 (2000).

32. Oscar S. Cisneros, "ICANN't Believe that Domain Name," *Wired News*, 27 July 2000, at wired.com/news/print/0,1294,37801,00.html.

33. *National Cable Satellite Corporation* v. *Telmex Management Services*, National Arbitration Forum, No 102820 (2002).

34. *Ank of America* v *Bank of America*, National Arbitration Forum, No 105891 (2002).

35. *Bank of America* v. *Ban of America*, National Arbitration Forum, No 105885 (2002).

36. *Neiman-Marcus* v. *Tumay Asena*, National Arbitration Forum, No 99711 (2001).

37. *Neiman-Marcus* v. *Music Wave*, National Arbitration Forum, No 135020 (2003).

38. *Neiman-Marcus* v. *Lorna Kang*, National Arbitration Forum, No 109722 (2002).

39. *Williard C. Smith III* v. *Vip Mangalick*, National Arbitration Forum, No 156844 (2003).

40. *Michael Andretti* v. *Alberta Hot Rods*, National Arbitration Forum No 99084 (2001).

41. *CMG Worldwide* v. *Alessandro Bottai*, National Arbitration Forum No 94661 (2000).

42. *Garth Brooks* v. *Commbine.com*, National Arbitration Forum, No 96097 (2001).

43. *Celine Dion* v. *Jeff Burgar*, WIPO, No D2000-1838 (2000).

44. *Mick Jagger* v. *Denny Hammerton*, National Arbitration Forum, No 95261 (2000).

45. *Emeril Lagasse* v. *VPOP Technologies*, National Arbitration Forum, No 34373 (2000).

46. *Dan Marino* v. *Video Images*, WIPO, No D2000-0598 (2000).

47. *MPL* v. *Denny Hammerton*, National Arbitration Forum, No 95633 (2000).

48. *Julia Roberts* v. *Russell Boyd*, WIPO, No D2000-0210 (2000).

49. *Kevin Spacey* v. *John Zuccarini*, National Arbitration Forum, No 96937 (2001).

50. *Heidi Fleiss* v. *Tricky Web*, National Arbitration Forum, No 103136 (2002).

51. Leah P. Falzone, "Playing the Hollywood Name Game in Cybercourt," *Loyola of Los Angeles Entertainment Law Review* 21, no. 1 (2001): 289–325.

52. *Madonna* v. *Dan Parisi*, WIPO, No D2000-0847 (2000).

53. See, for example, dispute over walmartcanadasucks.com in *Wal-Mart Stores* v. *Walsucks*, WIPO, No D2000-0477 (2000).

54. *Compusa Management* v. *Customized Computer Training*, National Arbitration, No 95082 (2000).

55. *Channel D* v. *Channel-D*, National Arbitration Forum, No 94298 (2000).

56. *Victoria's Secret* v. *National Rag*, National Arbitration Forum, No 96492 (2001).

57. *Mark Warner 2001* v. *Mike Larson*, National Arbitration Forum, No 95746 (2000).

58. *Gordon Sumner* v. *Michael Urvan*, WIPO, No 2000-0596 (2000).

59. *Mick Jones* v. *Stephen Gregory*, National Arbitration Forum, No 125747 (2003).

60. *Dog.com* v. *Pets.com*, National Arbitration Forum, No 93681 (2000).

61. *UltraFem* v. *Warren Royal*, National Arbitration Forum, No 97682 (2001).

62. *Penguin Books* v. *Anthony Katz*, WIPO, No D2000-0204 (2000).

63. *Prom Software* v. *Reflex Publishing,* WIPO, No D2001–1154 (2001).
64. *Familiar Limited* v. *CTD Technologies,* WIPO, No D2001-1009.

CHAPTER 12

1. 17 USC. § 102 (a).
2. *Eldred* v. *Ashcroft,* 123 S Ct 769 (2003).
3. *Los Angeles Times* v. *Free Republic,* 2000 US Dist Lexis 5669 (CD Cal 2000).
4. FreeRepublic.com, "The Free Republic Legal Defense Fund," at freerepublic.com/forum/a3/b3290e42e6f.htm (accessed June 2002).
5. *Playboy Enterprises* v. *Frena,* 839 F Supp 1552, 1558 (MD Fla 1993).
6. Steven Bonisteel, "Pamela Anderson Wins One in Sex Video Fight," *Washington Post* [Newsbytes], 25 April 2002, at newsbytes.com/cgi-bin/ . . . story.id=176130.
7. *Wall Street Journal,* "Web Software Pirate Is Given 46 Months in Federal Prison," 20 May 2002, p. B4.
8. Jennifer Sullivan, "MP3 Pirate Gets Probation," *Wired News,* 24 November 1999, at wired.com/news/print/0,1294,32276,00.html.
9. "Big Music Fights Back," *Economist,* 16 June 2001, 61–62.
10. *Sony* v. *Universal City Studios,* 464 US 417 (1984).
11. Matt Richtel, "Napster Case: Hard Queries on Copyrights," *New York Times* [online], 3 October 2000, at nytimes.com/2000/10/03/technology/03musi.html.
12. *A&M Records* v. *Napster,* 239 F 3d 1004 (9th Cir 2001).
13. Chris Taylor, "The Next Napsters," *Time,* Fall 2001, 34.
14. Ariana Eunjung Cha, "File Swapper Eluding Pursuers: Unlike Napster, Kazaa's Global Nature Defies Legal Attacks," *Washington Post,* 21 December 2002, p. A1.
15. *Recording Industry Association of America* v. *Verizon Internet Services,* 2003 US Dist Lexis 681 (DDC 2003).
16. *Universal* v. *Reimerdes,* No 00–9185, oral argument (2d Cir, 1 May 2001).
17. Christopher Conte, "The Privacy Panic," *Governing,* December 2000, 20–26.
18. Keith H. Hammonds, ed., "Online Insecurity," *Business Week,* 16 March 1998, 102.
19. Pew Internet & American Life Project, *Trust and Privacy Online: Why Americans Want to Rewrite the Rules* (Washington, D.C.: Pew Internet & American Life Project, 2000), 25.
20. FTC, "Privacy Online: A Report to Congress," June 1998, at www.ftc.gov/reports/privacy3/toc.htm.
21. FTC, "Fair Information Practices in the Electronic Marketplace," May 2000, at www.ftc.gov/reports/privacy2000/privacy2000.pdf.
22. Brock N. Meeks, "Federal Sites Score Poorly on Privacy," *MSNBC News,* 6 September 2000, at msnbc.com/news/45637.asp?cp1=1.
23. Declan McCullagh, "Whitehouse.gov No Place For Kids?" *Wired News,* 7 October 2000, at wired.com/news/print/0,1294,39334,00.html; Meeks, "Federal," msnbc.com.
24. Christopher Conte, "Privacy Panic," 24.
25. Richard Raysman and Peter Brown, "Update on On-Line Privacy," *New York Law Journal,* 9 November 1999, 3.
26. FTC, "Self Regulation and Privacy Online," at www.ftc.gov/os/1999/9907/privacy99.pdf (accessed June 2002).
27. See *In re Geocities,* FTC No 9823015 (1998).

28. Declan McCullagh and Ryan Sager, "Privacy Laws: Not Gonna Happen," *Wired News*, 2 March 2001, at wired.com/news/print/0,1294,42123,00.html.

29. Declan McCullagh, "Making an E-Contract with America," *Wired News*, 23 June 2001, at wired.com/news/print/0,1294,44753,00.html.

30. Omnibus Appropriations Bill FY99, PL105–277.

31. FTC, "Fair Information," ftc.gov; Pew Internet, *Trust and Privacy*, 2.

32. Molly M. Peterson, "A Tangled Web," *National Journal*, 5 May 2001, 314–18.

33. Chris Oakes, "Tackling E-Privacy in New York," *Wired News*, 3 June 1999, at wired.com/news/print/0,1294,19991,00.html.

34. Reuters, "AGs Eye Privacy," *Wired News*, 23 March 2000, at wired.com/news/print/0,1294,35175,00.html.

35. Dick Kelsey, "Gov. Ventura Signs Internet Privacy Bill," *Washington Post* [Newsbytes], 23 May 2002, at newsbytes.com/cgi-bin/ . . . story.id=176737.

36. C-SPAN, Fleishman-Hillard Forum, 26 February 2001.

37. *ACLU of Georgia* v. *Miller*, 977 F Supp 1228 (ND Ga 1997).

38. American Management Association, "2003 E-Mail Rules, Policies and Practices Survey," at amanet.org/research/pdfs/Email_Policies_Practices.pdf (accessed July 2003).

39. *Timothy McVeigh* v. *William Cohen*, 983 F Supp 215, 220 (DDC 1998).

40. House Report, 103–827 (1994).

41. Donald M. Kerr, "Testimony before the U.S. Senate Judiciary Committee," 6 September 2000, at www.fbi.gov/congress/congress00/kerr090600.htm.

42. Alan B. Davidson, "Testimony before the House Committee on the Judiciary Subcommittee on the Constitution," 24 July 2000, at cdt.org/testimony/000724 davidson.shtml.

43. Jim Wolf, "'Carnivore' Gets a New Name," *MSNBC News*, 14 February 2001, at msnbc.com/news/530857.asp.

44. Kerr, "Testimony," fbi.gov.

45. David S. Fallis and Ariana Eunjung Cha, "Agents Following Suspects Lengthy Electronic Trail," *Washington Post*, 4 October 2001, p. A24.

46. Patrick Thibodeau, "Clarke: Terrorists Used Net for Info on Targets," 15 February 2002, at cnn.com/2002/tech/internet/02/15/terrorists.internet.idg/index.html.

47. George W. Bush, "Remarks on Signing the USA Patriot Act of 2001," *Weekly Compilation of Presidential Documents* 37, no. 43 (October 2001): 1550–52.

48. Declan McCullagh and Ben Polen, "DOJ's Already Monitoring Modems," *Wired News*, 28 November 2001, at wired.com/news/print/0,1294,48711,00.html.

49. Declan McCullagh, "Terror Law Foes Mull Strategies," *Wired News*, 3 November 2001, at wired.com/news/print/0,1294,48120,00.html.

50. Pew Internet & American Life Project, *Fear of Online Crime: Americans Support FBI Interception of Criminal Suspects' Email and New Laws to Protect Online Privacy* (Washington, D.C.: Pew Internet & American Life Project, 2001), 5.

CHAPTER 13

1. International Telecommunications Union (ITU), "Cellular Subscribers," at itu.org (accessed November 2002).

2. Peter Lennon, "From Finland to Phoneland," *The Guardian* (Manchester, U.K.), 3 June 1999, p. O2.

3. Lennon, "Finland," O2.

4. William Shaw, "In Helsinki Virtual Village," *Wired*, March 2001, 156–63.

5. Pippa Norris, *Digital Divide: Civic Engagement, Information Poverty, and the Internet Worldwide* (Cambridge: Cambridge University Press, 2001), 63.

6. Norris, *Digital Divide*, 59–60.

7. European Commission, *Measuring Information Society 2000* (Brussels: European Commission, 2000), 13; Department of Commerce, "Falling through the Net II: New Data on the Digital Divide," at www.ntia.doc.gov/ntiahome/net2/falling.html (accessed July 1998). Combined categories are unweighted averages of component categories with the exception of U.S. income categories, which are averages of categories refined by allocating categories to their percentage in the population based on census data from U.S. Bureau of the Census, *Money Income in the United States: 1997* (Washington, D.C.: GPO, 1998), B3, B6.

8. European Commission, *Europe 2002 Benchmarking: European Youth into the Digital Age* (Brussels: European Commission, 2001), 11.

9. Associated Press, "EU Plans to Tax Internet Sales," *New York Times* [online], 8 May 2002, at nytimes.com/technology/ . . . 1-tax.html.

10. Christina Holtz-Bacha, Lynda Lee Kaid, and Anne Johnston, "Political Television Advertising in Western Democracies: A Comparison of Campaign Broadcasts in the United States, Germany, and France," *Political Communication* 11, no. 1 (January–March 1994): 67–80.

11. William T. Stanbury, "Financing Federal Politics in Canada in an Era of Reform," in *Campaign and Party Finance in North America and Western Europe,* ed. Arthur B. Gunlicks (Boulder, Colo.: Westview, 1993), 68–120.

12. 1997 party sites are labourwin97.org.uk and conservative-party.org. The 2001 party sites are conservatives.com and labour.org.uk.

13. Holtz-Bacha, Kaid, and Johnston, "Advertising," 75.

14. Peter Golding, David Deacon, and Michael Billig, "Dominant Press Backs 'On Message' Winner," *The Guardian,* 5 May 1997, p. A4.

15. Martin Harrison, "Politics on the Air," in *The British General Election of 1992,* ed. David Butler and Dennis Kavanagh (New York: St. Martin's, 1992), 155–79.

16. Stephen Clarkson, "Securing Their Future Together: The Liberals in Action," in *The Canadian General Election of 1997,* ed. Alan Frizzell and Jon H. Pammett (Toronto: Dundurn, 1997), 39–70.

17. Parties include Liberal (liberal.ca), New Democratic Party (fed.ndp.ca/fndp/election97), Progressive Conservatives (pcparty.ca), and Reform (reform.ca).

18. Doug Struck, "Internet Changed Culture of S. Korean Vote," *Washington Post,* 15 April 2000, p. A14.

19. Reform Party, at reform.ca (accessed May 1997).

20. "Serious Stuff," at nocrap.org.nz/serious/serious.htm (accessed October 1999).

21. One News, "National Website Branded a Dirty Trick," 21 October 1999, at onenews.co.nz.

22. Kim Griggs, "Kiwis Want You@Army.Mil.NZ," *Wired News,* 29 September 2001, at wired.com/news/print/0,1294,4718,00.html.

23. European Commission, "Commission Publishes First Survey on eGovernment Services in Europe," 30 November 2001, 1.

24. John Stackhouse, "Canberra's Electronic Vote an Australian First," *Washington Post* [Newsbytes], 23 October 2001, at newsbytes.com/cgi-bin/ . . . story.id=171393.

25. Sonni Efron, "Online Is Off Limits to Japan's Politicians," *Los Angeles Times,* 19 June 2000, p. A1.

26. Alan Abrams, "'Pardon My English,' Georgia Tech Tells French Organizations," *Journal of Commerce,* 12 June 1997, p. B2.

27. Wendy R. Leibowitz, "National Laws Entangle the 'Net: It's a Small, Small Litigious Web," *National Law Journal,* 30 June 1997, p. B7.

28. Jeffrey Benner, "EU Drives Privacy Global," *Wired News,* 16 July 2001, at wired.com/news/print/0,1294,44922,00.html.

29. Paulo Rebelo, "Casting a Wider Net in Brazil," *Wired News,* 30 July 2001, at wired.com/news/print/0,1294,45526,00.html.

30. Glyn Moody, *The Rebel Code: The Inside Story of Linux and the Open Source Revolution* (Cambridge, Mass.: Perseus Publications, 2001), 317.

31. Michelle Delio, "Norge: Where Technology Rules," *Wired News,* 10 July 2001, at wired.com/news/print/0,1294,45130,00.html.

32. Alan Garcia, "Presidente," at alanperu.com (accessed June 2001); Alejandro Toledo, "Democracie en el Peru," at alejandrotoledo.com (accessed June 2001).

CHAPTER 14

1. John Davidson, "Secret It Business," *Australian Financial Review,* 30 April 1999, 38.

2. Andrea Goldstein and David O'Connor, *E-Commerce for Development: Prospects and Policy Issues* (Paris: OECD, 2000), 4.

3. Frances Harrison, "Malaysia Casts Legal Eye Over Net," *The Guardian* (Manchester, U.K.), 2 April 1999, p. 18.

4. Reporters Without Borders, "The Twenty Enemies of the Internet," 9 August 1999, at rsf.org.

5. The twenty are Azerbaijan, Belarus, Burma, China, Cuba, Iran, Iraq, Kazakhstan, Kirghizia, Libya, North Korea, Saudi Arabia, Sierra Leone, Sudan, Syria, Tajikistan, Tunisia, Turkmenistan, Uzbekistan, and Vietnam.

6. Christophe De Roquefeuil, "Iran Veils Internet in Islamic Code," *The Globe and Mail* (Toronto), 14 January 1999, p. C2.

7. Reporters Without Borders, "Internet: A Chronicle of Repression," 18 April 2002, at rsf.fr/article.php3?id_article=1290.

8. Reuters, "China Shuts Down Internet Cafes," *Wired News,* 17 June 2002, at wired.com/news/print/0,1294,53232,00.html.

9. Brian Whitaker, "Saudis Claim Victory in War for Control of Web," *The Guardian,* 11 May 2000, p. 17.

10. King Abdulaziz City for Science & Technology, "Internet Regulations and Policies," at www.isu.net.sa/regulations.html (accessed May 2001).

11. Jennifer Lee, "Companies Compete to Provide Saudi Internet Veil," *New York Times,* 19 November 2001, p. C1.

12. King Abdulaziz, "Internet," isu.net.

13. Lee, "Companies Compete," C1.

14. Louise Williams, "Web of Intrigue," *Sydney Morning Herald* [online], 29 April 2000, at smh.com.au/news/0004/29/spectrum/spectrum1.html.

15. Reuters, "S. Africa Battles over Internet Control," *MSNBC* News, 13 June 2002, at msnbc.com/news/766560.asp.

16. Jonathan Evans, "Turkey Passes Strict Net Law," *Wired News,* 15 May 2002, at wired.com/news/print/0,1294,52558,00.html.

17. Reporters Without Borders, "Internet," rsf.fr.

18. Reporters Without Borders, "Internet," rsf.fr.

19. Natalia A. Feduschak, "FBI Probe Blocked in Ukraine Murder," *Washington Times,* 22 April 2002, p. A14.

20. Reporters Without Borders, "Tunisian Cyber-Dissident Sent to Prison for Two Years," 21 June 2002, at rsf.fr/article.php3?id_article=2633.

21. Williams, "Web of Intrigue," smh.com.

22. Rick Perera, "The Internet Revolution: Serbia and the Web," *IDG.net,* 16 October 2000, at idg.net.

23. Harry M. Cleaver Jr., "The Zapatista Effect: The Internet and the Rise of an Alternative Political Fabric," *Journal of International Affairs* 51, no. 2 (Spring 1998): 621–40.

24. Juanita Darling, "Mexico Accused of Human Rights Abuses during Revolt Report: Amnesty International Says Soldiers Terrorized Indian Villagers," *Los Angeles Times,* 25 January 1994, p. A10.

25. Julia Scheeres, "Faint Voices Rise from Cuba," *Wired News,* 29 May 2001, at wired.com/news/print/0,1294,44045,00.html.

26. Matthew Forney, "How China Beat Down Falun Gong," *Time Atlantic,* 2 July 2001, 26–29.

27. Neil MacFarquhar, "For First Time in War, E-Mail Plays a Vital Role," *New York Times,* 29 March 1999, p. A12.

28. MacFarquhar, "First Time," A12.

29. Associated Press, "China Solicits Comments Via Internet," *New York Times* [online], 9 December 1998, at nytimes.com/library/tech/98/12/biztech/articles/09internetchina.html.

30. Clay Chandler, "For Chinese Pilot, Martyrdom on Earth and in Cyberspace," *Washington Post,* 18 April 2001, p. A15.

31. King Abdulaziz, "Internet," isu.net.

32. Williams, "Web of Intrigue," smh.com.

CONCLUSION

1. Markle Foundation, *Report on the Global On-Line, Direct Elections for Five Seats Representing At-Large Members on the Board of Directors of the Internet Corporation for Assigned Names and Numbers* (New York: Markle Foundation, 2001), 28.

Index

Note: Italicized page numbers identify those entries that are referring to information in tables or figures.

About the Author

Robert J. Klotz is assistant professor of political science at the University of Southern Maine. A leader in the field of Internet politics, he authored several of the earliest systematic studies of Internet politics, which appeared in *Political Communication* and in other peer-reviewed journals. His essay on future agendas in political communication was included in *Communication in U.S. Elections*, also published by Rowman & Littlefield.